REIMAGINING THE CREATIVE INDUSTRIES

This book documents the rise in youth creativity, entrepreneurship, and collective strategies to address systemic barriers and discrimination in the creative industries and create an expanded, more diverse, inclusive, equitable, and caring field.

Although the difficulties of entering and making a living in the creative industries—a field which can often perpetuate dominant patterns of social exclusion and economic inequality—are well documented, there is still an absence of guidance on how young creatives can navigate this environment. Foregrounding an intersectional approach, *Reimagining the Creative Industries* responds to this gap by documenting the work of contemporary youth collectives and organizations that are responding to these systemic barriers and related challenges by creating more caring and community-oriented alternatives. Mobilizing a care ethics framework, Miranda Campbell underscores forms of care that highlight relationality, recognize structural barriers, and propose new visions for the creative industries. This book posits a future where creativity, collaboration, and community are possible through increased avenues for co-creation, teaching and learning, and community engagement.

Anyone interested in thinking critically about the creative industries, youth culture, community work, and creative employment will be drawn to Campbell's incisive work.

Miranda Campbell is an Associate Professor in the School of Creative Industries at Ryerson University in Toronto, Canada. Her research focuses on creative employment, youth culture, and small-scale and emerging forms of creative practice. Her book, *Out of the Basement: Youth Cultural Production in Practice and in Policy*, was shortlisted for the Donner Prize for the best public policy book by a Canadian. Her involvement with creative communities includes coordination and Board of Director roles with Rock Camp for Girls Montreal, a summer camp dedicated to empowerment for girls through music education, and with WhipperSnapper Gallery, an artist-run centre focusing on emerging artists in Toronto.

REIMAGINING THE CREATIVE INDUSTRIES

Youth Creative Work, Communities of Care

Miranda Campbell

Routledge
Taylor & Francis Group
NEW YORK AND LONDON

First published 2022
by Routledge
605 Third Avenue, New York, NY 10158

and by Routledge
2 Park Square, Milton Park, Abingdon, Oxon, OX14 4RN

Routledge is an imprint of the Taylor & Francis Group, an informa business

Library of Congress Cataloguing-in-Publication Data
A catalog record for this title has been requested

ISBN: 978-0-367-46821-7 (hbk)
ISBN: 978-0-367-46815-6 (pbk)
ISBN: 978-1-003-03133-8 (ebk)

DOI: 10.4324/9781003031338

Typeset in Bembo
by MPS Limited, Dehradun

CONTENTS

List of figures vii
Acknowledgements ix

Introduction 1

1 Creative Industries as Discourse: Changing the Frame 24

2 Care Ethics for the Creative Industries 43

3 The "Diversity" Response 66

4 From Margins to Centre: Building Inclusion through Pedagogical Encounter 94

5 Youth Creative Work and Community Arts 120

6 Collaborative Production, Communities of Practice, and Communities of Care 148

7 Inclusive Spaces for Small-Scale Cultural Production 173

Conclusion: Towards a Collaborative Future 194

Index 204

FIGURES

3.1	*Clear Expectations: Guidelines for Institutions, Galleries and Curators Working with Trans, Non-Binary and Gender Diverse Artists* cover image	84
3.2	"What Is the Need for This Resource" from *Clear Expectations*	85
3.3	*Agenda for Change* Cover Image from Equity UK	86
3.4	"Introduction" from *Agenda for Change*	87
3.5	Elements of "What Makes for a Responsible Creative Collaboration" from *Think Before You Appropriate: Things to Know and Questions to Ask in Order to Avoid Misappropriating Indigenous Cultures—A Guide for Creators and Designers*	89
3.6	Further Elements of "What Makes for a Responsible Creative Collaboration" *Think Before You Appropriate*	90
4.1	"Damned if You Do" Event Flyer from PEERS Program	109
4.2	"Safer Bars and Spaces" Program Flyer from the Dandelion Initiative	112
4.3	"Now Serving: Education in 2020" Flyer from the Dandelion Initiative	115
5.1	SKETCH Working Arts' Theory of Change	130
6.1	*Rock Camp for Girls Montreal Volunteer Handbook* Cover Image	155
6.2	"Best Practices for Band Coaches and Band Managers" from *Rock Camp for Girls Montreal Volunteer Handbook*	159
6.3	Further elements of "Best Practices for Band Coaches and Band Managers" from *Rock Camp for Girls Montreal Volunteer Handbook*	160
7.1	The Dynamic Triangle by David Panton, Acme U.K.	189
8.1	"Towards a Collaborative Future" Flyer from CCC Research Lab	195

8.2 "Butterfly Hands" Event Flyer from Tea Base Collective 201
8.3 "AGO Is in Chinatown, Chinatown Is on Stolen Land" Banner from Tea Base Collective 202

ACKNOWLEDGEMENTS

This book is the culminating point of various research projects. The research funding I have received—including from the Social Sciences and Humanities Research Council, and at Ryerson University, from the Faculty of Communication and Design (FCAD) small grant, travel grant, and creative innovation grant—funded research assistance from Celeste Ali-Akow, max cotter, Jesse Cumming, Calla Evans, Anna Frey, Nataleah Hunter-Young, Kait Kribs, Johannes Valdes, and Lucy Wowk. I am grateful for this support, and for all of the insights and hands-on work that has helped shape the research and enabled its completion.

Thank you to friends and colleagues who reviewed chapters and provided feedback in particularly busy times. Raphaëlle Aubin, Cheryl Thompson, Benjamin Woo, and Lucy Wowk, thank you for your outside eyes, insight, and expertise.

Thank you to all the undergraduate and graduate students I have taught and mentored over the years, who have worked through some of the ideas presented in this book with me. In particular, thank you to the students in the School of Creative Industries "Care Ethics for the Creative Industries" class and in the Communication and Culture program "Research and Care Ethics" class, who went through first entirely remote learning classes in Summer 2020. I have never met most of these students in person and I hope our paths will cross one day!

Thank you to all of the research participants who agreed to be interviewed in various research projects and for this book. Thank you for your time and for sharing your stories.

Thank you to Emma Sherriff at Routledge for stewarding this book from its proposal to its final publication. Thank you to Lucy Wowk for the beautiful cover design, and for research assistance and support to get this book through its final stages.

Some of the material published in this book was originally published elsewhere. Chapter 5, "Youth Creative Work and Community Arts" was originally published as two articles:

Miranda Campbell, 2021. "Reimagining the Creative Industries in the Community Arts Sector." *Cultural Trends*, DOI: 10.1080/09548963.2021.1887702

Miranda Campbell, 2019. "From Youth Engagement to Creative Industries Incubators: Models of Working with Youth in Community Arts Settings." *Review of Education, Pedagogy, and Cultural Studies* 41 no. 3: 164–192.

Chapter 6, "Collaborative Production, Communities of Practice, and Communities of Care," was originally published as:

Miranda Campbell, "'Girls Rock!': Best Practices in Collaborative Creative Processes at Rock Camp for Girls Montreal." *Collaborative Production in the Creative Industries*, eds. Alessandro Gandini and James Graham (London: University of Westminster Press, 2017): 177-196.

Some of the data from Chapter 2, "Care Ethics for the Creative Industries" was originally published in:

Miranda Campbell, 2020. "'Shit is Hard, Yo': Young People Making a Living in the Creative Industries." *International Journal of Cultural Policy* 26, no. 4: 524–543.

I am grateful to Taylor & Francis journals and to the University of Westminster press to reproduce versions of those works here.

Lastly, thank you to my cozy family, Adam Waito and Elinor Mae Campbell Waito. In the Introduction of this book, I discuss writing this book through COVID-19—to be clear this was not a pandemic writing holiday as we adjusted and coped with working, parenting, and being a kid through lockdown(s). Still my family has always been an anchoring point for me. Thank you, Adam and Elinor for keeping me grounded through tough times. Thank you to all of Elinor's teachers and caregivers doing the hands-on work of caring for her while I have been researching and writing this book.

INTRODUCTION

On December 2, 2016, an electronic dance music party at a warehouse in Oakland, California, called Ghost Ship, ended tragically with 36 deaths when a fire broke out. Most of these victims were young artists and musicians, but victims ranged in age from 17 to 61. The Ghost Ship warehouse did not have permits for residential or entertainment use, but was operating as a live-work space. In addition to known electrical problems in the building, the space did not have fire sprinklers or smoke detectors, and the space has been described as cluttered with wooden furniture. This clutter likely accelerated the fire, but also caused difficulty for partygoers in finding the exits, and contributed to the number of casualties. Reporting on the fire, the *Los Angeles Times* calls Ghost Ship "a 10,000 square foot tinderbox."[1] In his response to the event, President Obama noted that "Oakland is one of the most diverse and creative cities in [the United States]," and the fire was "one of the worst ... in the state's history,"[2] situating the impact of the destruction of this fire in the context of diversity, creativity, and urban life. I discuss the details of the Ghost Ship fire in relation to the role of small-scale spaces in incubating cultural production in further detail in Chapter 7, but I open with this incident to situate myself, my research, some of the limitations I have encountered with creative industries discourses, and the impact of these limitations at the level of my own lived experience.

I have never been to the Ghost Ship warehouse, but I have spent a lot of time in small-scale spaces and venues like Ghost Ship, attending art and music shows as a fan. I moved to Toronto, Canada, in 2015, to start the professor position that I am currently in, in the School of Creative Industries at Ryerson University. Before that, I lived in Montreal, Canada, for about 13 years, from my early 20s to my mid-30s. Those were good years, and I felt embedded in Montreal's vibrant art and music scenes. For Halloween, in 2014, I went to an over-capacity event at

DOI: 10.4324/9781003031338-101

an afterhours club to see a Talking Heads cover band. The Talking Heads is one of my all-time favourite bands, and the band that was playing were some people I knew, who are amazing musicians, so this set was really tight and beautifully performed. It took a long time to be able to get inside to see the show. From the street level, there is a long narrow staircase going up to the second-floor venue entrance, and there was a bottleneck of people trying to pay and get inside the venue for this event. The venue felt more like a residential apartment than an official club or venue space.

Because the room was so full, I wedged myself in and stood on the armrest of a couch to see. Though I was having a really good time, I remember having a clear thought that night that we could all die if something like a fire broke out. The entrance was the exit, and that was so jammed to get in, and there were so many people inside. This particular experience and many others like it may have led to the news of the Ghost Ship fire hitting me hard. When I heard about the Ghost Ship fire, I thought, that could have been me or my friends who perished.

Beyond the tragedy itself, the Ghost Ship news was also hard for me because conceptually, I have been in this space for some time, researching and documenting the importance of small-scale and emerging forms of cultural production. I sometimes doubt calling attention to and documenting these spaces: some do not publish their names or addresses officially to avoid trouble from the police. As I detailed above, they can be physically unsafe, not adhering to fire codes or permitted use. But these are often vital spaces, incubating the very kinds of creativity that have been so celebrated with the rise of creative cities and creative industries discourses. After my first book, *Out of the Basement*, came out, I was running a blog called *Every Day We're Hustling* (which became the title of a podcast I made), specifically addressing the dynamism and the hustle of small-scale creative work, which often does not register officially in policy structures, and can be denigrated in public consciousness with common but limited ways of thinking about young creatives as lazy or as members of a privileged elite demographic. Some of my work with *Out of the Basement* and *Every Day We're Hustling* was drawing attention to the question of scale in the creative industries. In Montreal, a "creative city" policy was adopted in 2007, but this policy did not register or celebrate the small-scale places that allowed the city to become known internationally as a vibrant place of creativity. Through the lens of noise complaints, I profiled what has become a common issue in many cities: people moving into trendy neighbourhoods but then being bothered by loud noise from music venues and making complaints to the police, who then give fines to music venues for this noise, which can result in venues having to close. Beyond official venues, this is also a problem faced by after-hours or unofficial loft spaces, and I have also drawn attention to these kinds of places and their importance. These places are even more precarious, sometimes ad-hoc, or makeshift, but can house and enable forms of creativity that exist on the margins.

Interrogating the Ordinary

Raymond Williams' work and thinking from the mid-20th century is now chronicled as contributing to and catalyzing the field of cultural studies as an academic discipline and a method of inquiry to understand culture. Williams' 1958 essay "Culture is Ordinary" offers inroads to question what we accept as "ordinary" as it relates to culture; in this essay, he asserts "culture is ordinary: that is where we must start," and this invocation has led me to open this book by interrogating what has been taken for granted as "ordinary" in the creative industries.[3] The Ghost Ship warehouse operating as a live-work artist space without proper permits or zoning is actually quite ordinary for DIY, or small-scale, do-it-yourself spaces. These spaces often not having fire sprinklers, smoke detectors, or adequate fire exits is also quite ordinary. That this warehouse and the creative projects and people it housed was located in Oakland, a relatively more affordable city about 30 minutes from the inflated to the point of unlivable costs of San Francisco and Silicon Valley, is also quite ordinary. These DIY small-scale spaces are sometimes called safe spaces for the inclusive cultures they can foster, but often can be quite physically unsafe, which highlights tensions in notions of creative cities and creative economies. When we celebrate creative cities or the creative industries more generally, we might ask, creative for whom, and at what cost? Creative industries inequities have been well traced by many critical creative industries scholars, especially with regards to working conditions, including precarity, low and no pay, necessity of networks and of networking, instability and insecurity, and so on, and so my purpose is not to retrace this work here, but instead to begin to query what alternatives exist or could be possible.

It is not entirely fair to place these questions about the fallout of contemporary creative industries discourses at the feet of Williams, but still, it is useful to look at the origins of how we come to understand and study cultural production today. Culture and media studies scholars Kate Oakley, Mark Ball, and Malaika Cunningham outline that some contemporary cultural studies work picks up concerns of "everyday culture" and has recuperated Williams and his insistence on the importance of the everyday as a form of culture, as distinct from elite or high culture.[4] Williams outlines two ways of understanding the meaning of culture: the everyday, a "whole way of life—the common meanings" and "the arts and learning—the special process of discovery and creative effort." Rather than locate a definition of culture in one of these two meanings, Williams insists "on both, and on the significance of their conjunction."[5] Foregrounding his working-class background and identity, Williams is wary of a "cultural dupes" argument that positions working-class people as uninformed, uncritical, uneducated masses, and instead showcases the importance of everyday working-class forms of culture. In contrast, he positions a newer category of workers, "new advertising men, publicity boys, names in the strip newspapers" as a "new, dangerous class." The contemporary historical moment brings a different context than the 1950s Welsh working class politics that Williams is speaking to. But, like Williams, if I were to identify danger in the creative industries, I also would locate it in a proliferation of discourses that champion economic growth without investigation of social and environmental costs, rather than in the physically dangerous DIY creative spaces of my youth.

Following Williams, in this book I explore multiple meanings of culture to find frameworks for bridging cultural participation and cultural production and develop a more holistic approach to understand the creative industries. I turn to the inroads offered by feminist care ethics that highlight relationality, recognize structural barriers, and propose new visions for a more caring and inclusive society. I gather insights from the models and working practices of youth and emerging cultural producers and collectives. To begin, though, I want to spend a bit more time in "the ordinary," or my "ordinary" everyday of the last few years, suggestive of how the "ordinary" can also be deeply disquieting. In some ways, Williams' essay is in praise of the ordinary or the everyday as embodying valuable ways of being, working, and relating to others, recuperating value in forms of culture that were denigrated or not even seen as culture in his era. In this vein, a cultural studies approach has also taught us to query what becomes accepted as common sense or "ordinary" as ideologically driven; what we take for granted embodies hegemonic values and norms. So here, I am calling attention to what has become ordinary in the creative industries and the limitations of the economic emphasis in this field.

"Ordinary" in the Workplace: Tolerance of Abuse

My department at Ryerson University, the School of Creative Industries, is a relatively new one, responding to the increased interest in the student body for interdisciplinary study of the creative industries and is intended for students who want to work in creative industries, but not necessarily as artists or makers. In Winter 2018, I was teaching a course called Creative Collaboration for the first time, a fourth year required course taught in smaller seminar sections. One of the final weeks of the semester in this course, week ten, was about conflict and conflict prevention when working in teams. In the School of Creative Industries, we have a majority female student body, and as is typical in many teaching contexts, week ten of the 12-week semester had dwindling numbers in attendance. In one of the sections of this course, Creative Collaboration, there were about eight or ten young women in the room for my conflict prevention class, creating a more intimate and informal environment. Led by student questions and comments, what we ended up talking about was harassment and abuse, and how this is different than conflict. During that class, students predominantly wanted a space to share their stories and raise their concerns. In subsequent years of this course, I have sought to clarify the difference between conflict and abuse, guided by Sarah Schulman's book of the same title, *Conflict Is Not Abuse: Overstating*

Harm, Community Responsibility, and the Duty of Repair. Schulman's argument in this book is that those in positions of power often "confu[se] doing nothing, normative conflict, and resistance with actual abuse, [producing] a wide practice of overstating harm." This practice of overstating harm, "overreaction to conflict," or resistance to feedback or concerns being raised, exists alongside "a culture of underreaction to abuse," or normalization of harmful working conditions.[6] With students, I aim to clarify what types of conflict and clash of ideas can enable creativity in the workplace, and what experiences of abuse violate workplace norms and the right to a safe working environment.

But in that class, in 2018, I was gutted by one student's questions about whether or not being berated by her boss, an experience I would characterize as verbal abuse, was ordinary. Her question was whether or not she just needed to get thicker skin to survive and have a career in the creative industries. After class, I followed up privately with this student to learn more about the context of her employment situation and to offer support. This teaching moment came on the heels of the #MeToo movement in 2017, which began as a social media movement and exposed to mainstream consciousness widespread experiences of sexual violence[7] across industries, but in particular in the creative industries, galvanized by but extending far beyond allegations about Hollywood film producer Harvey Weinstein. After several years of investigation, on October 5, 2017, *New York Times* journalists Jodi Kantor and Megan Twohey published an article titled "Weinstein Paid Off Sexual Harassment Accusers for Decades." As the title suggests, this article details Weinstein's longstanding pattern of sexual violence in the workplace with actresses, employees, and film industry workers. In 2015, one former employee wrote an internal memo addressing Weinstein's actions and the accompanying "toxic environment for women at this company."[8] Kantor and Twohey's book, *She Said: Breaking the Sexual Harassment Story That Helped Ignite a Movement* further details their journalistic investigation into the Weinstein case, highlighting the difficult process of encouraging women to speak on record about Weinstein's abuse, both because of the stigmas and penalties associated with speaking up, and because of Weinstein's use of nondisclosure agreements with settlement payments to women whom he sexually harassed, which contained conditions which prevented them from speaking about their experiences. Alongside these silencing settlement payments, *She Said* illuminates a broader culture of knowledge of Weinstein's pattern of abusive behaviour within his company, but a lack of effective intervention to curtail his workplace misconduct.

After 2017, we can note a shift in the normalization of the ordinariness of this abuse, and increased conversation about lack of inclusion in creative industries workplaces. Following Kantor and Twohey's 2017 article, many more women came forward to share their stories of workplace sexual violence from Harvey Weinstein. *USA Today* kept an ongoing tally of these reports, totalling more than 80 women by June 2018.[9] Alongside the proliferation of accounts of sexual violence being committed by Weinstein, many more stories of sexual violence committed by powerful men in the entertainment industries emerged, largely through social media, and the proliferation of the #MeToo hashtag. On October 15, 2017, the phrase "me too," which was coined by Black feminist and social activist Tarana Burke in 2006, was tweeted by actress Alyssa Milano, "If you've been sexually harassed or assaulted write 'me too' as a reply to this tweet," igniting what we now call the #MeToo movement.[10] Though shared experiences were vast, the media story of #MeToo largely surfaced and centred the experiences of white women, in particular Hollywood actresses. Cultural and gender studies scholar Carly Gieseler characterizes the #MeToo phenomenon as the "Weinstein effect climate," which marks a shift in proliferation of accounts of sexual violence alongside increased public credibility given to these accounts, but we can also query how public credibility is ushered in through white women speaking about their experiences of sexual violence.[11]

The viral spread of the #MeToo hashtag in 2017 and the subsequent consciousness raising and discussions of widespread sexual violence was enabled by decades of prior feminist work and organizing, even if feminism and feminist legacies were often not specifically invoked in the #MeToo conversation.[12] Burke coined the "me too" phrase on the social media platform Myspace to spread solidarity amongst survivors of sexual assault. Burke says she developed this phrase after a disquieting experience of having a young teen survivor of sexual assault disclose her experience. Upon reflecting on not knowing what to say in this moment to console this survivor, Burke says she wishes she had the courage to say, "me too." Burke's organizing work is based in what she terms "empowerment empathy", where survivors of sexual assault feel empowered to share their experience, rather than feeling shame or stigma, and instead can empathize, validate, and support each other's experiences.[13] On October 17, 2017, Burke tweeted, "It's beyond a hashtag. It's the start of a larger conversation and a movement for radical community healing. Join us. #metoo."[14] Here Burke underscores community, or collective-based responses, rather than individual ones. This larger conversation about sexual violence is an ongoing one, not only on the topic of consent, but also on the challenges of diversity and inclusion within the creative industries that result in a lack of representation of people from equity-deserving groups, including people of colour, LGBTQ+ people, people with disabilities, and women, and in a lack of safe and inclusive working conditions.

In my class in 2018, I would have liked to tell that student her boss' behaviour was unusual, or that she would never again face a circumstance like that, or that there would always be clear channels to report and have misconduct taken seriously. Here, I want to tell her instead that this kind of behaviour can be ordinary but it should not be, and that everyone should speak up about it when they see it, but the problem is not individuals and whether or not individuals are speaking up—a deeper source of the problem is an industry that often profits from and enables abuse. This classroom experience made me deeply question my role in preparing students for work in the creative industries, and what teaching and training for these industries should look like in the 21st century.

Racism in the Creative Industries

In my teaching practice in classes like "Building Inclusive Spaces and Scenes," later called "Diversity/Creative Industries," I have engaged with students about the challenges of lack of diversity in creative industries, alongside discussions about how to develop more inclusive alternatives. Some of the challenges are systemic and cyclical. For example, in 2015, after all 20 actors nominated for Academy Awards in leading and supporting roles were white, the #OscarsSoWhite hashtag was created by BroadwayBlack.com managing editor April Reign and rapidly circulated.[15] Despite this public conversation, the 2016 Academy Award nomination produced the same outcome, with all-white nominees in all acting categories, again sparking a renewed public conversation, and high-profile Black celebrities boycotting the 2016 Academy Award ceremony, including Spike Lee and Jada Pinkett Smith.[16] In response to this problem, the Academy of Motion Picture Arts and Sciences announced changes to its voting members, seeking to diversify voters and its executive and Board committees, while also limiting appointment terms (instead of lifetime appointments). Despite these changes, in 2020, this conversation about lack of diversity in the Academy Award nominees surfaced again. Commentators noted that only 2 of 20 acting nominees were people of colour, and that no female director was nominated in the Best Director category.[17]

As I write this book through the summer of 2020, with the rise of attention to the Black Lives Matter movement, it has become all the more apparent that attention to fostering equity and inclusion is urgently needed in light of heightened awareness of pervasive systemic racism, discrimination, and inequality in all aspects of society and industry, including in the creative industries. For example, in 2020, *The New York Times* ran a piece titled "Just How White is the Book Industry," finding that 89% of books in their sample from 2018 were published by white people; people working in the publishing industry acquiring and editing books were 85% white.[18] Findings from outside of the United States about race and publishing are similar. In the Canadian context, creative industries and Black visual culture scholar Cheryl Thompson writes, "I believe that the structure of the Canadian publishing industry has a lot to do with the dearth of Black writing about Black people, places, and spaces in Canada. According to a 2018 Canadian Book Publishing Diversity Baseline Survey of 372 anonymous respondents, published by the Association of Canadian Publishers (ACP), which represents 115 Canadian-owned and controlled English-language book publishers, 78 percent of book publishing heads are white, while only 2 percent are Black. Of the nineteen different possible responses to the question of race, 82 percent of respondents identified as white, and only 3 percent identified as Black." Thompson reflects on the broader implication of this underrepresentation of Black people in publishing, including "what stories are understood to be important and what stories are not."[19]

These kinds of critical questions about demographic representation and implications of underrepresentation are increasingly being urgently asked across sectors of the creative industries; questions and conversations about racist and toxic work cultures are also coming to the fore. For example, in 2020, Black employees spoke up about anti-Black racism at feminist-branded digital media company Refinery29. One employee, Ashley C. Ford, characterized a "toxic company culture where white women's egos ruled."[20] Williams' essay "Culture is Ordinary" speaks to the importance of valuing working-class forms of culture; in the 60 years since the publication of this essay, popular culture has largely been accepted as a worthy pastime and area of academic study, but a culture of discrimination, including along the lines of socio-economic status, race, gender, and other structural factors, remains. Discussing the all-too common practice of appropriation of Black culture in music and fashion, Johanna Yaovi, the founder of The Curl Project, defines "blackfishing" as "picking and choosing common black traits and characteristics for one's benefit … while we continue to face discrimination on a day to day basis."[21] Blackfishing occurs when limited and often stereotypical tropes of Blackness become appropriated and commodified in the creative industries, revealing anti-Black racism at play.

Commenting on tensions between hip hop and Canada's music industry for the "Toronto Was Always a Hip-Hop City" episode of the *This is Not a Drake Podcast*, hip hop studies scholar Mark V. Campbell comments that anti-Blackness also manifests in rigid archetypes for Black artists, leading to safe and knowable tropes. He says, "those tropes are not just about a record label archetype. It's really about race, and about how Blackness can be known and commodified and managed." In this podcast, Toronto-based hip hop artist Kardinall Offishall further comments on the failure of the Canadian music industry to celebrate, incubate, support, and champion Black Canadian hip hop artists, despite a wealth of talent and creativity. Commenting on "Black music currently in this country," Offishall says, "the numbers are there as proof. We are a viable commodity. We are something you can sell. We are something that can be successful. So either you're not an astute businessman or you're inherently racist when it comes to Black music in this country."[22] Indeed, anti-Black racism produces this failure to support emerging Black artists, even as these artists become profitable and change the music industry. These accounts of lack of diversity, anti-Black racism, appropriation, and sexual violence suggest the urgent need for transformation in creative industries. In Chapter 2, I question an overarching and narrow focus on economic values in the creative industries, but questions of economics—who and what is seen as profitable, and who is extracted from—are also shaped by structural factors, including race. In *Reimagining the Creative Industries*, I explore more inclusive working practices for the creative industries, and gather learnings from already-existing alternatives to dominant patterns of exploitation and inequity.

Community and Wellbeing

My final opening anecdote about the disquieting nature of the ordinary or the everyday in this Introduction comes from Fall 2018. At the time, I was in this last phase of a research project called "Community Youth Arts Programs as Creative Industries Incubators," which I will discuss more fully in Chapter 5 of this book. In this last phase of the research project, my research team was running a program with research participants, co-creating an art exhibit to take place at Ryerson University. We were several weeks into this program when one afternoon I got a call from one of my research assistants telling me that someone who had been a participant in a previous phase of the research project had died by suicide, and that participants from our current program would likely not be attending that evening, as they knew and had deep ties with this person, as did my research assistant from an extended period of participant observation. I had gone into that research project seeking to assess how community youth arts program incubate creative careers. Community youth arts programs can and do scaffold economic self-advancement for young people, but they are also spaces of healing, becoming, exploring, sharing, and learning in ways that transcend the economic.

Creative industries frameworks that privilege economic advancement lack the means to capture these important values, and I have sought to have these personal, social, and cultural values register within a creative industries framework. While community arts can enable wellbeing, there are also limits to the capacity of the arts in this regard, and limits to research to be able to assess or intervene into systemic issues. That afternoon, when I got that call and in the weeks that followed, I fumbled with how to run my research program, how to meaningfully address this loss, and how to engage with the research participants who were affected. In this book I suggest a rearticulation of social, economic, and cultural values for the creative industries, but this rearticulation must exist in a larger framework that is aware of structural realities and barriers that culture and creativity cannot remedy. I am opening this Introduction by noting ordinary moments in my life—going to music shows, teaching, running research projects—that made me feel quite out of my depth, as a community member, as a teacher, as a researcher, as I think this is actually a good place to start the work of reimagining. With this feeling I am thinking and rethinking how to be in and do my work. I have deep investment in the creative industries, as a fan, teacher, and researcher—music, film, television, books, art, theatre, dance, and so many other interdisciplinary emerging creative activities have shaped so much of who I am, how I see the world, the teaching I do, and the research and writing I undertake. Here, I am also trying to think through and reimagine what that creative industries are and what they could be. This book follows from this urge.

So, how did we get here?

Background on the Research of This Book

Contemporary work in the creative industries is rife with contradictions: seemingly both a source of economic growth while also driving growing economic inequality, seemingly open and talent-led while perpetuating if not worsening patterns of social exclusion.[23] While these labour patterns in the creative industries have been well documented, and young people are aware of these challenges, youth still increasingly seek to work in these fields. These contradictions of creative labour suggest the need for new conceptual models beyond a creative economy model, which has celebrated the creative industries as a source of economic growth that is purportedly inclusive and socially cohesive. Issues of sexual violence, lack of diversity, precarious, low-paid, and unpaid work, especially at the entry-level, call into question these celebratory accounts of the creative sector. Much of my research agenda has attended to the labour dynamics in the creative industries, as a growing area of employment that is increasingly sought out. Working primary qualitatively, in my research I have profiled entry-level creative labour through the lens of youth cultural production. Using ethnographic methods based in oral history and life story methodologies, in addition to community participatory action research, my research has found that young people spend substantial amounts of time in community-oriented ways, working to redress structural problems, exclusion, and inequity, often alongside multiple jobs to pay the bills.

Defining Creative Industries, Youth Creative Work, and Emergence

In order to register these community-oriented values and pursuits, I operate from expansive definitions of creative practice and of labour. Through this Introduction and in Chapter 1, I query and probe how this term "creative industries" has been defined, but these industries are largely known to create products with cultural, expressive, and symbolic values. Many scholars in the field use the term "cultural industries" to retain both the cultural and the collective basis of these industries, as these industries have opened up to include anything and everything that might be deemed "creative."[24] While I am cognizant of the potential dangers of the dilution of "cultural" to "creative" industries, my research has employed the term "creative industries" to signal expanded forms of creative practice undertaken by youth and emerging cultural producers. Nonetheless, as detailed below, my use of care ethics as a theoretical framework for the creative industries similarly underscores a collective, relational underpinning for the term "creative industries."[25] I am aware that there is slippage between the terms cultural and creative industries and they are not necessarily always the same thing; nonetheless, I use the term creative industries but draw on literature from the field of cultural industries (amongst other fields). Despite the challenges of nomenclature, I see my work as still embedded within this field of cultural industries (or critical creative industries studies), and I aim to expand hegemonic definitions of art and culture as well as a primary focus on economic output for the creative "industries." For example, in my "Young People Making a Living in the Creative Industries" research project, I outlined an expansive definition of creative pursuits: music, performance, visual arts, fashion, design, writing and publishing, film, photography, or new and/or interdisciplinary forms of creative work, either through self-employment or working for a creative industries company. I solicited participants who may not pursue their creative projects on a full-time paid basis, given that contemporary economic realities mean needing to sometimes pursue several lines of paid work alongside developing a creative industries career.[26]

For many young people, choosing to work in the creative industries means an expansion of how entrepreneurship is defined, and what and who it looks like, given that entrepreneurship is still normatively perceived as the provenance of white men. For youth and emerging cultural producers, entrepreneurial capacity does not only include business acumen, but also includes a range of soft skills, such as collaboration, listening and amplifying the voices of others, improvising, innovating, taking initiative, mutual support, and collective action, and many young people are providing support to one another to gain these types of skills and experience. These soft skills suggest an expansion of entrepreneurship, alongside an expansion of what an "industry" is in the creative industries. In my research, I have also used an expansive definition of youth, aged 18 to 35, understanding youth as an extended period of transition in the life course, and I have chronicled the contemporary fluctuating economic and social conditions that give rise to the extension of this youth period.[27] In *Reimagining the Creative Industries*, I dive less into youth as a demographic category than in my previous work, and instead foreground these conditions of flux, transition, and emergence that give rise to an extension of youth, and investigate what the creative industries might look like through this lens, of cultural production from the margins. Conversations about the problems of age-based demographics to define the category of emerging artists are also happening in the creative industries. For example, in 2021, the Writers' Trust of Canada removed their age cap of 35 years for their award for emerging writers, responding to an open letter criticizing the "inequitable" eligibility of this award due to barriers for BIPOC, 2SLGBTQIA+, disability, immigrant, and other marginalized communities and women to "participating fully in the literary community."[28] I am also increasingly wary of age-based demographics, and instead of discussing the social and economic constraints that underly this demographication, I highlight the category of emergence here.[29]

For social justice facilitator and author adrienne maree brown, "emergence is the way complex systems and patterns arise out of relatively simple interactions."[30] In order to appraise emergence, we attune our attention to the relatively simple or mundane in the search for new patterns or systems; emergence is what is arising. Similarly, for art theorist Natalie Loveless, emergence is an approach that is "rooted in process, multiplicity, context specificity, and contingency."[31] Building her discussion of emergence, Loveless draws on Donna Haraway, who in her book *The Companion Species Manifesto,* comments, "situated emergence of more livable worlds depends on that differential sensibility."[32] In this light, I define youth creative work here less in a demographic, aged-based bracket, and more in "that differential sensibility" of emergence. In this book, I locate this "differential sensibility" of youth creative work in the social realm, involving reflexivity on people and processes, including autonomy, access, and balance in cultural production, with emphasis on diversity, equity, and inclusion.

Locating Myself

My research is also informed by my context, including my social and geographic location. I am Canadian, a cisgender straight middle-class white woman and mother; I spent a lot of time working and living in Montreal, and now live in Toronto. In Montreal in particular, I was embedded in a community of artists and cultural producers; in Toronto some of my involvement with creative communities has developed through my role on the Board of Directors at Whippersnapper Gallery, an artist run-centre focused on supporting under-represented emerging artists, and through my various research projects, discussed in this book. My Canadian context of the creative industries means that I am from a country where cultural policy provides grants and subsidies for arts and culture; however; many of my youth research participants have voiced alienation, marginalization, and exclusion from mainstream granting structures and institutional arts education contexts. While Canada on the whole and our arts infrastructure in particular is sometimes favourably compared to the United States, I caution against any facile celebration of our national context, or our national commitment to arts and culture.[33] In Toronto, our official city motto is "diversity is our strength," though as will be discussed in Chapter 3, the use of diversity discourse often obfuscates underlying realities of racism and inequality. Nonetheless, Toronto is one of, if not the most multicultural city in the world, depending on how forms of diversity are measured. In 2016, 46% of Toronto's population was classified as immigrants and 50% of the city's racial composition was non-white.[34] Also in 2016, *BBC Radio* named Toronto the most diverse city in the world, with the greatest number of different nationalities represented (230).[35]

Writing this book through the summer of 2020 and through the lockdowns of COVID-19 changed my plans for international case studies for this book due to the impossibility of international travel. Instead, I have further situated myself in my local context, one of the most international cities in the world, and have mobilized an intersectional approach, centring the margins, and spotlighting underrepresented forms of cultural production. With this methodology, I suggest that the work that I am presenting here is illustrative of emerging trends in communities of care through youth creative work, without being representative of all youth in the creative industries. The particular working practices and organizational cultures of the youth and grassroots collective profiled here may change over time or respond to new issues and challenges that arise; as discussed in Chapter 2, a care ethics framework suggests ongoing reflexivity rather than a one-size-fits-all or universal, unchanging model. In many cases, when I profile or spotlight particular youth projects or collectives in this book, these research participants have agreed to publish their names and the names of their projects, as these projects are public-facing. In other cases, in some chapters in this book, when I have done larger scale research projects about experiences working with particular organizations, research participants have opted for pseudonyms or have been anonymized. In presenting these experiences in this book, I have chosen to follow the particular circumstances of the original interviews (presenting participants either with their names or anonymized), rather than opting for consistency across the board, with this aim of being illustrative rather than being representative.

As such, I write from where I am, who I am, and the research I have done, informed by an ethics of care, as will be discussed in Chapter 2. I suggest the process of locating myself strives for specificity through relationality, rather than attempting to be all-encompassing or universal. It is my hope to see emerging researchers similarly work from their own contexts, under the mantle of rearticulated forms of social, economic, and cultural value for the creative industries, to expand what the "creative industries" means and looks like, drawing attention to important forms of emerging creative practice in local contexts. With a sole focus on economic or industry values for the creative industries, we miss diverse forms of cultural production and further reify a narrow, exclusionary view of what this field is. I desire this expanded, more vibrant, more inclusive, and more creative vision of the creative industries for myself to inhabit, too, as a fan, teacher, and researcher. Discussing limited models for conceptualizing the cultural/creative industries, cultural industries scholar Mark Banks suggests, "properly understood—and socially supported—cultural industries are not merely industries, but forms of social practice that can challenge accepted orthodoxies and provide the conceptual resources for creating images of alternative possible worlds—'dream factories' in the broadest possible sense."[36] Below, I investigate how pedagogy can be an inroad to understanding social practice in the creative industries, including forms of imagining and dreaming alternatives. In *Reimagining the Creative Industries*, I understand pedagogy expansively, not specifically tied to classroom instruction or didactic forms of depositing knowledge. Rather, I understand teaching and learning as ongoing and relational processes in many contexts, angling towards humanization, and forward pedagogy as a connector of rearticulated values in a creative industries context. This book follows the thread of the pedagogical through youth/emerging forms of creative work that open expansive pedagogical spaces for teaching and learning through relationality, which fosters inclusive cultures.

Imagining Alternatives through Pedagogy and Care

Much research in the creative industries stems from a political economy approach, documenting vertical and horizontal integration and other conglomerations of power, prestige, and profit in these industries that give rise to the systemic social inequality noted above. In my research, I forward a creative ecology framework for the creative industries, providing the conceptual means to make bridges across sectors (economy, culture, social life); to highlight the instrumental and the intrinsic values of culture; to map the relationships and tensions between sectors of the creative economy (large vs. small; established vs. emerging); and to register the lived experiences and embodied processes of engaging with culture.[37] Creative industries scholars Jonathan Gross and Nick Wilson suggest that an "ecological" approach to the creative industries examines the interdependencies between cultural resources and reveals key political questions like who stewards these resources, with what values and to what aims.[38] The focus on creative industries as an ecosystem offers avenues to investigate access and equity in cultural participation and cultural production, alongside questions about the experience of working in this sector. Through my ecological approach, I suggest a rubric of *decoupling* an instrumentalized economic growth imperative from cultural production; *recuperating* cultural and social value; and *rearticulating* the relations between economic, social, and cultural value within a creative ecology framework.

Articulating his concept of creative justice, Banks moves past the so-called "business case" for diversity, which suggests that more diverse products reach a more diverse audience and increases revenues, and instead forwards an argument about access to economic resourcing, cultural expression and recognition, and political participation. Banks suggests a lack of equal opportunity to cultural work "creates a broader democratic deficit, since the range of voices and perspectives that circulate in the cultural arena is diminished," which is detrimental to society.[39] Investigating the question of "why do the cultural industries matter?", cultural industries scholar David Hesmondhalgh asserts that "the cultural industries are involved in the making and circulating of products that, more than the products of any other kind of industry, have an influence on our understanding and knowledge of the world."[40] Diversity, equity, and inclusion matter in all sectors of work, and are even more pressing in the cultural/creative industries, which are industries that circulate meaning and views of the world, alongside developing new labour patterns and modes of working. Hesmondhalgh sketches an overview of media studies scholars' debates about the nature and extent of this influence, but concludes "there can be no doubt, the media do have an influence."[41] At the far end of this influence spectrum, the communicative capacities of the creative industries are propagandistic or didactic, and it is true that there are cultural works that are intended to convince or to instruct. Rather than resort to a simplistic or causal argument about the impact of the cultural industries, Hesmondhalgh conceptualizes a view of the cultural industries and the texts they produce as "complex, ambivalent, and contested."[42] This complexity of creative industries products is pedagogical: enabling teaching and learning in ambivalent and contested ways that go beyond the didactic.

Moments of Rupture

For Cree scholar, artist, and writer Karyn Recollet, moments of rupture can be generative and pedagogical. Speaking at the "When the World is Ending… Strategies and Practices of Care within Indigenous Futurist Research and Pedagogies" roundtable event in 2021, Recollet highlights the historical context of dislocation of Indigenous peoples, including the Sixties Scoop and residential schools in Canada, commenting that rupture can also enable alternatives focused towards decolonization. The description for this event queries how apocalypse is normatively presented: "an apocalypse is usually defined as an ending, a final destruction. Yet the word itself suggests a very particular point of view. If the apocalypse means the end of capitalism, the demise of nation-state sovereignty, and the collapse of colonial law, then we need to ask, apocalypse for whom?" Recollet comments that "apocalyptical narratives devalue and don't highlight the process of care and mutual aid and support that communities are practicing in these particular moments in time." She foregrounds the kinds of sociality, community organizing, gathering, relationality, and survivance that are emergent through these moments. Drawing on religious studies and African American and African Studies scholar Ashon Crawley's concept of "otherwise movements,"[43] Recollet forwards the concept of "architecture otherwise," asking, "what kinds of architectures of being together and hosting each other and thinking about how to be in good relation, what are these architectures otherwise?"[44] Through this book, I trace care as "architecture otherwise," a pedagogical and expansive space for reimagining the creative industries, given the rupture of our times.

Discussing and trying to make sense of new forms of social organization that emerged through the Greek economic crisis of 2008, urban studies and degrowth scholar Angelos Varvarousis foregrounds the philosophy of Serge Latouche, who suggests that new ways of thinking, being, and relating to others can emerge from the "pedagogy of disasters," or the learning experience of living through moments of crisis. Varvarousis outlines that "crisis opens up a stage of suspension—a liminal stage—in which experimentation with new personal and collective experiences can transform the destabilization of the social imaginary."[45] Emphasizing the "social" aspects of the social imaginary, Varvarousis draws on Cornelius Castoriadis' articulation of this concept, which Varvarousis emphasizes is "the shared collective imagination distilled in specific institutions, which operates as the 'glue' that holds a society together by being a representation of it."[46] As discussed above, the creative industries can operate as a pedagogical vehicle for this "glue," the social imaginary. Though Varvarousis' work is situated in the specific context of the Greek economic crisis of 2008, many 21st century moments internationally have given rise to the pedagogy of disaster: the 2008–2009 financial collapse, rising unemployment rates, in particular global youth unemployment, climate crisis, COVID-19, heightened awareness of systemic racism and the resurgence of attention to the Black Lives Matters movement, and so on. Varvarousis' framework invites us to consider how crisis can open alternative ways of imagining society, pedagogically.

For Varvarousis, crisis may open up new possibilities, but this is "not a linear and gradual process. On the contrary, it involves ruptures, asymmetries, accelerations and moments of stagnation and reversal." In *Reimagining the Creative Industries*, I turn to emergent youth creative workers and collectives to illuminate what these pathways of possibility can look like. I profile this search for expansion, where social change may be non-linear or gradual. I document some of this movement, where the pedagogical enacts an opening for more space for care, understanding that this movement might be small, partial, or asymmetrical. As much as individuals, collectives, or societies might not be able to smoothly enact personal or social change, the movement is important, and in this book, I note a shifting social imaginary, in particular around reflexivity on diversity, equity, and inclusion in the creative industries. I locate the pedagogical not only in moments of crisis and in the teachings of these crises, but also in the response to these crises. These responses are also pedagogical, in that they open up possibilities while working to develop new social imaginaries. However, the pedagogical does not only need to be ushered in through disaster or crisis. In his book *Pedagogy of Hope*, educational theorist Paulo Freire seeks to restore the value of hope in times of struggle as a necessary component of striving toward improved realities, asserting that "hope is an ontological need" which "demands an anchoring in practice."[47] Through this book, I examine this anchoring in practice, through profiles of youth collectives, spaces, and organizations, revealing a shifting social imaginary through developing more caring forms of social relations in and through creative work.

Hope and Imagination

Care and hope can be modes of imagining alternatives to neoliberal competition and self-interest. These impulses are social concerns, and are part of developing a new social imaginary. In *Freedom Dreams: The Black Radical Imagination*, professor of history and Africana studies scholar Robin D.G. Kelley seeks to recuperate the power of the imagination in striving for social change, centring Black experience and examining these questions of imagination from the perspective of marginalized and underrepresented communities. He writes, "there are very few contemporary political spaces where the energies of love and imagination are understood and respected as powerful social forces," but "the map to a new world is in the imagination." Naming what "imagining a different future" might look like, Kelley invokes "new social relationships, new ways of living and interacting, new attitudes toward work and leisure and community."[48] A profoundly unequal and racist historical context means that the social fabric has been discriminatory; Kelley centres Black imagination as a mode of developing a better future.

Freire describes this work of dreaming the future as the pedagogical work of "humanization," teaching and learning towards liberation and fully realized human selves. He writes:

> the dream of humanization, whose concretization is always a process, and always a becoming, passes by way of breach with the real, concrete economic, political, social, ideological, and so on, order, moorings that are condemning us to dehumanization. Thus the dream is a demand or condition that becomes ongoing in the history that we make and that makes and remakes us.[49]

As Freire notes, economic, political, social, and ideological contexts shape the social imaginary, but this process is dynamic, not static, and it is not linear, as history is ongoingly shaped through the process and the dream of humanization. In this dynamic, the creative industries can have a key role to play, as these industries both reflect these contexts, and further shape the social imaginary. Exploring the capacity to imagine alternatives to the harmful status quo, adrienne maree brown identifies the power of art to shape perceptions of acceptable or unacceptable ways to live: "art is not neutral. It either disrupts or upholds the status quo, advancing or regressing justice. We are living now inside the imagination of people who thought economic disparity and environmental destruction were acceptable costs for their power. It is our right and responsibility to write ourselves into the future."[50] To this end, brown calls for collaborative ideation, and dreaming a collective future. She acknowledges that the capacity for radical imagination—the capacity for imagining differently—is shaped and limited by lived experience, naming collective trauma and colonization as factors that can reduce the scope of imagining what is possible. Nonetheless, brown asserts imagination is a muscle to be exercised, collaboratively:

> Right now we are living inside the results of other peoples' imaginations—people who couldn't imagine Black people being free, fat girls being sexy, disabled people being leaders. People who could only imagine their own power and dominance. When more people imagine together, and then step from imagining into thinking through the structures and protocols of a society together, then more needs get attended to.[51]

In *Reimagining the Creative Industries*, I explore some youth-led examples of collaborative creative imagining of alternative visions of what the creative industries could look like, that centre care and relationality while striving towards more inclusive cultures.

Outline of the Book

Above all, this book demonstrates an argument in favour of an interdisciplinary approach to creative industries scholarship, as I seek to recuperate and rearticulate economic and non-economic forms of value in the creative industries context. Communication and media studies scholar Eleonora Belfiore provides an overview of "renewed interest in articulating the non-economic value of culture and advocating for more 'holistic' approaches," in light of economic value "overshadow[ing] other forms of value—cultural, social, aesthetic," in particular in policy discussions in relation to creative industries contexts. Belfiore notes that "cultural economists have been themselves at the forefront of resistance to the excessive predominance of economistic notions of value within cultural policy debates."[52] In addition to echoing this need for more holistic approaches to value beyond the economic for the creative industries, in this book I map alternatives. Discussing small-scale and craft-based forms of cultural production, cultural and creative industries scholar Susan Luckman asserts that "models for reimagining capitalism in an age of climate crisis exist; the challenge now is their accessible mainstreaming into the broader social and economic landscape."[53] Despite the now well-documented shortcomings in creative industries working environments, there is a gap in the research literature concerning models of inclusive cultures for reimagining the creative industries. Following Luckman, I suggest that models for reimagining the creative industries do exist, but empirical knowledge about their characteristics is lacking, and this lack of knowledge presents challenges for mainstreaming these models to the broader landscape. In this book, I turn to guidance from theorists outside of the discipline of "creative industries" alongside practice-led examples from my research and research participants, to explore what alternative and more caring visions for creative work can look like.

In Chapter 1, "Creative Industries as Discourse: Changing the Frame," I investigate where this narrow and economic vision for the creative industries came from, examining policy and academic framings of the creative industries as a discourse. I discuss cultural mapping methodology as an alternative to creative industries mapping, which has narrowed in on economic values. In contrast, cultural mapping can inventory community characteristics and values. In Chapter 2, "Care Ethics for the Creative Industries," I explore the framework of feminist care ethics, identifying a typology of care thinking that involves relationality, recognizing structural barriers, and committing to transformative action for a more caring society. I explore care thinking in my investigation of modes of youth creative work, highlighting the characteristics of autonomy, access, and balance. I forward these characteristics as a more expansive and more inclusive vision of the creative industries, in opposition to the narrower, economically-driven proliferation of creative industries discourse. In Chapter 3, "The 'Diversity' Response," I draw on and extend Sara Ahmed's work on diversity discourses in a creative industries context, contrasting how large creative industries corporations pay lip-service to a sanitized facade of diversity with the ongoing work of fostering inclusion. I examine the genre of the "diversity report" from large, "top six" creative industries companies while analyzing how "diversity" gets used as a response to moments of crisis in the creative industries. I explore an alternative genre emerging from not-for-profit organizations, foundations, research labs, and unions that I term the "inclusion action plan", which is more carefully committed to the process of naming problems in creative industries workplaces, defining them, and developing strategies to move forward and take action to remediate these problems.

In Chapter 4, "From Margins to Centre: Building Inclusion through Pedagogical Encounter," I continue to document this work of fostering inclusive working practices through the lens of centring marginalized voices, and foreground Black intellectual thought, including Stuart Hall and bell hooks' discussions of margins and centre. In these discussions, I also underscore the concept of pedagogy, highlighting critical pedagogy scholarship by Paulo Freire and bell hooks alongside design justice and disability justice scholarship from theorists including Sasha Costanza-Chock and Leah Lakshmi Piepzna-Samarasinha. I explore the work of fostering inclusion and centring difference in the creative industries through profiles of the PEERS program, a peer-led support program to incubate marginalized and underrepresented artists, without an emphasis on output or producing, and the Dandelion Initiative, an organization that aims to combat sexual violence and create safer cultures, including in the nightlife, entertainment, and arts industries. In Chapter 5, "Youth Creative Work and Community Arts," I turn to the community youth arts sector and the work of this sector in supporting marginalized youth. I sketch on overview of goals, purposes, and definitions of "community arts," and identify different models of working with youth in this sector, identifying the *youth engagement* model and the *social justice* model, ultimately proposing the *incubator* model. From my case study of three community youth arts programs, I identify best practices and challenges in scaffolding youth creative careers through the community arts, including anti-oppressive practice; employing and funding emerging artists to support their skill and goal development; fostering relationships; and attention to pedagogical practice.

In Chapter 6, "Collaborative Production, Communities of Practice, and Communities of Care," I examine the possibilities and limitations of Étienne Wenger's concept of communities of practice (CoP) to foster community engagement through his identified CoP characteristics of joint enterprise, mutual engagement, and shared repertoire. Discussing limits of access to CoPs and problems of exclusion through the lens of women in music, I profile Rock Camp Montreal (RCFG*) as a community of care, as an alternative to the concept of a CoP. I discuss RCFG*'s strategies for widening access to participation through collaboration in music making. In Chapter 7, "Inclusive Spaces for Small-Scale Cultural Production," I continue this exploration of supportive and inclusive conditions for incubating marginalized forms of cultural production, spotlighting the role of physical space. Here, I draw on Edward Soja's concept of "third space" and Hannah Arendt's concept of the "space of appearance," in order to explore and extend the understanding of how "safe space" functions. I investigate advocacy models for creating and preserving space for artists from Acme Studios in the U.K. Finally, in the concluding chapter, "Towards a Collaborative Future," I end by highlighting the deep and ongoing challenges of diversity, equity, and inclusion in the creative industries, and the need for alternative, collaborative models to imagine a better future. I conclude with a profile of Tea Base collective in Toronto, Canada, which is creating a community of care through and beyond its physical space. Writing this book, I am galvanized by this collection of theorists and collectives, and I hope readers are as well. This is the vision of the creative industries that I want to partake in as fan, a teacher, and a researcher—vibrant, fresh, joyful, engaging, cutting edge, thought provoking, stimulating, and just fun. I look forward to your examples of what the creative industries looks like from a care ethics perspective.

Notes

1 Paige St. John, Jack Dolan, Phil Willon, and Anna M. Phillips, "Before Deadly Oakland Fire, Ghost Ship Warehouse Was Scene of Legal Sparring and Tenant Drama," *Los Angeles Times*, December 5, 2016, accessed January 4, 2016, https://www.latimes.com/local/lanow/la-me-oakland-fire-probe-20161205-story.html

2 ABC News, "President Obama Releases Statement on Oakland Ghost Ship Warehouse Fire," December 5, 2016, accessed January 4, 2016, https://abc7news.com/president-obama-statement-on-oakland-fire-ghost-ship-in-white-house/1640551/

3 Raymond Williams, "Culture Is Ordinary," in *The Everyday Life Reader*, ed. Ben Highmore (New York: Routledge, 2001), 91–100, 92.

4 Kate Oakley, Mark Ball, and Malaika Cunningham, *Everyday Culture and the Good Life* (CUSP Working Paper Series No 9) (Guildford: Centre for the Understanding of Sustainable Prosperity, 2018), https://www.cusp.ac.uk/wp-content/uploads/WP09-Everyday-Culture-and-the-good-life.pdf

5 Williams, "Culture Is Ordinary," 93.

6 Sarah Schulman, *Conflict Is Not Abuse: Overstating Harm, Community Responsibility, and the Duty of Repair* (Vancouver: Arsenal Pulp Press, 2016), 21.

7 Following the grassroots advocacy group, #AfterMeToo, I use the broad, non-legal term sexual violence to cover both sexual harassment (unwanted sexualization or sexual comments) and sexual assault (unwanted sexual touching or sexual activity) in this book. For more information on terminology, see *AfterMeToo Report*, available at https://a085d11e-6d13-4974-83f0-d75131b04e1c.filesusr.com/ugd/1766c7_398ee90fdbb047af951203f20a5f3db3.pdf

8 Jodi Kantor and Megan Twohey, "Harvey Weinstein Paid Off Sexual Harassment Accusers for Decades," *The New York Times*, October 5, 2017, accessed April 20, 2021, https://www.nytimes.com/2017/10/05/us/harvey-weinstein-harassment-allegations.html
9 Sara Moniuszko and Cara Kelly, "Harvey Weinstein Scandal: A Complete List of the 87 Accusers," *USA Today.com*, updated Jun 1, 2018, accessed October 26, 2020, https://www.usatoday.com/story/life/people/2017/10/27/weinstein-scandal-complete-list-accusers/804663001/
10 Alyssa Milano, Twitter post, October 15, 2017, https://twitter.com/alyssa_milano/status/919659438700670976?lang=en
11 Carly Gieseler, *The Voice of #MeToo: From Grassroots Activism to a Viral Roar* (Lanham, MD: Rowman & Littlefield, 2019), 18.
12 Milena Popova, *Sexual Consent* (Cambridge, MA: MIT Press, 2019), 170.
13 "Tarana Burke," *me too*, accessed October 26, 2020, https://metoomvmt.org/get-to-know-us/tarana-burke-founder/
14 Tarana Burke, Twitter post, October 17, 2017, https://twitter.com/taranaburke/status/919704949751255040?lang=en
15 Erica Vella, "Meet the Woman Behind 'OscarsSoWhite Hashtag'," *Global News*, February 24, 2016, accessed April 9, 2021, https://globalnews.ca/news/2537616/meet-the-woman-behind-oscarssowhite-hashtag/
16 Brandon Griggs, "Jada Pinkett Smith, Spike Lee to Boycott Oscars Ceremony," *CNN*, January 19, 2016, accessed April 9, 2021, https://www.cnn.com/2016/01/18/entertainment/oscars-boycott-spike-lee-jada-pinkett-smith-feat
17 Emily VanDerWerff, "The Lack of Diversity Among the 2020 Oscar Nominees Feels Disappointingly Familiar," *Vox*, January 13, 2020, accessed April 9, 2021, https://www.vox.com/culture/2020/1/13/21063505/oscars-2020-nominations-nominees-so-white-oscarssowhite-diversity-greta-gerwig
18 Richard Jean So and Gus Wezerek, "Just How White Is the Book Industry," *The New York Times*, December 11, 2020, accessed March 15, 2021, https://www.nytimes.com/interactive/2020/12/11/opinion/culture/diversity-publishing-industry.html
19 Cheryl Thompson, "On Fighting for Space in the Literary World as a Black Canadian Writer," *Literary Hub*, March 22, 2021, accessed April 20, 2021, https://lithub.com/on-fighting-for-space-in-the-literary-world-as-a-black-canadian-writer/
20 Kerry Flynn, "Refinery29 Is Reeling from Claims of Racism and Toxic Work Culture. Employees Say It's Even Worse Behind the Scenes," *CNN Business*, June 11, 2020, accessed March 15, 2021, https://www.cnn.com/2020/06/11/media/refinery29-workplace-culture/index.html
21 Priya Elan, "Blackfishing: 'Black Is Cool, Unless You're Actually Black,'" *The Guardian*, April 14, 2020, accessed March 15, 2021, https://www.theguardian.com/fashion/2020/apr/14/blackfishing-black-is-cool-unless-youre-actually-black
22 CBC Radio podcasts, "Episode 1: Toronto Was Always a Hip-Hop City," *This is Not a Drake Podcast*, July 7, 2020, https://www.cbc.ca/listen/cbc-podcasts/423-this-is-not-a-drake-podcast/episode/15782312-ep-1-toronto-was-always-a-hip-hop-city
23 For discussion of this point, see for example Mark Banks, *Creative Justice: Cultural Industries, Work and Inequality* (London, UK: Rowman & Littlefield International, 2017); Bridget Conor, Rosalind Gill, and Stephanie Taylor, eds., *Gender and Creative labour, Sociological Review Monograph Series* (London, UK: Wiley-Blackwell, 2015); David Hesmondhalgh and Sarah Baker, *Creative Labour: Media Work in Three Cultural Industries* (London, UK: Routledge, 2011); Anamik Saha, *Race and the Cultural Industries* (Cambridge, UK: Polity Press, 2018).
24 On this point, see for example Kate Oakley and Justin O'Connor, "The Cultural Industries: An Introduction," in *The Routledge Companion to the Cultural Industries* (London: Routledge, 2011).

25 I discuss this distinction between cultural and creative industries at greater length in my previous work. For further discussion, see "Defining the Cultural / Creative Industries" in my book *Out of the Basement: Youth Cultural Production in Practice and in Policy* (Montreal: McGill Queen's University Press, 2013).

26 Miranda Campbell, "'Shit Is Hard, Yo': Young People Making a Living in the Creative Industries," *International Journal of Cultural Policy* 26, no. 4 (2020): 524–543.

27 For a further discussion of these conditions resulting in the extension of youth, see my article, "Downward Mobility and the Individualization of Youth Struggle: *Girls* as Public Pedagogy," *Jeunesse: Young People, Texts, Cultures* 8, no. 1 (2016): 180–201.

28 K.J. Aiello, "The Writers' Trust of Canada Removes 'Discriminatory' Age Cap on Prestigious RBC Bronwen Wallace Award for Emerging Writers," *The Globe and Mail*, January 22, 2021, accessed January 28, 2021, https://www.theglobeandmail.com/arts/books/article-the-writers-trust-of-canada-removes-discriminatory-age-cap-on/

29 For a discussion of the "demographication" of youth unemployment, or the bulging category of "youth" that does not contextualize other structural factors that impact youth experience, see Ross Fergusson and Nicola Yeates, "Business, as Usual: The Policy Priorities of the World Bank's Discourses on Youth Unemployment, and the Global Financial Crisis," *Journal of International and Comparative Social Policy* 29, no. 1 (2013): 64–78.

30 adrienne maree brown, "Additional Resources for Facing Coronavirus / COVID-19," March 10, 2020, accessed January 5, 2020, http://adriennemareebrown.net/tag/grace-lee-boggs/

31 Natalie Loveless, *How to Make Art at the End of the World: A Manifesto for Research Creation* (Durham, NC: Duke University Press, 2019), 25.

32 Cited in Loveless, Ibid.

33 For a history of Canadian cultural policy, see "Federal Cultural Policy in Canada: Past, Present, Future" in my book *Out of the Basement*. My current focus here is not to trace the impact of cultural policy on cultural production; instead, my focus is to situate myself and the context of my work.

34 Statistics Canada. *Focus on Geography Series, 2016 Census*. Statistics Canada Catalogue no. 98-404-X2016001. Data products, 2016 Census (Ottawa: Statistics Canada, 2017), https://www12.statcan.gc.ca/census-recensement/2016/as-sa/fogs-spg/Facts-cma-eng.cfm?LANG=Eng&GK=CMA&GC=535&TOPIC=7

35 BBC Radio, "The World's Most Diverse City," *More or Less*, May 13, 2016, https://www.bbc.co.uk/programmes/p03v1r1p

36 Mark Banks, "Creative Economies of Tomorrow? Limits to Growth and the Uncertain Future," *Cultural Trends* 2, no. 5 (2018): 367–380.

37 For further discussion and use of the term creative / cultural ecology, see for example Mirjam Gollmitzer and Catherine Murray, *From Economy to Ecology: A Policy Framework for Creative Labour* (Ottawa: Canadian Conference of the Arts, 2008); Kate Oakley, "The Disappearing Arts: Creativity and Innovation After the Creative Industries," *International Journal of Cultural Policy* 15, no. 4 (2009): 403–414; David Throsby, *Economics and Culture* (Cambridge, UK: Cambridge University Press, 2001).

38 Jonathan Gross and Nick Wilson, "Cultural Democracy: An Ecological and Capabilities Approach," *International Journal of Cultural Policy* 26, no. 3 (2020): 328–343, 7.

39 Banks, *Creative Justice*, 3.

40 David Hesmondhalgh, *The Cultural Industries*, 4th ed. (London: Sage, 2019), 7.

41 Ibid.

42 Ibid., 8.

43 Ashon Crawley, "Otherwise Movements," *The New Inquiry*, January 19, 2015, accessed March 15, 2021, https://thenewinquiry.com/otherwise-movements/

44 UBC Learning Circle, ""When the World is Ending… Strategies and Practices of Care within Indigenous Futurist Research and Pedagogies," February 21, 2021, available at https://learningcircle.ubc.ca/2021/01/13/when-the-world-is-ending/
45 Angelos Varvarousis, "Crisis, Liminality and the Decolonization of the Social Imaginary," *Environment and Planning E: Nature and Space* 2, no. 3 (2019): 493–512, 500. For further discussion of the term "social imaginary," see for example Charles Taylor, *A Secular Age* (Cambridge, MA: Harvard University Press, 2007); Benedict Anderson, *Imagined Communities: Reflections on the Origin and Spread of Nationalism* (London: Verso, 1983).
46 Ibid., 499.
47 Paulo Freire, *Pedagogy of Hope: Reliving Pedagogy of the Oppressed*, trans. Robert R. Barr (London: Bloomsbury Academic, 1992), 2.
48 Robin D. G. Kelley, *Freedom Dreams: The Black Radical Imagination* (Boston, MA: Beacon Books, 2002), 2, 5.
49 Freire, *Pedagogy of Hope*, 2, 89.
50 adrienne maree brown, *Emergent Strategy: Shaping Change, Changing Worlds* (Chico, CA: AK Press, 2017), 123.
51 Ibid., 151.
52 Eleonora Belfiore, "Whose Cultural Value? Representation, Power and Creative Industries," *International Journal of Cultural Policy* 26, no. 3 (2018): 383–397, 383.
53 Susan Luckman, "Craft Entrepreneurialism and Sustainable Scale: Resistance to and Disavowal of the Creative Industries as Champions of Capitalist Growth," *Cultural Trends* 27, no. 5 (2018): 313–326, 324.

1

CREATIVE INDUSTRIES AS DISCOURSE: CHANGING THE FRAME

My intention here is not to write a comprehensive history of creative industries as a discourse, but to establish creative industries as a *discourse*, with a particular set of discursive focuses. The creative industries as a cohesive object or entity has been heralded into being through policy and through academic analysis. In order to investigate creative industries as a discourse, we can turn to Norman Fairclough's rubric of critical discourse analysis (CDA). Fairclough suggests that power operates opaquely, and his methodology seeks to explore discursive practices, events, and texts, investigating how forms of discourse arise out of and are ideologically shaped by relations of power and struggles over power. He suggests that the opacity of these relationships between discourse and society is itself a factor that secures power and hegemony.[1] Here, I turn to cultural and creative industries policy documents and to academic texts to analyze what is foregrounded or what is most prominent in the assumptions of these document and texts, in order to assess how the creative industries came to be known as a thing. In itself, that the creative industries became known as a thing is an enactment of power, and these definitions inform what registers, what counts or is visible, what is valued and valorized. Following this analysis of creative industries as a discourse, I explore alternative definitions and possibilities, turning to cultural mapping methodology.

Creative Industries as Discourse: Policy Proliferation

To begin, I examine creative industries policy at the national level, to then consider how these national policies diffused globally. Creative industries policy picked up locally through the "creative cities" concept, but here I start with larger, broader strokes, to understand how creative industries became established

DOI: 10.4324/9781003031338-1

as a discourse with a particular kind of focus. In 1998, the Department of Culture, Media and Sport (DCMS) in the United Kingdom produced the *Creative Industries Mapping Documents* in the United Kingdom; this mapping exercise was repeated again in 2001. These 1998/2001 documents mark the most crystallized first take ups of the cultural/creative sector and of the creative economy as a driver of the economy.[2] Prior to these mapping exercises, Australia had also focused on the cultural industries in the 1994 policy document *Creative Nation*. This Australian document emphasized cultural industries in broad terms, yet the emphasis remained on activities that might be more clearly and more historically defined as "cultural," including film, radio, and libraries.[3] The U.K. mapping exercises were rooted in an industry perspective, separating the creative industries into a variety of fields, with the stated goal of raising awareness about these industries and their overall contribution to the economy. In its toolkit that provides an overview of best practices in creative industries mapping, the British Council Creative Economy Unit defines mapping as "intended especially to give an overview of the industries' economic value, particularly in places where relatively little is known about them."[4] Primary emphasis in the 1998/2001 U.K. mapping documents includes employment indicators, reported in number of jobs and in value of exports, quantified in revenues as well as in percentage of total GDP in the U.K. In the 2001 *Mapping Documents*, the DCMS represents these indicators pictographically, with images of different types of pens to represent different creative industries sectors. Economic value is represented by the length of these different pens. The total revenues from each creative industries discipline and the total number of jobs in each sector are quantified. These pictures present a visual depiction of economic indicators as a yardstick, a means of comparing the relative impact of various sectors of the creative industries. In their analysis of the proliferation of creative industries mapping documents both in the U.K. and worldwide, Peter Higgs and Stuart Cunningham identify the reoccurrence of four types of mapping metrics, including 1) employment (primarily full-time employment within each discipline); 2) firm activity (primarily the number of firms in each discipline); 3) gross value added to the economy (revenues); and 4) exports.[5] Higgs and Cunningham's analysis identifies varied but persistent economic emphasis through various economic indicators for the creative industries as a way to map them.

Economic Emphasis in Creative Industries Policy

The nature of these economic indicators for the creative industries raises questions about definitions and disciplines: what is included, meaning what kinds of creative activities, by what is measured? Starting in 1998, the DCMS defined the creative industries to include the following disciplines: advertising; antiques; architecture; crafts; design; fashion; film; leisure software; music; performing arts; publishing; software; and TV and radio. These disciplines that were included have been debated and critiqued. For example, questions have been raised about whether or not software fits within a definition of creative industries, as most software development might stem from traditional business or IT focuses, rather than from "creative" purposes, such as video game development. This question about the IT sector is particularly apt, as it is profiled as the top leader in the creative industries in these *Mapping Documents* in its revenues, employment figures, and exports, bolstering the claim that the creative industries contribute sizeable impact to the economy. If the creative industries are deemed to be important because of economic impact, which disciplines are included in what counts as "creative industries" matters. Similarly, questions have been raised about antiques as a discipline of the creative industries, given that the trading of used objects does not generate new intellectual property. Given the more modest contribution of the antiques market to a definition of the creative industries, this particular debate has less of a pressing impact on whether or not the creative industries are considered economically important or worthy of support and celebration. Nonetheless, definitions and what is included have implications for the visibility of particular forms of cultural production, and hence different kinds of cultural producers.

This economic emphasis continues through the proliferation of U.K. DCMS Creative Industries policy, shifting from raising the visibility of the creative industries to celebrating their success and their contribution to the economy. The *2010–2015 U.K. Media and Creative Industries Government Policy* celebrates and quantifies the economic contribution of the creative industries to the GDP by the minute, declaring, "Our creative industries are a real success story. They are worth more than £36 billion a year; they generate £70,000 every minute for the U.K. economy; and they employ 1.5 million people in the U.K. According to industry figures, the creative industries account for around £1 in every £10 of the U.K.'s exports."[6] This excerpt demonstrates a rhetorical instantiation of the common phrase, time is money, and, in other words, money talks.

Beyond the realm of policy documents, the creative industries as a positive source of national identity have also been celebrated in the realm of popular culture. In the U.K., the mid to late 1990s was the era of resurgence of Brit Pop. Bands such as Blur, Elastica, Oasis, Pulp, and The Verve were topping international music charts, and there was hope that this rise of the British music industry would return the U.K. to a world leader in this regard, harkening back to the 1960s moment of Beatlemania. Musicians like Noah Gallagher from the band Oasis were photographed hanging out with British Prime Minister Tony Blair, ushering in what become known as "Cool Britannia" and "cool capitalism," where national identity, electoral politics, economic advancement, and cultural production via the creative industries could be conceptualized as complementary and mutually beneficial. Recall a different moment 20 years prior, with the mainstreaming of the British punk movement in the late 1970s. On their 1977 album *Never Mind the Bollocks, Here's the Sex Pistols*, British punk band the Sex

Pistols turned their noses up at the British monarchy, equating it with "a fascist regime." This moment displayed a different social imaginary, where music ostentatiously professed contempt for national identity, and cultural production and cultural policy were seemingly at odds. Fast forward and contrast this contempt with a 1997 moment when British band the Spice Girls performed their hit song "Who Do You Think You Are" at the Brit Awards. Band member Gerri Halliwell, also known as Ginger Spice, sartorially performed national identity with her "union jack mini dress," voted as the "most iconic dress of the past 50 years" by online respondents in a survey conducted by a British online fashion retailer in 2010.[7]

Here, I both interrogate and put aside dichotomies of authenticity and incorporation that have long been associated with in particular counter-cultural, youth-led, and grassroots forms of cultural production. I raise these examples of the Sex Pistols and the Spice Girls not to pit one against the other. Both bands were top-selling, popular artists; these examples illustrate a large shift in expression of the social imaginary of national identity and creative industries within a 20-year period in the U.K. In the late 1990s in the U.K., creative industries were seen as good, creative industries were seen as British, creative industries were seen as profitable, and creative industries were seen as a thing. Creative industries were seen as a good thing because they were seen as profitable. If we move forward another 20 years, we can take note of a further shift in the social imaginary, with questions of diversity, access, and inclusion coming to the foreground of the conversation about the creative industries. For example, in 2016, Black British actor Idris Elba delivered an impassioned speech to the U.K. Parliament about the need for greater diversity in representation in film and media, noting the "disconnect between the real world and the TV world. People in the TV world often aren't the same as people in the real world. And there's an even bigger gap between people who make TV, and people who watch TV." Elba notes that media shapes reality, and "the creative industries are the foundation of Britain's future economy," yet opportunities to enter into the creative industries are lacking for people from underrepresented groups.[8] These questions of equity and access to economic opportunity move beyond earlier celebratory rhetoric and economic indicators.

Creative Industries Development Model

The "creative industries" as an area of policy emphasis emerged in this late 1990s U.K. policy moment, but the creative industries as a discursive and policy entity has proliferated worldwide. Kate Oakley and Justin O'Connor trace the migration of the creative industries to East Asia in particular, including Singapore, South Korea, Hong Kong, Taiwan, and China.[9] Nancy Duxbury, Anita Kangas, and Christiaan De Beukelaer provide an overview of the rationales and deployments of culture and cultural policy through the lens of the United Nations.

The authors note the shifting and at times limited take up of culture in international development, for example noting the limited role of culture in the 2015 Sustainable Development Goals. At the same time, the authors note the instrumentalization of culture in the creative industries moment in the "'neoliberal tide' of the 1990s," when "a new policy discourse of 'creative industries' and a policy practice, known as the 'creative industries model' in the U.K. and Australia, became successful exports to other parts of the world, linking together a seemingly heterogeneous set of sub-sectors as the 'creative industries.'"[10] Surveying conceptual models of globalization and the rise of "creative cities," Terry Flew calls for nuanced analysis about how global trends play out in local contexts like cities, highlighting the "institutional contexts and constraints" that present themselves to multinational corporations.[11] Despite this call for nuanced attention to local take ups and context, "creative industries" has often been mobilized in simplified terms. Surveying the adoption of creative industries through policy emphasis, Oakley and O'Conner note "creativity as an input (rather than culture as an output) allowed the imaginative, dynamic, transformative and glamorous aspects of culture to be pressed into the service of an innovation machine. Questions of value other than innovation and other economic impacts were dropped."[12] Oakley and O'Connor note the widening discourse of "creativity" to include disciplines not traditionally thought of as "cultural." This widened discourse also reveals a narrowed focus on the economic, which then gets exported worldwide as "the creative industries."

This creative industries-as-export model also reached the developing world through the United Nations, via the United Nations Conference on Trade and Development (UNCTAD).[13] Within UNCTAD creative industries policy documents, there is not necessarily an attempt to export a British or Australian model of the creative industries wholesale. Conversely, culture and creativity are seen as bottom-up resources for local development, and mapping exercises survey existing creative sectors in each country, rather than suggesting the need to import the DCMS definition of which creative disciplines count as creative industries. For example, in the UNCTAD document titled *Strengthening the Creative Industries for Development in Mozambique*, policy emphasis includes attention to microfinancing and skills development and paying attention to local context. But these UNCTAD documents also suggest that the creative industries are a means to foster social development and sustainability alongside economic development, suggesting that the creative industries promote gender equality, social cohesion, and are compatible with environmental protection. Creative industries are seen as a good thing because they are seen as profitable, but here the primacy of economic concerns assumes that social and environmental development will also necessarily follow. Returning to a critical discourse analysis frame, the hegemonic power of an economic framework is evident when social, cultural, or environmental considerations are assumed to naturally emerge from economic development.

Local Creative Industries Policy Emphasis

As discussed in the Introduction, in this book and in my research more broadly, my view and understanding of the creative industries is shaped by my context and location. In Canada, we have not had a "creative industries" moment or celebration comparable to the U.K. or Australian uptake of the creative industries, or comparable to the export/development-focused model of the creative industries internationally. Nonetheless, discussing Canada's 2017 national *Creative Canada Policy Framework*, Mariane Bourcheix-Laporte asserts, "this new framework crystalizes a neoliberal turn in Canadian cultural policy that has been taking place since the 1980s and marks a transition from cultural industries to creative industries discourse. As such, it testifies to an ideological shift in the valorization of culture, one that emphasizes culture's potential to bolster economic growth by harnessing the promises of digital and creative economies."[14] In Canada, individual provinces retain responsibility for aspects of cultural and economic development. The province where I currently live, Ontario, makes reference to the economic impact of the creative industries in its 2019 budget document, *Protecting What Matters Most*, which states "Ontario's cultural media industries contributed almost $7 billion to provincial GDP in 2016, and represented 27 per cent of the overall culture sector. These industries, which include film and television production, interactive digital media, book and magazine publishing and sound recording, are an important and growing segment of Ontario's economy."[15] These metrics correspond with Higgs and Cunningham's rubric of common economic indicators for the creative industries, including revenues, alongside a discipline-based focus, of what constitutes a creative industry. These various policy documents discussed in this chapter display commonalities across how the creative industries are presented and discussed when economic values are quantified and valorized.

This 2019 Government of Ontario budget document replaced a previous document, the province's first cultural policy strategy, released in 2016, entitled *Telling Our Stories, Growing our Economy*.[16] Here, there was some gesture towards non-economic value for culture, and this policy document targeted both cultural production and cultural participation. Though the creative industries are championed as a source of economic growth, this is not the sole focus of this document. The first half, "telling our stories" targets cultural participation, with a recognition of the importance of engaging with culture for non-economic reasons including wellbeing and a sense of self. Moreover, there is a recognition of barriers to cultural participation, especially with regards to youth and Indigenous communities. For example, there are discussions of working towards reconciliation with Indigenous communities, given the history and legacy of colonization and cultural genocide in Canada. When this document turns to a discussion of "growing our economy," there is a noticeable shift towards celebrating the virtues of the creative economy as a source of economic growth, without substantively addressing barriers, challenges, or inequity. The bulk of this second half of the document, entitled "Fuel the Creative Economy," consists of discussions of creativity and innovation. Interestingly, Strategy 1 in the "Fuel the Creative Economy" section, "Make Ontario a Culture Leader at Home and Internationally" features a photo of female film director Sara St. Onge on set, shooting her feature film *Molly Maxwell.* This image might call something into being, and visually depict female film directors as leaders "at home and internationally," but there is no discussion of gender or barriers for women or any other underrepresented people or communities in entering or accessing leadership positions in the creative industries. When this "Fuel the Creative Economy" section discusses the economic impact of innovation, scaling-up companies, and the competitiveness of Ontario's creative industries, we can ask who benefits from these initiatives and who is excluded. These critical questions highlight power relations alongside recuperating the importance of social values that impact people and processes in the creative industries. Centring social and cultural values raises a different set of questions, such as: beyond economics, why might the creative industries be good? Why might they be important, other than making money? Further critical questions include: who and what is seen as profitable, and why? Who is seen as a safe bet and who and what is seen as a risk or liability? Who and what is supported and championed and who and what is marginalized in the creative industries?

Creative Industries as Discourse: Academic Model Proliferation

Alongside the proliferation of the creative industries as an area of cultural-as-economic policy emphasis, the "creative industries" has also proliferated as an academic discourse, as theorists have sought to grapple with and make sense of what constitutes the "creative industries." Reflecting back on 20 years of academic creative industries scholarship, Mark Banks and Justin O'Connor note the celebratory tone of some of this early scholarship, "There was a tremendous amount of excitement about the creative industries.... In some sense, we shared in this nascent optimism—the research institute in which we worked had developed its reputation not simply by documenting but by participating actively in some of the popular cultural projects and initiatives then being identified as central to Manchester's cultural and economic renewal. As much as we were researching and evaluating change, we were also involved in manifesting it, at least to some minor degree."[17] Academics working in the area of creative industries/media studies can sometimes identify as fans or participants in the thing they are analyzing and calling into being as a thing; the creative industries have sometimes also been identified as a source of renewal or growth in positive or progressive ways by academics working in the field. Some of this early optimism later migrated into caution and critique, with widespread criticism from critical creative industries scholars of the neoliberal take up of the creative industries and of the creative industries leading a neoliberal entrepreneurial approach to work across fields.[18] Cognizant of the early celebration of the creative industries "moment," or as Banks and O'Connor put it, the celebration of the creative industries as a "positive new direction,"[19] I am wary of taking on a celebratory tone about alternative forms of social practice or models for reimagining the creative industries. In this book, I also seek to engage with the messiness of these forms and models, including the challenges of performing unseen, devalued, and often unpaid forms of care labour to foster inclusion. Here, I first draw attention to early academic models of the creative industries, and then explore methods for identifying alternative models.

Cores and Rings

Some of the early academic discussions of cultural/creative industries took up the question of definition and produced models to visualize or otherwise register distinctions between cultural and creative industries. Cultural economist David Throsby discusses the "concentric rings" model for the cultural industries, retaining cultural value alongside economic value in this model. The concentric rings model radiates outwards from "core creative arts," including literature, music, performing and visual arts; to "other core cultural/creative industries," such as film, museums, and photography; "wider cultural industries" like heritage services and publishing and print media; then finally "related" industries including design and fashion.[20] Throsby comments that foregrounding and retaining cultural value at the core is a way to "strengthen the cultural orientation of cultural policy" and thereby "counteract a tendency towards interpreting cultural policy simply as an arm of economic policy and nothing more." At the same time, Throsby notes "there is no 'right' or 'wrong' model of the cultural industries, simply a range of alternative constructions based on different sets of assumptions and employing different mechanisms for putting the parts together. But the choice of a model by means of which to interpret the structural characteristics of cultural production has important implications for the formulation of cultural policy."[21] In short, the model matters for what gets seen, supported, and emphasized. While Throsby's model suggested retaining and valuing the cultural core, policy emphasis became placed on the movement outwards to broader activities as "creative."

Assessing the articulation of economic and cultural values, Jason Potts and Stuart Cunningham forward "Four Models of the Creative Industries," charting the relationship between the creative industries and the economy from various perspectives, asking "what is the dynamic relation between the creative industries and the rest of the economy?"[22] They provide an overview of four possible models: 1) welfare model: the creative industries as worth supporting despite a net drain on the economy because of their effects on the "welfare" of the public; 2) competition model: the creative industries are like any other industry, contributing no more or no less to technological change, innovation, or productivity growth in the economy; 3) growth model: the creative industries promote economic growth, either through increasing supply or increasing demand; 4) innovation model: the creative industries evolve the economy through transfers of knowledge due to their contribution to the coordination of new ideas or technologies. These four possible creative industries models emphasize the relationship between the creative industries and other industries; Potts and Cunningham's framing question is an economic one. Some of these early creative industries models might also gesture towards the intrinsic value of culture and creativity, but the main emphasis is on the relationship between cultural input and economic output. As such, what "counts" as a cultural or creative industry, and how to define these industries, remains an economic "counting."

Academic theoretical work and policy discourse are also co-constitutive, as both academic and policy models attempted to define cultural/creative industries, and in doing so, assert their existence as an entity, and as a worthwhile entity for academic research and for policy attention. We can see the "concentric rings" model, and variations on it, proliferating in policy and think tank documents that sought to define and champion the creative industries. For example, Swedish think tank the Knowledge Foundation produced the ERIBA model (Education; Research; Industry; Business; Arts/Culture) for "an effective and successful policy framework for the creative industries." Like Throsby's model, this ERIBA circle model positions the arts as a core centre, radiating out to "the creative sector" then "creativity/innovation as an economic activity."[23] Similarly, in Switzerland, the Creative Economies Research Venture think tank also has a concentric-rings based "creative economies model," highlighting "core" and "extended" forms of value creation in the creative industries.[24] In these early models, questions of economic and cultural value are articulated in various definitions and conjunctions, often with an emphasis on the movement outwards to economic value.

Appraising the Social

In some of these creative industries models, social values are alluded to via the cultural, including questions of identity, belonging, quality of life, and collective experience, but social values were largely under-investigated and under-represented in core/ring models and as such are a missing piece of how the creative industries are understood. Assessing which artistic/creative disciplines "count" as creative industries does not offer a lens to appraise these social concerns. Avenues into the social, which foreground people and their practices, have largely been made through research on labour practices in the cultural/creative industries, highlighting these industries not only as areas of the economy, but also as area of employment, often with poor employment standards and quality of employment. When the number of jobs in the creative industries is touted as an indicator of the success of these industries, we can ask critical questions about the quality of these jobs. Through the inroads of practitioner/employee experience, we can also consider questions of scale in the creative industries and interrogate how various cultural/creative disciplines have been grouped together to form a coherent entity called "the creative industries." For example, we might ask, do large, globalized creative industries firms have anything in common with a small company employing one or two people? Does the experience of a salaried IT professional at a company like Google have anything in common with the experience of a freelance ballet dancer? Both the IT professional and the freelance ballet dancer might "count" as creative industries workers in various models, but do their experiences differ *in degree* (across a spectrum of creative industries workforce experiences) or do their experiences differ *in kind* (categorical difference)? Does it make sense to discuss the creative industries as a coherent object of analysis at all?

Some discussions about cultural policy metrics highlight the political nature of what and how quantification takes place with regards to culture, and the lack of consensus about cultural measurement methods.[25] These discussions are accompanied by a questioning of the very nature of the "creative industries" as a coherent category of analysis, and suggestions that investigations into the nature of this sector might be better accomplished through "disaggregating" the creative industries into different sectors or occupations, or through returning to sociological, qualitative, or other ethnographic means of analysis.[26] I take up this call in this book, examining the creative industries from the perspective of how they are experienced by participants or by practitioners from care-based perspectives.

Cultural Mapping and the Politics of Visibility

Reimagining the creative industries necessitates paying attention to and recuperating forms of value in the creative industries beyond economic value. This process means rethinking overarching capitalistic values, and also means paying attention to the politics of visibility. In a superstar creative industries economy, large revenues streams and other large-scale indicators (for example, audience numbers or other attendance metrics, views, streams, "likes," or hits, etc.) typically correlate with conventional indicators of success. What other forms of value and other indicators might register as meaningful in a creative industries context? In order to register small-scale forms of creative practice, my research methodologies stem from a cultural mapping framework, attuned to emergence. As a researcher, I have drawn attention to emerging forms of creative practice, as they have implications for the ways we work and live, but we often lack the lenses and capacity to see and understand change as it is unfolding. In the discussion of cultural mapping methodology below, I differentiate between cultural mapping as an alternative discourse and the creative industries mapping discussed above, which was oriented around economic indicators and discipline distinctions.

In their edited collection *Cultural Mapping as Cultural Inquiry,* Nancy Duxbury, W. F. Garrett-Petts, and David MacLennan provide an overview of this methodology as a "emerging field of practice" and describe cultural mapping methodology as a way of "describing, accounting for, and coming to terms with the cultural resources of communities and places."[27] The need for a refreshing of economic indicators of success and registering or coming to terms with social, cultural, and other resources is particularly important within a dominant neoliberal framework for the creative industries. For example, other resources or strengths might include models of inclusive working practices, pedagogical practices, and other forms of care that are more difficult to quantify as output. Duxbury, Garrett-Petts, and MacLennan open their collection with key questions about the politics of visibility, acknowledging that mapping has "a long history, entangled with exploration, colonialism, and political control." In these contexts, mapping has been done *on* communities and land, rather than *with* communities. In light of this history, Duxbury, Garrett-Petts, and MacLennan position cultural mapping as "an alternative discourse," one that works with communities to inventory community characteristics.[28] The authors draw on the Creative City Network of Canada's definition of cultural mapping as "a process of collecting, recording, analyzing, and synthesizing information in order to describe the cultural resources, networks, links and patterns of usage of a given community or group."[29] Working with cultural mapping methodology, I aim as much as possible to collaboratively engage with research participants, striving to work reflexively with an ethic of care, while also recognizing that ultimately as a researcher and a writer I am in a position of power and responsibility.

Maps and Stories

Cultural mapping can inventory both quantitative and qualitative resources; as such, the output of this methodology can be varied. Nigel Crawhall defines cultural mapping as "the exercise of representing a previously unrepresented world view or knowledge system in a tangible and understandable geo-referenced medium."[30] Indeed, many cultural maps take the form of literal, geo-referenced maps. For example, Tobias Plieninger, Sebastian Dijks, Elisa Oteros-Rozas, and Claudia Bieling's research study conducted mapping exercises and interviews with 93 people in Eastern Germany in order to map the local "cultural ecosystem." The collected data was processed with a geographical information system (GIS). Participants were asked to represent the landscape by "delineating sites on the map with pencils or markers," using sticker dots to locate sites on the map, and identify/number sites and then annotate them in a questionnaire.[31] The CBC's "Did You Live Near a Residential School" map from 2018 offers a further example of a geo-located map, locating residential schools on a map of Canada and inviting users to enter the postal code of the community where they grew up to determine distance to the closest residential school.[32] In this case, cultural mapping delivers a personal impact. Map users may be familiar with the longstanding abuse of Indigenous peoples through residential schools in Canada, but geo-locating these schools in this instance makes this history of genocide more immediate rather than distant or quantified, as users are invited to physically situate themselves in this legacy.

While there is a rise in these kinds of geo-referenced maps, cultural mapping can take on other forms to inventory qualitative cultural values and resources, such as oral histories and storytelling, or artistic forms of expression through community collaborations, though these intangible forms of value can pose challenges for representation and communication.[33] M. Sharon Jeannotte's cultural mapping project with communities in Ontario attempted to register and represent spiritual values, cultural identity, social cohesion, and heritage; she concludes that "there is some way to go before community story-telling can successfully capture the intangibles of place."[34] The CBC "Residential School" map also features testimony from survivors of residential schools in the form of short video clips. In this book, I primarily turn to profiling stories and experiences in order to map and recuperate creative industries values beyond the economic. I employ cultural mapping through life stories and oral histories by interviewing cultural producers about their experiences, and aim to represent some of the nuances and intricacies of these experiences.

Tensions of Scale

Cultural mapping can be used to illustrate the tensions of scale in the creative industries through the lens of lived experience. For example, one way I have employed cultural mapping methodology though life stories is through a collaborative photo essay with friend and photographer Johanna Heldebro, in order to shine a light on particular artist experiences. These experiences illuminate broader and common trends, but I also sought to register and do justice to particular individuals and experiences. In this piece, titled "Art Work," I profiled artists facing eviction at one particular location, a four-storey building at 224 Wallace Street in Toronto.[35] As will be further discussed in Chapter 7, a now-familiar narrative about gentrification is that it is artist-led. In this narrative, artists move into affordable neighbourhoods to find space to live and work. Then these neighbourhoods become trendy, developers and corporations become interested in these neighbourhoods, resulting in real estate and rental prices increasing, artists moving elsewhere to further find affordable areas, and the cycle starting again. This narrative of gentrification obscures the role of policy, lobbyists, and corporations in shaping city landscapes, in particular in the development of "creative cities" and creative economies.

This tension in scale of the creative industries (large vs. small) and the lack of visibility of small-scale creative industries drove my interest in the building featured in the "Art Work" article and photo essay. When video game company Ubisoft arrived at 224 Wallace on the second floor of this building in 2016, artists and small business owners started getting 30-day eviction notices from the building management because Ubisoft sought to expand and rent out more space for their offices and their employees. This expansion occurred physically upwards, taking over the third floor and then the fourth floor, and I wanted to document the remaining artists on the first floor, in their studio spaces, while they were still there in 2018. These first-floor tenants were evicted in 2019; at the time of our photo essay in 2018, artists were cautious about the likelihood they would remain in their space long term, though some were optimistic.

In Canada, the province of Ontario invested $263 million in Ubisoft to attract the French company to Toronto, a move meant to create jobs—but independent artists and business owners at 224 Wallace felt the brunt of the company's expansion. For them, eviction can mean the closure of their businesses: new affordable space is hard to come by, and suddenly, work projects that are already underway cannot be completed. When I spoke to artists and small business entrepreneurs on the first floor at 224 Wallace in 2018, they highlighted the irony of cultural policy investment in the creative industries in Ontario. According to the province, the cultural sector in 2014 supported nearly 280,000 jobs, contributing about $25.3 billion, or nearly 4%, to Ontario's GDP. Small independent creatives are part of this ecosystem, but where artists can sometimes get small grants, large corporations like Ubisoft receive major subsidies. These major subsidies help attract large corporations like Ubisoft, rather than anchor artists and small businesses in the communities that they have helped to build. Discussing the development of "creative cluster" and cultural district policies, Flew highlights how some of these policies have been directed to groups of buildings for a range of activities ("avoiding the 'all eggs in one basket' problem"), noting research from Allen Scott that suggests that "top-down approaches based upon directive planning are most likely to fail, particularly in cities and regions that lack a strong, pre-existing base of cultural production."[36] Some of the conflict and tensions at 224 Wallace emerged from the lack of visibility and attention to the pre-existing cultural production and the range of activities already at this site, not adequately valorized within the dominant neoliberal creative industries paradigm. One tenant, Charlotte Blake, who co-runs an art production studio that specializes in custom art installations called Kolectiv, says many of the tenants at 224 Wallace "work big"—doing projects on a large scale, or several at the same time for different clients on tight deadlines. The large studios they had at 224 Wallace allowed them to accommodate these demands of their working lives. Her partner, Maciek Balmas, felt like the remaining independent artists at 224 Wallace were viewed as obstacles in the way of development. Balmas wondered what coexistence between big and small might look like. "We're all here for the same reason," he said. "We want to make a living." The particularities of 224 Wallace highlight the discrepancy of visibility between large scale and small-scale forms of the creative industries, with large-scale being perceived as more worthwhile of support and investment, but Balmas' comment suggests economic commonality around the shared experience of making a living.

Extraction and Community Knowledge

Cultural mapping methodology can be used to draw attention to under-represented forms of cultural production, but this research lens needs to be used reflexively with care when highlighting small-scale, emerging, and sometimes underground forms of creative practice. In their book *Scenescapes: How Qualities of Place Shape Social Life*, authors Daniel Aaron Silver and Terry Nichols Clark discuss how "scenes" shape social and economic realities and transform geographies. They assert that the practices and amenities that make up scenes "are listed in the yellow pages, pay taxes, have conventions, and sometimes are even counted in national censuses. You can look them up on Google Maps to get a feel for what types of activities characterize a place. And the social scientist can document and analyze them."[37] They write "how one conceives something shapes how one measures it," and their research methods for documenting and analyzing scenes include gathering data from the Yellow Pages (YP) and the U.S. Census Bureau Zip Code Business Patterns (BIZZIP). The authors state, "despite their limitations, BIZZIP and YP are among the best data sources we have found for measuring scenes."[38] These measurement methods document and analyze what exists in public listings; small-scale forms of creative practice can often occur in places without official permits or sanctioned uses, and might not register in business or Census listings. For these reasons, people and organizations running these types of underground spaces might want to avoid above-the-board documentation and visibility, especially when visibility can mean surveillance and criminalization. Turning to data produced by official listings produces a limited view of the social and cultural life of a place, and one that may not be able to register small-scale and emerging forms of creative and social practice. These problems also suggest the limitations of geo-located forms of cultural mapping, as not all forms of social or creative practice can or want to be visible according to address or physical location.

On the other hand, large-scale creative industries can sometimes appropriate ideas, designs, and creative products from small-scale and independent cultural producers, which further raises ethical considerations when attempting to increase the visibility of less visible creative forms. For example, clothing and lifestyle retailer Urban Outfitters is well known for appropriating artists' designs, which often lack copyright protections. In one (of many) examples, from 2020, Urban Outfitters was accused of stealing the design from a painting by Australian-based Indigenous artist Mitjili Napurrula and selling it as an outdoor rug.[39] These practices of theft in the creative industries exist within the long-standing context of cultural appropriation of the culture and creativity of Black, Indigenous, and racialized artists and communities.[40] This history impacts cultural mapping as a research framework, suggesting caution about this research tool being redeployed as a means to surface, document, or exploit marginalized forms of creative practice. Returning to the discussion from Silver and Clark, the role of the social science researcher might not just be to document and analyze, but to attend to people and their practices instead of only gathering data from official listings, remaining sensitive to whether or not these people and practices want to be documented and analyzed, alongside ethical considerations of potential harm that can stem from documentation. At the same time, it is harmful to not think of the creative ecosystem and only focus on economics, to the detriment of the small scale. Care ethics can help bring this ecosystem into view alongside bringing reflexivity to research methods and approaches.

Thinking about the potential and limits of cultural mapping methodology can also shift the end goals and audience of this research practice. Theorizing Indigenous resurgence through the lens of "grounded normativity" or the localized and generative ways of knowing and being that come through the land, Michi Saagiig Nishnaabeg scholar, writer, and artist Leanne Betasamosake Simpson questions the limits of community participatory action research as an academic method to partner with communities to gather or produce knowledge. In the context of Indigenous resurgence, this concern is particularly acute, given the impact and legacies of colonial extraction of knowledge and land from Indigenous peoples. Simpson discusses her involvement as a research assistant through her graduate work in the Effects on Aboriginals from the Great Lakes Environment (EAGLE) project. This research project sought to document traditional knowledge of the land held by Indigenous Elders of the Great Lakes region: "the project was to gather the individual, cognitive, territorial maps Elders held in their heads into a collective, a visual mapping and translation of some aspects of Indigenous Knowledge into a form that would be *recognized* by industry and the state" (emphasis in original).[41] Simpson doubts that visually mapping and translating this knowledge to industry and the state is an effective change-making process. It would be unwise to hope that presenting this knowledge would catalyze industry and the state to recognize the errors of their colonial ways, to recognize that profound forms of knowledge pre-exist and supersede colonial contact and extraction, and to make reparations. If anything, visualizing these forms of knowledge could act as a tool and guide for further extraction of land, resources, and knowledge. To change the focus and purpose of this type of cultural mapping research, Simpson suggests that the end audience of this type of work is not external audiences like industry and the state, but is instead the communities themselves. She articulates community mapping as "a process that could be used as a tool to generate cohesion, pride, and rebuilding within our own communities when our own people saw visually and so clearly what dispossession, displacement, and encroachment, and industrial extractivism look like over our territories across time. Laid out in a visual way, the magnitude of loss cannot be ignored away, the strategic nature of colonialism cannot be ignored. The driving force of capitalism in our dispossession cannot be denied."[42] Importantly, Simpson speaks to Indigenous methodologies with Indigenous communities, where it is important to acknowledge a historical and ongoing role of research extractivism. Indigenous methodologies and the movement towards collaborative and ethical approaches that emphasize relationality and relationship building are important with all communities. In this light, cultural mapping can be a tool for communities to better know themselves, and to communicate their capacities and resources, on their own terms.

Visibility and Ethics of Care

There is not one easy answer about what or who cultural mapping is for, or whether or not it is always an ethically engaged mode of research; these tensions also arise when recuperating and rearticulating social values in a creative industries context. Discussing care ethics, Maria Puig de la Bellacassa raises the complexities of care, citing a question from Melissa Atkinson-Graham et al.: "the question, then, is not 'how can we care more' but instead to ask what happens to our work when we pay attention to moments where the question of 'how to care' is insistent but not easily answerable."[43] Puig de la Bellacassa further writes, "caring obligations that would enact nonexploitative forms of togetherness cannot be imagined once for all."[44] Instead, drawing on Donna Haraway, Puig de la Bellacassa suggests to "stay with the trouble." With this in mind, in this book I aim to stay with the trouble, working with youth and emerging cultural producers to register their forms of creative practice, mapping these forms while discussing tensions, challenges, and contradictions in these alternatives to mainstream creative industries discourse. Thinking with a creative ecology model for the creative industries, and highlighting relationships and relationality also invites some of this messiness; nonetheless, this is a more productive avenue for analysis than a tidier but also more reductive concentric rings model.

To return to the creative industries context, the politics of visibility informs who is and who is not found in official and public records, and whose forms of cultural production are marginalized, poorly known, misunderstood, exploited, or extracted from. Mainstream models of the creative industries have also been built around norms of cisgender, straight, thin and able-bodied white men as creators and audiences, fans, and consumers. These norms are now being questioned through the lens of diversity, equity, inclusion, and decolonization. Speaking to the context of the fashion industry and post-secondary fashion education, fashion scholar Ben Barry writes:

> The boundaries around what is and what isn't fashion are quickly and tightly established. Fashion history courses celebrate the 'birth' of fashion in Paris with the launch of the House of Worth by designer Charles Frederick Worth in 1858. With this single story, Paris and whiteness become the arbiters of fashion; European ways of understanding and practising fashion are the standard. Indigenous, African, East Asian and South Asian fashion design that has been practised since time immemorial are either erased from introductory fashion classes or demoted to 'ethnic dress' or 'world costume' elective courses... The bodies that make up these fashion history courses are mostly white, cis-gender men who design for white, thin, cis-gender women. Black, trans and disabled people rarely make an appearance. Fat and disabled people are notably absent. Students don't learn why only some bodies have been privileged—and how this has come at the expense of others—because most fashion history courses avoid teaching about the ways in which colonisation and the transatlantic slave trade have structured the fashion industry as we know it.[45]

Barry's comments suggest the need for contextual analysis, informed by awareness of historical and continued power imbalances that dictate how we define and conceive of the creative industries. In Chapter 2, I suggest care ethics as a holistic framework for the creative industries that is able to recognize historical context, power dynamics, and structural barriers while also striving for transformative action.

Notes

1 Norman Fairclough, "Critical Discourse Analysis and the Marketisation of Public Discourse: The Universities," *Discourse & Society* 4, no. 2 (1993): 133–168, 135.
2 Department for Culture, Media and Sport, *Creative Industries Mapping Documents 1998* (London, UK: Department of Culture, Media and Sport, 1998); Department for Culture, Media and Sport, *Creative Industries Mapping Documents 2001* (London, UK: Department of Culture, Media and Sport, 2001).
3 Department of Communications and the Arts, *Creative Nation: Commonwealth Cultural Policy 1994* (Canberra, AU: Department of Communication and the Arts, 1994).
4 British Council, *Mapping the Creative Industries: A Toolkit* (London, UK: British Council, 2010), 11, https://creativeconomy.britishcouncil.org/blog/10/04/08/mapping-creative-industries-toolkit/
5 Stuart Cunningham and Peter Higgs, "Creative Industries Mapping: Where Have We Come From and Where Are We Going?," *Creative Industries Journal* 1, no. 1 (2018): 7–30, 8.
6 Department for Culture, Media and Sport, *2010-2015 Government Policy: Media and Creative Industries* (London, UK: DCMS, 2015), https://www.gov.uk/government/publications/2010-to-2015-government-policy-media-and-creative-industries/2010-to-2015-government-policy-media-and-creative-industries
7 Hilary Alexander, "Online Poll Announces the Top Ten Most Iconic Dresses of the Past Fifty Years," *The Telegraph*, May 19, 2010, accessed January 14, 2020, http://

fashion.telegraph.co.uk/article/TMG7740201/Online-poll-announces-the-top-ten-most-iconic-dresses-of-the-past-fifty-years.html

8 Ali Jaafar, "Idris Elba Posts Full Text of Powerful Diversity Speech Online," *Deadline*, January 20, 2016, accessed January 14, 2020, https://deadline.com/2016/01/idris-elba-posts-full-text-of-powerful-diversity-speech-online-1201686614/

9 Kate Oakley and Justin O'Connor, "The Cultural Industries: An Introduction," in *The Routledge Companion to the Cultural Industries*, eds. Kate Oakley and Justin O'Connor (London, UK, Routledge, 2011), 1–32, 4.

10 Nancy Duxbury, Anita Kangas, and Christiaan De Beukelaer, "Cultural Policies for Sustainable Development: Four Strategic Paths," *International Journal of Cultural Policy* 23, no. 2 (2017): 214–230, 219.

11 Terry Flew, *The Creative Industries: Culture and Policy* (London: Sage, 2011), 142.

12 Oakley and O'Connor, "The Cultural Industries," 3.

13 See, for example, UNCTAD's documents *Strengthening the Creative Industries for Development in Mozambique* and *Strengthening the Creative Industries for Development in Zambia*, both published in 2011. For critical assessment of how the creative industries are envisioned by UNCTAD to contribute to economic development in developing nations, see Christiaan De Beukelaer, "Creative Industries in 'Developing' Countries: Questioning Country Classifications in the UNCTAD Creative Economy Reports," *Cultural Trends* 23, no. 4 (2014): 232–251.

14 Mariane Bourcheix-Laporte, "Creative Canada: A Critical Look at a "New" Cultural Policy Framework," *CRTC Prize for Excellence in Policy Research 2019 - Doctoral Award*, 2019, 1.

15 Government of Ontario, *2019 Ontario Budget: Protecting What Matters Most* (Toronto: Queen's Printer for Ontario, 2019), 221.

16 Government of Ontario, *The Ontario Culture Strategy: Telling Our Stories, Growing our Economy* (Toronto: Queen's Printer for Ontario, 2016).

17 Mark Banks and Justin O'Connor, "Inside the Whale (and How to Get out of There): Moving on from Two Decades of Creative Industries Research," *European Journal of Cultural Studies* 20, no. 6 (2017): 637–654, 638.

18 For a fuller discussion of key approaches to cultural / creative industries research, see for example Oakley and O'Connor, "The Cultural Industries"; David Hesmondhalgh, "Theories of Culture, Theories of Cultural Production," in *The Cultural Industries* (4th ed.) (London, UK: Sage, 2019), 47–80.

19 Ibid., 641.

20 David Throsby, "The Concentric Circles Model of the Cultural Industries," *Cultural Trends* 17, no. 3 (2008): 147–164.

21 Ibid., 156.

22 Jason Potts and Stuart Cunningham, "Four Models of the Creative Industries," *International Journal of Cultural Policy* 14, no. 3 (2008): 233–247, 233.

23 Tobias Nielsen, in collaboration with Carin Daal, Ingegerd Green, Lars-Erik Ronnlund, and Putte Svensson, *The ERIBA Model: An Effective and Successful Policy Framework for the Creative Industries* (Stockholm, SE: The Knowledge Foundation, 2008), 37, https://www.norden.ee/images/loomemajandus/info/loome/tobias_nielsen_eribamodel2008.pdf

24 Creative Economies Research Venture, *3rd Creative Economies Report* (Zurich, CH: Creative Economies Research Venture, 2018), http://archive.creativeeconomies.com/archive/www.creativeeconomies.com/downloads/creative-economy-report-switzerland-2018-de.pdf

25 For further discussion of the politics of cultural measurement, see for example Dave O'Brien, "Cultural Value, Measurement and Policy Making," *Arts & Humanities in Higher Education* 14, no. 1 (2015): 79–94; Lachlan MacDowall, Marnie Badham, Emma Blomkamp, and Kim Dunphy, eds. *Making Culture Count: The Politics of Political Measurement* (Basingstoke, UK: Palgrave MacMillan, 2015).

26 Peter Campbell, Dave O'Brien, and Mark Taylor, "Cultural Engagement and the Economic Performance of the Cultural and Creative Industries: An Occupational Critique," *Sociology* 53, no. 2 (2019): 347–367; Angela McRobbie, "Towards a Sociology of Fashion Micro-Enterprises: Methods for Creative Economy Research," *Sociology* 50, no. 5 (2016): 934–948.
27 Nancy Duxbury, W.F. Garrett-Petts, and David MacLennan, "Cultural Mapping as Cultural Inquiry: Introduction to an Emerging Field of Practice," in *Cultural Mapping as Cultural Inquiry*, eds. Nancy Duxbury, W.F. Garrett-Petts, and David MacLennan (New York, NY: Routledge, 2015), 1–42, 2.
28 Ibid., 1, 2.
29 Cited in Duxbury, Garrett-Petts, and MacLennan, "*Cultural Mapping*," 2.
30 Cited in Duxbury, Garrett-Petts, and MacLennan, "*Cultural Mapping*," 4.
31 Tobias Plieninger, Sebastian Dijks, Elisa Oteros-Rozas, and Claudia Bieling, "Assessing, Mapping, and Quantifying Cultural Ecosystem Services at Community Level," *Land Use Policy* 33 (2013): 118–129, 119, 120.
32 CBC News, "Was There a Residential School Near You? Find Out with Our Interactive Map." *CBC News,* June 18, 2018, accessed January 20, 2020, https://www.cbc.ca/news/indigenous/residential-school-interactive-map-beyond-94-1.4693413
33 Nancy Duxbury, W.F. Garrett-Petts, and Alys Longley, eds. *Artistic Approaches to Cultural Mapping: Activating Imaginaries and Ways of Knowing* (New York, NY: Routledge, 2019).
34 M. Sharon Jeannotte, "Story-telling about Place: Engaging Citizens in Cultural Mapping," *City, Culture and Society* 7, no. 1 (2016): 35–41, 41.
35 Miranda Campbell and Johanna Heldebro, "Art Work," *Maisonneuve Magazine* 69 (2018): 16–21.
36 Flew, *The Creative Industries*, 152, 154.
37 Daniel Aaron Silver and Terry Nichols Clark, *Scenescapes: How Qualities of Place Shape Social Life* (Chicago: University of Chicago Press, 2016), 9.
38 Ibid., 66, 73.
39 S.B. Williams, "Urban Outfitters Accused of Ripping Off Indigenous Artist Mitjili Napurrula," *The Brag*, April 17, 220, accessed January 21, 2021, https://thebrag.com/urban-outfitters-mitjili-napurrula-plagiarism/
40 For further discussion of these practices of appropriation, see for example Elizabeth Burns Coleman, *Aboriginal Art, Identity and Appropriation* (Aldershot: Ashgate, 2005); Jason Rodriquez, "Color-Blind Ideology and the Cultural Appropriation of Hip-Hop," *Journal of Contemporary Ethnography* 35, no. 6 (2006): 645–668; James O. Young, *Cultural Appropriation and the Arts* (Hoboken: Blackwell Publishing, 2008).
41 Leanne Betasamosake Simpson, *As We Have Always Done: Indigenous Freedom Through Radical Resistance* (Minneapolis: University of Minnesota Press, 2017), 12.
42 Ibid., 12–13.
43 Cited in Maria Puig de la Bellacassa, *Matters of Care: Speculative Ethics in More than Human Worlds* (Minneapolis: University of Minnesota Press, 2017), 7.
44 Ibid., 24.
45 Ben Barry, "How Fashion Education Prevents Inclusivity," *The Business of Fashion*, January 6, 2020, accessed January 18, 2021, https://www.businessoffashion.com/amp/articles/opinion/op-ed-how-fashion-education-prevents-inclusivity?__twitter_impression=true

2

CARE ETHICS FOR THE CREATIVE INDUSTRIES

When the COVID-19 pandemic struck in 2020, many people worldwide were caught offguard but also quickly mobilized caring and community-oriented responses based in mutual aid. In Toronto, the Caremongering-TO Facebook group began with offers of support to help others get groceries and supplies, but expanded to become a wide-ranging vehicle for support, including offers of home office IT support and addition recovery discussions. At the time of publication of this book in 2021, the Caremongering-TO Facebook group had over 25,000 members. One group member, Paula Toledo, comments that the development of the group suggests, "you're not alone in this, and if you can have the resources to reach out when you need help, and there are people there to respond and help you out in those times, I think we can make it through."[1] Reporting on this "caremongering" phenomenon, BBC News stated that "kind Canadians" had started a trend and coined the caremongering term, but forms of care based in mutual aid, solidarity, and sharing of resources have long existed, in particular in marginalized and underrepresented communities.[2] Through COVID-19, these groups and communities also mobilized and circulated resources and support. For example, the Portland-Oregon based PDX Non-Binary Community Effort group circulated a "collective cares" Google Document, which included information and resources on topics ranging from how to make a homemade mask, to mental health support, childcare, and houselessness.[3] Social justice activist and disability justice author Leah Lakshmi Piepzna-Samarasinha circulated the "Half Assed Disabled Prepper Tips for Preparing for a Coronavirus Quarantine" Google Document, similarly sharing information about food, sanitization, health, medical supplies, and mutual aid.[4] These quick responses emphasize community care, but also stand in contrast to the lack of policy and government preparation for this pandemic, which we can characterize as a care deficit.

DOI: 10.4324/9781003031338-2

Commenting on 21st century societal challenges, Nancy Fraser and Rahel Jaeggi state that "our crisis is not only economic. It also encompasses care deficits, climate change, and de-democratization."[5] Though these societal challenges are vast and urgent, my focus here is on the creative industries, where care deficits or a lack of care has meant willful inattention to create safer, more inclusive, and more representative workplace conditions these creative industries. Here, I begin by defining care and care ethics, exploring feminist scholarship in this area, and then turn to practice-led examples of care from youth creative workers and collectives.

Defining Care

In the Introduction, I outlined a creative ecology framework for creative industries research, and this framework can be further informed by care ethics, mobilizing feminist scholarship that highlights relational ontology and the work of social reproduction that underpins capitalism. Both of these interventions are important for reimagining the creative industries, where a dominant neoliberal, entrepreneurial model of self is pervasive, despite many creative industries scholars suggesting creative industries work is inherently collaborative, with much behind-the-scenes "backstage" labour, including that which is distributed to the Global South, being needed to support a "superstar" economy.[6] Furthermore, both of these components of care ethics can be inroads to develop frameworks for inclusive working practices, foregrounding how people relate to one another and the politics that underly these relationships.

Relational Ontology

Discussing and defining care through the lens of relational ontology, Bernice Fisher and Joan Tronto historicize a Western, individualized, autonomous self in the 19th century "cult of domesticity," enabled by and enabling "the entrance of white, middle-class men into the capitalistic marketplace."[7] Here, we can go further to name the conditions of colonialism and slavery that enabled the development of the capitalist marketplace, and enabled white men to enter and profit from this marketplace, based in the exploitation and enslavement of other people and of the environment. Discussing the emergence of capitalism as an "institutionalized social order" rather than a de-historicized economic inevitability, Fraser and Jaeggi name the conditions of exploitation, extraction, and expropriation that underpin capitalism.[8] While feminist interventions historicize and contextualize the emergence of a Western, individualized self, they assert that a relational ontology is a more expansive and caring grounding for the self. For feminist philosopher Nel Noddings, an ethics of care is based in relational ethics; caring is "rooted in receptivity, relatedness, and responsiveness."[9] Noddings asserts the primacy of relationality and care for ethical norms for society, outlining that "relation will be taken as ontologically basic and the caring relation as ethically basic." With this foundation, "our efforts must, then, be directed to the maintenance of conditions that will permit caring to flourish."[10] In this book this "maintenance of conditions" is appraised as the work of fostering inclusive cultures and working practices, through the lens of a relational rather than an entrepreneurial self.

Similarly, in an often-cited definition of care, Fisher and Tronto highlight the work of sustaining the "world"; they outline that care is "a species activity that includes everything that we do to maintain, continue, and repair our 'world' so that we can live in it as well as possible."[11] Though environmental concerns are important and vital for care ethics, the "world" invoked here highlights the social realm, including how people relate to one another, live together, and work to keep society afloat. This definition of care underscores the collective and relational subject of "we." Fisher and Tronto outline four phases of care: caring about (paying attention); caring for (taking responsibility); care giving (doing the hands-on work); and care receiving (the responses to the caring process of the care receiver). The authors identify the "asymmetry between responsibility and power" in these phases of care, and identify that the factors of time, resources, knowledge, and skill impact individuals' capacities to care.[12] While they recuperate care work as vital, the very work of keeping society afloat, it is also work that is divided, feminized, and devalued. Those expected to do the hands-on work of caregiving often have the fewest resources and power despite this great responsibility. Digging into these complexities of care, Maria Puig de la Bellacassa writes, "to care can feel good; it can also feel awful. It can do good; it can oppress." Puig de la Bellacassa defines care as "an affective state, a material vital doing, and an ethico-political obligation." Care involves emotional investment, hands-on work, and questions of what is right or wrong, what she terms the "triptych of care as 'ethics-work-affect.'"[13] Caring and caregiving can sometimes invoke dependent care, like child care and elder care, but these expansive definitions from Noddings, Fisher and Tronto, and Puig de la Bellacassa appraise care not only in its content (e.g. providing care), but also as an ethical framework and approach (e.g. repairing the world).

Separating care into phases and acknowledging its overlapping complexities also allows for a rubric of care that registers the presence of partial or fragmented care. In the mainstream creative industries, one way this fragmentation of different phases of caring manifests, with an accompanying devaluation of the hands-on work of caring, is in gender segregation in occupational categories. Creative industries research shows that women are often directed towards behind-the scenes forms of labour needing care work, including communication and coordination, while prestigious, creative positions, remain male dominated.[14] Nonetheless, defining care as a process creates a framework to register small acts as part of a larger caring cycle, and also envisions that one individual may not complete the whole cycle of care. In a context where care is not devalued, worthy parts of care include a sense of attentiveness or noting and paying attention to problems, and taking responsibility or caring for others who are affected beyond the self. In this context, collective and collaborative caring solutions are all the more vital, in order to more effectively mobilize the time, resources, knowledge, and skills that are unevenly distributed or spread across groups.

Social Reproduction

Further inroads in care ethics are made through the theorization of the work of social reproduction, which is the work of maintaining, repairing, or sustaining society, while highlighting the historical and continual feminization and devaluation of this form of labour. In *Care Work*, Piepzna-Samarasinha identifies care as "skilled labor," highlighting its vital importance despite its continued devaluation: "I want all genders of people to be receiving and providing that labor in our communities."[15] Beyond gender-segregation in job categorization in paid work, feminist care theorists identify that the overarching functioning of capitalism relies on behind-the-scenes care work that is devalued and invisible. For Fraser, the "crisis" of capitalism is one that divides and pits the work of economic reproduction against the work of social reproduction. Fraser argues that capitalism works towards financial gain, but is unsustainable without the caring work of social reproduction. Fraser defines social reproduction as "the work of birthing and socializing the young… caring for the old, maintaining households, building communities and sustaining the shared meanings, affective dispositions and horizons of value that underpin social cooperation."[16] In a creative industries context, a creative ecology framework offers a lens to register this work of social reproduction and to map the relationships and tensions between economic and social reproduction. The work of fostering inclusion falls within this work of social reproduction; crises in the creative industries that highlight sexual violence, racism, and lack of equity underscore the unsustainability of economic gain without addressing and fostering inclusive working environments.

As Fraser outlines, the work of social reproduction is capitalism's "economic subsystem," primarily non-market and non-waged labour that underpins "the existence of waged work, the accumulation of surplus value and the functioning of capitalism as such."[17] Fraser defines the historical but changing distinctions between economy and society; between production and reproduction; and between work and family as "boundary struggles." Similarly, Tronto notes that historically care has been "backgrounded" even if it is a critical part of human life because economic growth has been so "thoroughly foregrounded."[18] For Tronto, the project of democracy is to facilitate the conditions where collective caring is possible, such that care is no longer backgrounded and inequitable. In this book, I hope to contribute some elements of a vocabulary for a "vision of caring"[19] for the creative industries. In the profiles of youth and emerging cultural producers and collectives, we can note not merely a switching of the "backgrounding" and the "foregrounding" of the work of social reproduction and economic growth. Instead, we can note a shift in the work of social reproduction, of care work, from the private to the public sphere, reworking binary delineations of either/or, striving towards a both/and rearticulated conceptualization of the social and the economic through cultural work. This reflexivity on working practices is a boundary shift, envisioning care as a public and cultural good, where care is centred and valued for economic, social, and cultural reproduction. In practice, this means a navigation of the tensions between the social and the economic as the work of social reproduction moves into the public space. This boundary shift requires decoupling the sole primacy of economic growth from cultural production, recuperating the importance of social values, in particular inclusion, and rearticulating the value of inclusion within a relational creative industries ecosystem.

Communities of Care

In her discussion of organizational tools and responses to precarization in the creative industries, Angela McRobbie highlights the work of Isabell Lorey on the "care community." Lorey suggests that the care community "enhanc[es] the status of care," and foregrounds the activist work of the feminist collective Precarias a la Deriva in Spain, which focuses on "housework, nursing, child-raising and education… and also work in call centres and in sex work."[20] In the creative industries context with youth and emerging creators and collectives, raising and repositioning the status of traditional care work is not a specific concern per se, but there are rising efforts to respond to neoliberalism and precarity. Greig de Peuter and Nicole Cohen note that "across Europe and North America, cultural workers are responding to… strained conditions by experimenting with organizational forms and collective activities."[21] While de Peuter and Cohen examine the resurgence of trade unions, particularly amongst free-lance creative workers and in digital media journalism, Marisol Sandoval highlights worker co-operatives as "an alternative way of organising cultural work.[22] These formal initiatives are important to note and assess, but it is also important to take note of smaller-scale, emerging alternatives that may be exploratory or may not be addressing workplace realities head on.

Communities of care in the creative industries demonstrate a shift towards a collective impulse and suggest the resilience of alternative formations of social enterprise within the broader neoliberal uptake of the creative industries as economic driver. The neoliberal imperatives of the creative industries instrumentalize risk as an individual concern and suggest the need to compete for seemingly scarce resources. Communities of care foreground a collective rather than an individual response to mitigating and managing this risk, creating broader support structures in the absence of policy frameworks. In their exploration of creative labour, David Hesmondhalgh and Sarah Baker map the qualities of what they identify as "good work," including good wages, working hours and high levels of safety; autonomy; interest; sociality; self-esteem; security; self-realization; work-life balance; the production of excellent products; and the production of products that contribute to the common good.[23] Although the labour conditions and the self-exploitation found in creative industries work might locate it under Hesmondhalgh and Baker's rubric of "bad work," Hesmondhalgh and Baker seek to restore the promise and lure of creative industries work under their articulation of "good work."

Many young people are endeavouring to restore creative industries work, and more broadly work in general, as "good" work, through their efforts to transform what this work might look like, towards a more caring and collaborative mode. Tronto's work on care ethics critiques both the "bootstrapping" and the "charity" models of dealing with the economic struggles of others within a neoliberal paradigm; communities of care offer an alternative to these neoliberal models of extending help. Rather than offering help to others, communities of care emphasize relationality and mutual support. These responses, based in mutual aid, might take different forms and might go by different terms. Forwarding a definition of "care work" centred in disability justice, Piepzna-Samarasinha comments, "I first learned of the term 'mutual aid' as an anarchist teenager, in books like Ursula Le Guin's *The Dispossessed* and in a lot of zines that quoted white guy theorists like [Peter] Kropotkin. All of these writers, and many other anarchist and antiauthoritarian writers, use the term to mean a voluntary reciprocal exchange of resources and services for mutual benefit. Mutual aid, as opposed to charity, does not connote moral superiority of the giver over the receiver. White people didn't invent the concept of mutual aid—many precolonial (and after) Black, Indigenous, and brown communities have complex webs of exchanges of care."[24] This definition of mutual aid suggests looking to practice-led examples from marginalized and underrepresented communities to learn innovative, relational models of care, while recognizing that colonialism and capitalism have sought to extinguish these relational care webs.

Rather than positioning formal organizing in opposition to community-oriented values, we can recognize both of these responses as part of the work of fostering a caring culture and of social transformation. In youth creative work, the continued existence of social values within a creative industries paradigm includes respect, reciprocity, vulnerability, empathy, and mutual support. Centring these values is also part of restoring creative industries work as "good work." bell hooks highlights values such as friendship, talking together, trust, respect, care, knowledge, responsibility, as "the process of making community wherever we are," which is "unlike other movements for social change that require joining organizations and attending meetings."[25] These values offer a lens to note and foreground the importance of caring relations, as care often remains devalued and invisible in comparison to formal or public-facing initiatives. Similarly, Leah

Bassel offers a "defence of micropolitics" or a "reorientation of political practice toward one another, fellow citizens, alongside politics vis-à-vis formal institutions with power."[26] Here, Bassel suggests an articulation of the importance of how individuals interact with one another with formal organizing. She suggests "political practice" is also found in social relations, which locates power relationality in interactions, rather than only locating power with institutions.

Care Thinking

Care ethics in a creative industries framework can materialize in various ways, including both formal organizing and initiatives and informal social values and interactions. Both of these elements of care invoke relationality and the work of social reproduction and transformation. Here, I further define components of care through a typology of "care thinking" in order to mobilize care as a guiding framework, while also attempting to think with care. First, as discussed above, care thinking involves a relational ontology or theory of self. Care has been devalued, but all people give and receive care, even if their caring labour is delegated or forced onto others. Next, care thinking also involves an investigation of structural barriers and inequities related to giving and receiving care. Situating care in relational thinking and relational ontology can give rise to sentiments and expressions like "we are all in this together," which was, for example, popularly heard through early stages of the COVID-19 pandemic in 2020. Care thinking recognizes the historical, political, economic, and social factors that impact our lived experiences and how we relate to one another, including our capacities to meaningfully care for ourselves and others, rather than assume collective capacity exists, or that experiences are collective. Third, care thinking can involve utopian or transformative speculation, a commitment to recognizing barriers and developing alternatives. As discussed in the Introduction, radical imagination is central for care thinking. Fisher and Tronto conclude that "in order to reshape caring activities we ultimately need to reenvision social institutions… To build the feminist future we need to stretch our imaginations so that we can discover new visions of society in which caring is a central value and institutions truly facilitate caring."[27] Fisher and Tronto highlight the need to reconfigure caring activities, because of their current devaluation and divide, but also underscore building a future through imagination and "new visions." Similarly, Piepzna-Samarasinha's book *Care Work* is subtitled *Dreaming* Disability Justice; adrienne maree brown's book *Emergent Strategy* is subtitled *Shaping* Change, *Changing* Worlds; Maria Puig de la Bellacassa's book *Matters of Care* is subtitled *Speculative* Ethics (emphasis in these subtitles added).

As discussed above, in Fisher and Tronto's rubric of care-as-process, care involves paying attention. As such, a first step of care can be attuning the attention, considering that attention is often primarily directed towards economic value in a neoliberal paradigm. But beyond choosing to direct one's attention differently, paying attention, as a step of care, involves making choices. Fisher and Tronto write, "there are often more things to care about than we can comprehend, and we often care about more than that to which we can respond." Discussing this discrepancy between the many things that can pull our attention and the number of things we can reasonably respond to, the authors note that the Old Saxon etymological root of the word care is *sorrow*.[28] Following in this etymological thread, it is often now commented that the Latin root of the word curate is *curatus*, or to take care of, suggesting that acts of curation can be thought of as acts of care. In the creative industries context, curating can mean selecting which works or whose works to present: this raises ethico-political questions of whose forms of cultural production are foregrounded and whose are on the margins. In this book, I map care thinking around this ethico-political question, centring underrepresented forms of cultural production and forms of care work that imagine alternatives to dominant paradigms. Below, I begin this mapping by highlighting characteristics of youth creative work from my research projects.

Redefining the Creative Industries: Doing Differently

Given the continued desire to work in the creative industries, despite known challenges, ongoing assessments of how young people cope with and navigate these working realities is vital. In their analysis of exclusion in the creative industries labour market, Bridget Conor, Rosalind Gill, and Stephanie Taylor highlight the tension between the myth of the creative industries as open, diverse, Bohemian, cool, and egalitarian and the reality of creative industries work as precarious, unequal, and informal. In comparison to other labour market areas, creative industries labour in many sectors is often deregulated, with ambiguous and declining set qualifications and certifications. For example, in a digitized environment, anyone might call themselves a journalist, whether or not they went to journalism school. This differs from other employment sectors, for example nursing, though there may well be a push towards lowering standards and qualifications across industries. A deregulated creative industries environment might seemingly be more open to a wider array of people as creativity and cultural production become more widespread, but systemic social inequality and biases remain pervasive, which influence how talent and creativity are appraised. Conor, Gill, and Taylor note that problems with gender and racialized inequity and exclusion of visible minorities relate to 1) informal recruitment in hiring practices; 2) racism, sexism, and stereotypes; and 3) self-representation and the need to "look the part."[29] Discussing the pervasive problem of sexual violence in the creative industries, Sophie Hennekam and Dawn Bennett note elements of creative industries cultures that enable this abuse, including tolerance for sexual harassment; competition for work; industry culture; gendered power relations; and informal networks.[30]

These problems of entering and working in the creative industries urgently suggest the need for more inclusive alternatives. As discussed in Chapter 1, cultural mapping methodology can be used to attune to emergence and forms of social practice in the creative industries that are present, but might be outside of the dominant lenses used to frame these industries. Working from my research data about young people's experiences in the creative industries, here I forward autonomy, access, and balance as characteristics of creative work and as alternative means with which to understand the creative industries, beyond an overarching economic focus or discipline-based definition of these fields. What do the creative industries look like from the perspective of people, in practice, when characterized by the desire to work differently?

Autonomy

Many youth and small-scale cultural producers demonstrate a well-informed awareness of the challenges of creative industries work. The draw of this form of employment for many youth is not that it is lucrative; creative work can allow for a sense of autonomy and self-realization, which is even more appealing given the challenges of the labour market at large. Profiling the features of "good work" for the creative industries, Hesmondhalgh and Baker highlight the element of autonomy, which includes authenticity and freedom to self-direct within existing constraints. The authors highlight both *workplace autonomy*, "the degree of self-determination that individual workers or groups of workers have within a certain work situation" and *creative autonomy*, "the degree to which 'art' knowledge, symbol-making and so on can and/or should operate independently of influence of other determinants."[31] Discussing the drive for creative autonomy through artistic practice, Laikwan Pang criticizes the isolated, individualized vision of artistic autonomy, value-neutral and independent from "social interference" as a "fiction": "the discourse of the autonomy of art is a fiction... one heavily invested with the patriarchy's attempt to appropriate women. Postcolonial scholars and cultural anthropologists also remind us that arts are communally based in many places in the world, and that the 'autonomous' European arts were indeed invested with many racialized ways of looking at people."[32] Here, I build on this creative industries scholarship by foregrounding *relational autonomy* to recast a definition of autonomy in more communally-based ways. With contemporary youth creative work, there is a desire for creative work to be autonomous but not divorced from the social realm. With an awareness that neoliberal norms of economic competition are harmful and exclusionary, many young people strive to reimagine creative work differently and collectively, foregrounding collaboration instead of competition. Through communities of care, youth creative workers are charting their own pathways for what creative industries employment looks like, attempting to mobilize their own norms, including norms that expand the economic realm being a sole or primary driver of creative work. In practice, this means engaging with the realm of economic necessity, and developing nodes of rearticulated economic, social, and cultural values for the creative industries.

Cultural Production as Relational Response

Discussing the challenges of making a living as a young artist, one research participant pithily stated, "shit is hard, yo." In my research, I have gathered stories of young people making a living, or trying to make a living, in the creative industries, but I have also gathered stories about communal responses, re-imagining creative work with a renewed focus on the social realm, including taking care of one another, and developing collective strategies to develop new ways of living and working. As another research participant also pithily stated, "we are in this together. Like, shit is fucked. We need to come together."[33] Important here is not only the dire outline of the contemporary state of affairs, "shit is fucked," but also the repetition of the collective subject "we" and the call to "come together." Relational autonomy is not sdirected towards self-interest or an individualized self; a relational self contrasts a neoliberal or entrepreneurial model of self. This desire for autonomy in and through the creative industries also stems from an awareness of structural barriers, racism, and inequity, and a desire to reimagine creative work to centre underrepresented communities and people. Describing her creative projects, one research participant states, "my initiative prioritizes Black women in the wellness space because there isn't a lot of space for us. A portion of the initiative was to reach out to young Black girls and create a mentorship program for them, have a space for them to get together, and learn with each other… Some of the things that you don't really learn in school, anyways."[34] This research participant expresses the importance of fostering an inclusive environment or "just creating space that is comfortable for people" as "the basis of everything I do. I try to create that." The creation of this environment is prioritized more than particular artistic disciplines or outputs. Foregrounding a caring and relational mode of exchange, this research participant discusses her way of leading programs for youth but also engaging with others more generally: "[I] don't ever want to walk into a space and feel like: 'I'm going to teach you these things!' It's just like: 'let's learn from each other—this as an exchange.'" This research participant facilitated these types of exchanges across various artistic mediums and different projects and expressed a desire for "a physical space of my own where all of those things will come together." Relational autonomy can involve the desire for a space of one's own (material or immaterial), and for various creative and community-oriented projects to be able to come together.

Given a history of cultural appropriation and theft of the creative work of Black, Indigenous, and racialized artists, autonomy in creative industries pursuits has particular salience. Musician and artist Lido Pimienta, who identifies as Afro-Indigenous and Columbian-Canadian, articulates the desire to retain creative and economic autonomy in the music industry away from major record labels:

> For a massive distribution you need to sign your music away to a label. And I'm not ready to do that. I'm not ready to give control to a big label. That's another decision I'm making. I could reach out to these big labels and that means my album will be released in two years instead of [in a few months]. And you give them your masters. I don't have the patience to pursue a label that will fit to what I need. It's a true issue that we have to deal with. We need the protection of a label, whatever money they give upfront, but they will have control.[35]

Here, Pimienta speaks to balancing "money upfront" with control and ownership over one's own work, alongside the expediency and timeliness of pursuing an autonomous pathway. As will be further discussed below, autonomy often means balancing economic imperatives with creative and caring concerns, negotiating how to retain autonomy and community alongside economic survival.

For many youth creative workers, the desire for relational autonomy is expressed as a desire to carve out space for the self and others away from dominant models that do not see or support them. Artists Humboldt Magnussen and Marjan Verstappen met while doing their Master's degrees in Fine Arts—but even with their Master's degrees in hand, they reflected on the lack of opportunities and difficulties for emerging and young artists to make a living from their work. With this in mind, they started the Younger Than Beyoncé (YTB) gallery in 2015 in order to provide a space to showcase emerging artistic work. In 2015, "younger than Beyoncé" would have been for artists 35 years old or younger, based on Beyoncé's age at that time, but the gallery is focused on supporting emerging artists rather than operating with any strict aged-based cut off. With this reference to Beyoncé, there is a both/and articulation of recognition and celebration of a widely commercially successful Black artist, while at the same time working to carve out space for small-scale alternatives. Co-founder Humboldt Magnussen states, "this is about making our own opportunities for ourselves as a young group of people. It's really important to foster that." YTB develops group-based rather than individual opportunities.

Fostering opportunities for oneself and others also reimagines definitions of "success" that conventionally mean individual upward mobility or economic profit. Instead, Humboldt says, "it's really important to work in a team. I think the reward is so much greater. It's like sports, when you're on a team and you accomplish something you get to high five your teammates, but if you're by yourself and you win the medal, you only get to high five yourself."[36] Expressed in this way, "only high-fiving yourself" suggests the loneliness and isolation of neoliberal models: with care ethics and communities of care, autonomy is not forwarded in these isolated ways. In this context, communities of care carve out autonomy from more dominant systems of individualism and competition, making space instead for friendship and collaboration.

On the whole, young people are acutely aware of the economic challenges they face entering into the creative industries workforce, while also experiencing a disconnect between established and emerging forms of creative practice, and a lack of infrastructure and attention to emergence. Merray Gerges discusses co-founding CRITpaper, an art criticism magazine as follows:

> I was frustrated with the lack of publishing opportunities for people who are still trying to figure out how to write... My peers, who were in the same boat, and I weren't in a place where we could publish anything, we were just figuring things out… There was an absence so we devised something for ourselves to remedy that.

Here, the collective "we" subject references peers and being "in the same boat," alongside collaboratively working to redress the challenge of lack of opportunity. Merray also discusses CRITpaper as an autonomous platform for expression that is not directed by advertising dollars, but is instead directed by the writers: "because we don't have a style guide and we don't publish ads, people can say and do whatever they want. Oftentimes the essays and the criticism take on forms that other print publications wouldn't be conducive to or would be resistant to publish because it's not what their readership is accustomed to… We can do whatever the fuck they want."[37]

However, challenges of funding and financing emerging forms of creative practice remain. One research participant expressed, "It's fantastic being able to create. I would never want to work a 9–5 job but I have also come to the realization that I will probably never drive a Mercedes or live in a mansion. But, I don't need that. I am perfectly content with my work and I love it. The hardest part is a consistent money flow."[38] This respondent articulates benefits to creative work beyond profit or beyond a desire for extreme forms of material wealth, but at the same time does not completely absent economic considerations, with the closing reference to the "money flow." Similarly, in his study of young people and "DIY" careers in music, Andy Bennett highlights that in the context of economic downturn and lack of secure career paths for young people, the "self-chosen precarious pathway" provides a more gratifying sense of purpose, and can be motivated by non-economic goals of "creative or aesthetic gratification" or "civic engagement, participation and inclusivity."[39] These non-economic goals of inclusion and engagement can be part of the desire for relational autonomy, and part of a rearticulated alternative in the creative industries—a rearticulation that includes cultural and social values with economic ones. These modified rationales for creative work are also found in other studies of small-scale and emerging forms of creative practice. For example, one participant in Susan Luckman's study of craft and design workers states: "I probably am never going to be rich but that's okay because that's not what I want to be. I just want to make a full time living from my business."[40] In these comments from cultural producers, there is a differentiation between making a living and being rich; this suggests that economic necessity is not shunned, but is limited in scope, put into place alongside cultural/social values.

Beyond Privilege

Common ways of thinking about the rationales for setting oneself apart from the desire for material wealth (e.g. being rich, Mercedes, mansion) underscore class privilege and having the economic means to not be overly concerned with economic means. That is, this line of thought suggests it takes a certain amount of established class and economic privilege to be able to say, "I don't want to be rich." However, there is a growing body of empirical work with creative industries workers that identifies that this type of work is not only pursued by those with class or other forms of privilege. Through the expansion of post-secondary education, McRobbie identifies the expansion of creative industries employment beyond the traditional middle classes to those "coming from lower middle-class or upper working-class backgrounds."[41] Working with Gilles Deleuze's concept of the line of flight, McRobbie suggests that this rise in self-expressive or creative work is motivated by:

> the desire to escape a lifetime of routine work… From the point of view of the young black British woman from a working-class background who has graduated in media studies, the element of struggle to work in film and television is articulated through an often family based narrative of somehow not doing the menial and repetitive jobs that her mother had to do.[42]

Cast in this light, the desire for autonomy is intergenerational, stemming from a desire for self-realization and self-actualization, away from traditional expectations and associated perceptions of drudgery and servitude that have accompanied working class and racialized forms of labour. At the same time, family can also be a source of care and teaching, including about entrepreneurship and entrepreneurial values; some of my research participants centre family as a space of intergenerational knowledge transfer and support. Writing about the period following the financial crisis of 2008, McRobbie argues that the bubble of the high expectations about the creative industries as a driver of the economy "has burst," yet "young people cling on with more determination than ever to make a living in these alley-way micro economies."[43] McRobbie's work identifies that it is something other than the promise of material wealth or class privilege that is driving cultural production as a line of flight. This "clinging" is also a form of care, and a desire for working differently and relationally.

Through my research, I have profiled youth entry-level creative industries workers who have high levels of education; in open-ended survey questions and in semi-structured interviews, one way this education manifests is through an informed knowingness and resistance to elements of exploitation in the creative industries. As noted by McRobbie, expansion of post-secondary education means increasing segments of the general population are accessing and obtaining higher levels of education, but it is not necessarily formal education systems that are responsible for increased knowledge or resistance amongst young people. These orientations towards creative industries work can also be formed through self-education, engagement with these conversations online or in social media, with peers, or through practical, lived experience.

Nuances and tensions about the line of flight, or the quest for autonomy, emerge from the lived experiences that youth cultural producers articulate, and these tensions complicate the sometimes overly facile discussions of youth that emerge from the media and popular discourses. In viral articles like "Slaves of the Internet Unite," *New York Times* writer Tim Kreider delivers a "plea" to his younger colleagues to refuse unpaid work, providing an email template response to reply and turn down requests for uncompensated work.[44] In the *Jacobin* article "In the Name of Love," Miya Tokumitsu skewers the contemporary call to passion-led work, arguing that this erases labour and gives rise to "people persuaded to work for cheap or free, or even for a net loss of wealth. This has certainly been the case for all those interns working for college credit or those who actually purchase ultra-desirable fashion-house internships at auction."[45] These articles suggest that youth and those who are "persuaded" or are able to work for free are part of the problem of driving down labour standards in the creative industries. Indeed, studies of unpaid work in the creative industries have shown that youth and entry-level creative workers are more likely to accept the premise of working for free.[46] These continued practices of exploiting unpaid labour in entry-level creative industries pathways, including unpaid internships and other expectations to work for free, are important to register as part of the process of working towards collective change and improved working conditions in the creative industries. Tokumitsu's overarching argument is also important to preserve—that creative work is labour, and casting it only as a labour of love, or passion-led, minimizes the ability to intervene in and regulate labour conditions in this sector. However, the avenue for change in workplace practices is through policy change, or enforcement of existing labour codes and laws designed to regulate labour markets, rather than suggesting young people themselves are part of the problem. Here, I also seek to map other modes of engaging in the creative industries, beyond this thread of self-exploitation or an overarching generalization that creative industries employment necessarily correlates with privilege. One artist featured at a Younger than Beyoncé exhibit, Tau Lewis, references the labour and commitment in the work of developing alternatives to dominant creative industries models: "I don't like it when any of my friends or myself are called 'lucky' for our opportunities or successes. We are not lucky. We are strong; we are fighters."[47] Rather than echoing a mantra of "doing what you love" trumping the need for proper remuneration, youth respondents in my research highlight the challenges and inequities of their working lives, alongside the desire, labour, challenges, and joys of creating autonomous alternatives.

Widening Access: A Culture of Participation

Some theorizations of young people choosing to work for free in entry-level creative industries work have forwarded the concepts of "hope" or "aspirational" labour, or choosing to perform free labour in the goal that it will later convert into paid labour.[48] Here, I forward a sense of caring beyond a transactional desire to move from unpaid to paid labour, suggesting instead that communities of care are based in a desire for an enlargement of possibilities of what work in the creative industries might look like and who might work in the sector. Following from young people's informed awareness about labour challenges in the creative industries, there is also informed awareness about structural barriers and lack of diversity. To this end, I forward *access* as an emerging characteristic of how youth creative workers define their creative industries pursuits. If hope or aspirational labour remains within a neoliberal model of individual self-advancement, working towards widening access suggests a relational model of self, and an expansion of who works in these industries alongside moving towards more inclusive working practices. Recognizing these structural barriers and inequity in the creative industries and working to create change are also elements of care thinking.

Widening access to creative work in terms of diversity and equity has been expressed by my research participants as something they "care about," in the sense defined by Fisher and Tronto, something that they are paying attention to. Access is a framework that helps these research participants define and articulate their positionality and involvement in the creative industries. One research participant commented "school isn't important when it comes to preparing yourself for a career in the arts … some opportunities … will always necessarily be closed off to you because of who I am and how the arts are themselves structured by white supremacy and capitalism and patriarchy and hetero-patriarchy." Here, there is an expression of distance from formal education as the site of knowledge transfer and career incubation alongside an analysis of structural barriers, including systemic racism and patriarchy, that shape and limit access and opportunities in the creative industries. Another research participant spoke of their desire to "dismantle traditional structures of curating and criticism" as "there aren't a lot of young folks who are being represented a lot of the time, and there aren't a lot of women, there aren't a lot of people of colour, there aren't a lot of Indigenous folks." Another respondent expressed their desire to help the process of "underrepresented and marginalized peoples … express[ing] the conditions of their lives and seek change" through the arts.[49] With the awareness of inequity and a commitment to creating change to widen access, we can note "caring for" diversity and equity, in the sense of taking responsibility as defined by Fisher and Tronto. One research participant stated, "part of the reason I started to work as a critic and curator was because I didn't see other people really doing it in a way that supported young artists and I wanted to try to provide that a little bit myself."[50] Many research participants expressed a need and desire to work collaboratively towards common goals of increasing access, in response to a competitive neoliberal model that pits people against one another and is also exclusionary along the lines of race, gender, class, sexuality, disability, age, and other structural factors.

Mechanisms to move towards widening access with regards to underrepresented people and communities include sharing knowledge and time in order to combat secrecy and scarcity. For example, speaking about her record label Dap Records, musician, artist, and community organizer April Aliermo comments on sharing logistical information about how to navigate the music industry: "with our label the goal is to put out bands... to empower them with the know-hows of certain parts of the industry. A lot of bands just don't know. They just want to make music of course. But, they have no idea where to begin to set up a tour or—you should print your CDs out at this place and mail it out to all these college and radio stations. No one tells anyone that. Very simple basic knowledge. We want to give [this knowledge] to bands that we find interesting."[51] One research participant commented that they wished creative workers "talked more," and shared their experiences of how they make a living: "if artists have other jobs I want to know and I feel like it's not something you should be ashamed of, like it makes people feel solidarity and okay about how they are doing."[52] These open conversations about economic realities could lead to more transparency about rates of pay (which are often unequal with regards to race and gender) and the necessities of multiple income streams; more knowledge can demystify how and who is making a living through creative work and could lead to more access and equity.

Though I have defined my research participants as "youth" or emerging creative workers, many of these research participants also have an awareness of themselves as slightly more seasoned than someone just starting out. Many research participants also comment on offering support to younger or more entry-level creative workers. For example, one research participant comments, "overall I feel there were not enough resources for creative business mentorship available to young people, in particular young women who work in male-dominated industries. I know of a few creative entrepreneurs my age who are now volunteering their time to mentor young people seeking to professionalize their creative skills, myself included." Here, efforts to widen access for young women underrepresented in the creative industries are developed through the strategies of time and mentorship. Similarly, Luckman tracks a "a sense of solidarity" amongst her research participants, crafts-based creative workers, that is "a far cry from the combative competition that is such a feature of business enterprise television shows such as *The Apprentice*."[53] Luckman's comment suggests the difference and distance between more outlandish and public expressions of what creative industries and enterprise can look like (*The Apprentice*), and more typical working realities, including caring, cooperative, collaborative, and relational values, which can be less visible. These values are particularly important in the context of visibility and inclusion of underrepresented people and communities in the creative industries. Speaking about starting a modelling agency for people of colour, called Lorde Inc., Nafisa Kaptownwala comments, "we are missing people in this industry that look like me, and that look like my friends." Nafisa speaks to relationality with friends and community members as sparking her desire to create alternatives structures and a business focused on people of colour: "definitely there being a lack of diversity in fashion, but... I was more focused on the people in my community. Art photographers and editorial fashion photographers, I was like this is fucked, where are all the people of colour?"[54] Nafisa's comments underscore the importance of moving past a deficit model, that suggests underrepresented people lack entrepreneurial knowledge or lack connections or social capital. The absence of people of colour in creative industries also highlights problems of systemic racism and discrimination, and the need to create change in industry structures.

Balancing Community and Economic Needs

Above, I framed reduced material aspirations as the desire to put economic values in their place, in order to make space for other social, cultural, and collaborative values. In practice, this means navigating the tensions between community and economic values, as the pressing need to make a living remains: people still want and need to make a living, including being fairly compensated for their work. Because they are often less visible, in this book I seek to map the existence and persistence of these community-oriented values as rationales for creative work and as a defining characteristic of what the creative industries looks like for many emerging cultural producers. Preserving community-oriented values is part of care thinking, working toward a new vision for the creative industries. Developing strategies to find *balance* between community and economic needs is challenging within an overarching capitalistic framework. Discussing founding her recording studio, Sandbox Studios, Kiana "Rookz" Eastmond highlights business opportunities and the creativity involved in developing new business initiatives: "it's the ideation into the creation piece of building a business, thinking about how things will connect to other people and shooting the gaps in the market."[55] Rookz speaks to gaining this entrepreneurial mindset through her family upbringing, "I grew up with a mother who was an entrepreneur. My mother owned many businesses since I was a young child." Describing finding and building Sandbox, she highlights racist stigmas against hip hop music:

> I had gone to so many studios. And speaking of entrepreneurship, and to touch on other intersectionalities, and different things that happen being a young Black female queer entrepreneur—I'd gone to a lot of spaces and spoken to them over the phone, and I was like I want to open a recording studio, and they'd be like 'Yep, yep come by' and then I would come by and they would be like 'No we're not even renting the space out anymore.' Or some people would just straight up say 'I don't want rappers here.' So I was really discouraged after about a month. I'd gotten all these 'yesses' over the phone and I went to ten spaces and every time I'd show up with first and last [month's rent] and they'd be like, 'no.' People have their own ignorance around what they probably think happens in a studio. One day I was going to give up and then I got on the phone with somebody they were like 'yeah forget this,' and I was like 'no I'm not going to forget this'—it was that disbelief. Like, 'just quit,' and I was like 'that's not who you are.'

Here, Rookz highlights the resilience and determination of continuing to pursue entrepreneurial goals in the face of discrimination and hostility. Through these experiences, Rookz also speaks to community values, such creating inclusive spaces for Black LGBTQ+ youth through her recording studio.

One balancing strategy between economic and community-oriented values voiced by my research participants is limiting performing unpaid work for larger or established organizations. "Just say no" was a common response to the question of how respondents navigate the expectation that they work for free or give away their creative work for free; one research participant commented "I would just say no" and another responded with a resounding "hell no." Other respondents commented that working for free was a more common part of their experience when they were younger, and they have learnt the skill of saying no. At the same time, my research participants also voiced the strategy of taking on free and community-oriented labour through the lens of fostering diversity and inclusion, and also through the lens of friendship and peer support. "Now, I don't [work for free] unless it's an organization that I know has no money and I think it'll be really fun or a really good experience for me, or I'm doing it for a friend, but I know in the past I've definitely done a lot more," says one research participant, both voicing distance from past unpaid work, and also choosing to do this form of labour through the rationales of pleasure and enjoyment, friendship, and knowledge of organizations having limited financial means. Similarly, another research participant highlights the social rationale of friendship, alongside the cultural rationale of supporting emerging art: "Yeah. I definitely get asked, [and] I definitely do a lot of free publicity work for friends. Just because, if I don't do it, no one else will, and because I like the work that they do, or the art they create. I want to make sure it's getting the attention it deserves." The absence of broader support systems or structures is noted with the reference to "no one else" to do the work, alongside an expression of desire to fill these gaps. Another research participant highlights feeling part of a creative community as an artist: "I... do a ton of volunteer work that can sometimes lead to paid work and sometimes doesn't—I think a big part of being an artist is also being a citizen of that community, and that involves time and effort."[56] Here, there is reference to the transactional element or the conversion of unpaid labour into paid work, but this is not the only expressed rationale behind choosing unpaid work. The reference to being a citizen of a community also speaks to community-oriented values, and a balance between community and economic needs.

This nuance about when, how, and if to work for free expands a simple dichotomy of volunteerism vs. paid work in creative industries settings. Although "just say no" to unpaid work is expressed by my research participants, this nuance also expands an either/or approach to paid or unpaid work, suggestive of a rearticulation of economic, social, and cultural values. However, because of the challenges of making a living, some research participants voiced their inability and lack of desire to perform unpaid, community-oriented forms of labour. Speaking about providing mentorship to others, one research participant stated that "I enjoy doing [it]... But at the same time, I really need the income. I would love to be able to do that in a paid situation," expressing the need for compensation to be able to have time and capacity to take on care labour. Asked about working in community-oriented ways, one research participant stated: "I find that I'm doing that less and less, I've been on boards of directors and all that stuff, but my own expansion in terms of my own practice and my paid work as well [is what I'm now emphasizing]." Alongside the economic considerations of paid work, this research participant foregrounds their own personal development, highlighting the importance of centring the self even within contexts of care and relationality.

In their study "Unemployed by Choice: Young Creative People and the Balancing of Responsibilities Through Strategic Self-Management," Sven Mørch and Sabina Pultz, assess the rationales of Danish youth aspiring to creative careers who choose unemployment to access welfare benefits to financially underwrite their creative practices. The authors profile the conflicting justification strategies that youth deploy to make sense of their choice, which is an illegal practice. Justifications include intensified work ethic and increased individualization through self-management alongside what they characterize as civil disobedience and societal critique, including critique of the (un)employment and education systems; critique of lack of support for creative careers; and critique of capitalism, despite a lack of collective organizing. The authors characterize this tension between individualized self-management and societal critique to stem from "the inherent contradictions of late modern demands,"[57] highlighting the tensions in balancing social and economic rationales for cultural/creative work. They note the high levels of education, social, and cultural capital amongst their research participants, raising questions of how these young people's experiences of unemployment differ from other populations; nonetheless, these identified strategies offer inroads for rethinking either/or binaries of economic vs. social rationales for creative work.

Through my research, I highlight communities of care as the creation of infrastructure and support systems to bolster making a living in the creative industries while pursuing community-oriented goals. While some examples raised in my research interviews, like drinking wine and discussing work as a group, may not appear as overtly politicized activities, communities of care can nonetheless be understood as a response that fosters collective solidarity with regards to common struggles in the creative industries. This is a form of collective organizing, even if it does not necessarily mobilize in politicized or publicly activist expressions. These support systems range from loose or ad-hoc groups to creating new organizations or structures to serve others. For example, one research participant commented that "me and some of my peers, we've formed these support systems where we have regular critiques with each other and just sending each other links and stuff." Another research participant spoke to developing a collective: the group of four running the collective has a range of backgrounds in theatre, comedy, and community organizing and one project that this collective undertakes is a program providing training in comedy to youth. When commenting on the "male-dominated" nature of the music industry, one research participant referenced the informal mentorship and mutual support of a secret Facebook group for women and gender non-conforming people in music with hundreds of members: a space for asking questions, sharing information about jobs, getting supporters to come to shows, and organizing in-person meet-ups. "I really wish this community existed a long time ago [because] it would have helped all of us along the way," says this research participant. With this balance of community and economically oriented work, many young people are aiming to create systems to help themselves while also helping others, in their process of navigating the creative industries and negotiating what these industries are and can be.

In Chapter 3, I turn my attention to diversity work more specifically. Limited ways of conceptualizing the creative industries, discussed in Chapter 1, are not only reductive, as they have also created harm by enabling toxic and abusive work environments in these industries. While "diversity" has become celebrated as a positive value for companies and organizations, this celebration is often hollow and does not confront the realities of discrimination or commit to meaningful inclusion work. The elements of care thinking established in this chapter—relationality, recognizing barriers, and developing new visions—and the characteristics of youth creative work—autonomy, widening access, and balancing community and economics—offer important interventions of care ethics for the creative industries.

Notes

1 Heather Wright and Brooklyn Neustaeter, "'You're Not Alone In This': Canadians Are 'Caremongering' through the COVID-19 Pandemic," *CTV News*, March 19, 2020, accessed March 16, 2021, https://www.ctvnews.ca/health/coronavirus/you-re-not-alone-in-this-canadians-are-caremongering-through-the-covid-19-pandemic-1.4859369
2 Tom Gerken, "Coronavirus: Kind Canadians Start a 'Caremongering' Trend," *BBC News*, March 16, 2020, accessed March 16, 2021, https://www.bbc.com/news/world-us-canada-51915723
3 PDX Non-Binary Community Effort, "Collective Cares," accessed March 16, 2021, https://docs.google.com/document/d/1XBDKJjQsSQOCT64ADuuCaPognKHUT-ZD7syc_RIiGg3o/edit
4 Leah Lakshmi Piepzna-Samarasinha, "Half Assed Disabled Prepper Tips for Preparing for a Coronavirus Quarantine," accessed March 16, 2021, https://docs.google.com/document/d/1rIdpKgXeBHbmM3KpB5NfjEBue8YN1MbXhQ7zTOLmSyo/edit
5 Nancy Fraser and Rahel Jaeggi, *Capitalism: A Conversation in Critical Theory* (Cambridge: Polity, 2018), 3.
6 Mark Banks, "Craft Labour and Creative Industries," *International Journal of Cultural Policy* 16, no. 3 (2010): 305–321; Alessandro Gandini and James Graham, eds., *Collaborative Production in the Creative Industries* (London: University of Westminster Press, 2017).
7 Bernice Fisher and Joan Tronto, "Toward a Feminist Theory of Caring," in *Circles of Care,* eds. Emily Abel and Margaret Nelson (Albany, NY: SUNY Press, 1990), 36–54, 38.
8 Fraser and Jaeggi, *Capitalism*, 2.
9 Ned Noddings, *Caring: A Relational Approach to Morals and Ethics Education* (2nd ed.) (Berkeley: University of California Press, 2013), 2.
10 Ibid., 3, 5.
11 Fisher and Tronto, "Towards a Feminist Theory," 40.
12 Ibid., 44.
13 Maria Puig de la Bellacassa, *Matters of Care: Speculative Ethics in More than Human Worlds* (Minneapolis: University of Minnesota Press, 2017), 1, 90, 13.
14 Brigid Conor, Rosalind Gill, and Stephanie Taylor, eds., *Gender and Creative Labour, Sociological Review Monograph Series* (London: Wiley-Blackwell, 2015); David Hesmondhalgh and Sarah Baker, *Creative Labour: Media Work in Three Cultural Industries* (London, UK: Routledge, 2011).
15 Leah Lakshmi Piepzna-Samarasinha, *Care Work: Dreaming Disability Justice* (Vancouver, BC: Arsenal Pulp Press, 2018), 141, 139.
16 Nancy Fraser, "Contradictions of Capital and Care," *New Left Review* 100 (2016): 99–117, 101.
17 Ibid., 102.
18 Joan Tronto, *Caring Democracy: Markets, Equality and Justice* (New York: New York University Press, 2013), 139.
19 Fisher and Tronto, "Towards a Feminist Theory," 56.
20 Isabell Lorey, *State of Insecurity: Government of the Precarious* (London, UK: Verso, 2015), 91, 94.
21 Greig de Peuter and Nicole Cohen, "Emerging Labour Politics in Creative Industries," in *The Routledge Companion to the Cultural Industries*, eds. Kate Oakley and Justin O'Connor (London: Routledge, 2011), 305–318, 305, 307.
22 Nicole Cohen and Greig de Peuter, *New Media Unions: Organizing Digital Journalists* (New York: Routledge, 2020); Marisol Sandoval, "Fighting Precarity with Co-operation?" *New Formations* 88 (2016): 51–68, 52.

23 David Hesmondahlgh and Sarah Baker, *Creative Labour: Media Work in Three Cultural Industries* (London: Routledge, 2011), 39.
24 Piepzna-Samarasinha, *Care Work*, 42.
25 bell hooks, *All About Love* (New York: Harper, 2000), 143.
26 Leah Bassel, *The Politics of Listening: Politics and Challenges for Democratic Life* (London: Palgrave Pivot, 2017), 11.
27 Fisher and Tronto, "Towards a Feminist Theory," 56.
28 Ibid., 42.
29 Bridget Conor, Rosalind Gill, and Stephanie Taylor, "Introduction," in *Gender and Creative Labour* (Hoboken, New Jersey: Wiley Blackwell, 2015).
30 Sophie Hennekam and Dawn Bennett, "Sexual Harassment in the Creative Industries: Tolerance, Culture and the Need for Change," *Gender, Work & Organizatio*n 24, no. 4 (2017): 417–434.
31 Hesmondhalgh and Baker, *Creative Labour*, 40.
32 Laikwan Pang, "Art and Cultural Industries: Autonomy and Community," *The Routledge Companion to the Cultural Industries*, eds. Kate Oakley and Justin O'Connor (London: Routledge, 2011), 45–55, 47.
33 Miranda Campbell, "'Shit Is Hard, Yo': Young People Making a Living in the Creative Industries," *International Journal of Cultural Policy* 26, no. 4 (2020): 524–543.
34 Personal interview, May 22, 2018.
35 Miranda Campbell, "Shifting Gears," *Every Day We're Hustling* podcast episode 4, October 5, 2016, https://soundcloud.com/everydaywerehustling/04-episode-four
36 Miranda Campbell, "Crewing Up," *Every Day We're Hustling* podcast episode 3, September 28, 2016, https://soundcloud.com/everydaywerehustling/03-episode-three
37 Miranda Campbell, "Making Space," *Every Day We're Hustling* podcast episode 5, October 12, 2016, https://soundcloud.com/everydaywerehustling/05-episode-five
38 Campbell, "'Shit Is Hard.'"
39 Andy Bennett, "Conceptualising the Relationship Between Youth, Music and DIY Careers: A Critical Overview," *Cultural Sociology* 12, no. 2 (2018): 140–155, 147, 149, 152.
40 Susan Luckman, "Craft Entrepreneurialism and Sustainable Scale: Resistance to and Disavowal of the Creative Industries as Champions of Capitalist Growth," *Cultural Trends* 27, no. 5 (2018): 313–326, 317.
41 Angela McRobbie, *Be Creative: Making a Living in the New Culture Industries* (London, UK: Polity Press, 2016), 35.
42 Ibid., 38–39.
43 Ibid., 34.
44 Tim Kreider, "Slaves of the Internet Unite," *The New York Times*, October 26, 2013, accessed January 21, 2020, https://www.nytimes.com/2013/10/27/opinion/sunday/slaves-of-the-internet-unite.html
45 Miya Tokumitsu, "In the Name of Love," *Jacobin,* January 12, 2014, accessed January 21, 2020, https://www.jacobinmag.com/2014/01/in-the-name-of-love/
46 Neil Percival and David Hesmondhalgh, "Unpaid Work in the UK Television and Film Industries: Resistance and Changing Attitudes," *European Journal of Communication* 29 (2014): 188–203.
47 Amanda Parris, "In the Flesh: Younger than Beyoncé Gallery Puts the Focus on Emerging Talent," *CBC Arts*, June 2, 2016, accessed January 21, 2020, https://www.cbc.ca/arts/exhibitionists/in-the-flesh-younger-than-beyonc%C3%A9-gallery-puts-the-focus-on-emerging-talent-1.3611664
48 Kim Allen and Sumi Hollingworth. "'Sticky Subjects' or 'Cosmopolitan Creatives'? Social Class, Place and Urban Young People's Aspirations for Work in the Knowledge Economy," *Urban Studies* 50, no. 3 (2013): 499–517; Kathleen Kuehn and Thomas F.

Corrigan, "Hope Labor: The Role of Employment Prospects in Online Social Production," *The Political Economy of Communication* 1, no. 1 (2013): 9–25; Brooke Duffy, *(Not) Getting Paid to Do What You Love: Gender, Social Media, and Aspirational Work* (New Haven, CT: Yale University Press, 2017).

49 Campbell, "'Shit is Hard.'"

50 Ibid.

51 Campbell, "Making Space"

52 Campbell, "'Shit is Hard.'"

53 Luckman, "Craft Entrepreneurialism," 320.

54 Miranda Campbell, "Breaking Out," *Every Day We're Hustling* podcast episode 2, September 21, 2016, https://soundcloud.com/everydaywerehustling/02-episode-two

55 Ibid.

56 Campbell, "'Shit is Hard.'"

57 Sven Mørch and Sabina Pultz, "Unemployed by Choice: Young Creative People and the Balancing of Responsibilities through Strategic Self-Management," *Journal of Youth Studies* 18, no. 10 (2015): 1382–1401, 1397.

3

THE "DIVERSITY" RESPONSE

In 2019, the Annenberg Inclusion Initiative, partnering with the Time's Up organization, issued the "4% challenge" to increase the number of women film directors, and specifically women directors of colour, working for major film corporations. The challenge, announced during the 2019 Sundance Film Festival, invited industry leaders to commit to announcing one project with a female director in the following 18 months. Dr. Stacy L. Smith, director of the Annenberg Inclusion Initiative, based in the Annenberg School for Communication and Journalism at the University of Southern California, announced this challenge at a panel titled "Making the (In)visible: Radical Transparency in the Data-Driven Age" at Sundance. She shared that she had enlisted her fellow panelists, including film executives and producers Nina Jacobson, Angela Robinson, and Franklin Leonard to participate in this challenge prior to the event, and they had all agreed "with an enthusiastic 'hell yes!'"[1] Under Smith's leadership, the Annenberg Inclusion Initiative has tracked diversity statistics in the form of demographic representation, primarily in film and television, but also in music. This work involves large-scale quantitative content analysis, or counting, of representation of women, people of colour, LGBTQ+ people, and people with disabilities, as well as those employed behind the scenes. For example, in reports such as *Inequality in 1,200 Popular Films: Examining Portrayals of Gender, Race/Ethnicity, LGBTQ & Disability from 2007 to 2018*, the Annenberg Inclusion Initiative has counted the number of female characters who have speaking roles in top-grossing films, alongside numbers of racialized, LGBTQ+, and disabled characters in these films, while also tracking numbers of people from underrepresented groups working behind the camera in key creative positions, such as director, writer, producer, or composer. According to this research on the 1,200 top-grossing films from 2007 to 2018, just 4% of the directors of these films were women.[2] The work of the Annenberg Inclusion

DOI: 10.4324/9781003031338-3

Initiative has catalyzed an important public conversation about lack of representation in the film and TV industries by naming and quantifying the problem. The partnering organization for the 4% challenge, Time's Up, was formed in response to the #MeToo movement, and its organizational mandate addresses issues of sexual violence in the workplace. Their website states, "we're here to accomplish three goals." These goals include 1) safety (insisting everyone is safe at work); 2) power (disrupting the status quo); and 3) equity (levelling the playing field for women).[3]

The 4% challenge was launched via Twitter with the accompanying hashtag, #4PercentChallenge. The response to this challenge largely emerged from Twitter, and on the whole was positive and enthusiastic. Universal Filmed Entertainment Group (Universal Pictures, Focus Features, and Dreamworks Animation) was the first to accept this challenge, followed by STX Entertainment, MCM studios, and Paramount. Via Twitter, Walt Disney Company Chairman and CEO announced, "I'm proud to say 40% of @DisneyStudios' upcoming movie slate is being directed by women and we are striving for more! Individual actors also pledged their commitments to work with a female director in the following 18 months."[4] Kerry Washington tweeted "ABSOLUTELY! YES!!!!!!!!!" Olivia Wilde wrote, "Hell yes I'm in."[5] The format of the Twitter platform, with limited space and characters available, produces the need for short and punchy posts. Nonetheless, a celebratory and affirmative tone emerged from these responses. This 4% challenge offers a very small and a localized response to the systemic issues of lack of representation and lack of inclusion: a commitment to hiring one female film director. Increased representation and movement towards gender parity in employees is important across all industries, including the creative industries. Naming a problem can be part of the process of developing strategies to redress a problem, and campaigns such as the 4% challenge can raise awareness and create mainstream or mass conversations about the importance of these issues, but further work and strategies are needed to both foster improved representation and improved working conditions. In this chapter, I question if the increased conversations about representation and inclusion in the creative industries mark a shift towards an understanding of the systemic nature of underrepresentation and exclusion.

While the terms diversity and inclusion are often used synonymously or in tandem, distinguishing between them allows for a discussion of opportunities for success, mobility, fairness, and learning within a work environment. While diversity can refer to demographic difference (including race, gender, social class, sexuality, disability, age, and so on), inclusion characterizes the nature of the working environment, including a feeling of belonging alongside difference being recognized and valued.[6] Locating "diversity" as demographic *difference* is an important first step in critically appraising workplace environments, as "diversity" as a term can be used to connote an array or a mix: "diverse" offerings, meaning "varied." In mainstream workplace environments, research on the efficacy of diversity practices, such as affirmative action, highlight continued challenges for women and people of colour to reach senior management positions within organizations, suggesting the need for examination of internal workplace environments and mobility within career trajectories.[7] Amy Edmondson's research on psychological safety, the quality of a "climate where people feel safe enough to take interpersonal risk by speaking up and sharing concerns, questions, or ideas," identifies that this quality of a workplace helps to facilitate a "continuous loop of learning."[8] Edmondson notes that "hiring for diversity is not enough," as inclusion and belonging also need to be targeted.[9] Important to note in these discussions of the differences between diversity and inclusion is that inclusion is an active process that needs to be fostered through reflexivity on working practices—a focus on diversity alone cannot ensure equitable or inclusive experiences in the workplace. Given the normalization of sexual violence in the creative industries, discussed in the Introduction, bodily safety is also an important element for inclusive environments, to facilitate speaking up and sharing concerns. Mark Banks outlines a range of harms in creative industries workplaces, including "exploitation (or self-exploitation), overworking, stress, bullying, intimidation, domination, aggression or violence."[10] As such, harmful working environments can affect both physical and psychological safety, and both need to be present for meaningful inclusion.

In this chapter, I turn to Sara Ahmed's work on diversity discourse, or what she characterizes as a shallow lip-service celebration of diversity, in order to assess the possibilities and limitations of mobilizing "diversity" as a response to lack of representation and lack of inclusion in the creative industries. To begin, I offer some critical questions: does increased diversity discourse signal change in the creative industries? Why and when does diversity become important, and how is diversity defined? How is diversity discourse used, and what are its effects on workplace culture? Can diversity discourse lead to more equitable opportunities or work experiences? In this chapter, I attempt to disentangle diversity discourse in the creative industries, assessing both change and continuity in these industries' engagement with diversity and inclusion.

Defining Diversity Discourse and Critical Diversity

Sara Ahmed's research draws attention to the proliferation of diversity discourses, highlighting that the language of diversity, as distinct from the language of equity or anti-racism, is often seen as positive. Ahmed draws on Nirmal Puwar's work on race and gender in *Space Invaders*, which analyzes the mobility of racialized and gendered bodies into historically white male spaces. Puwar asserts: "The language of diversity is today embraced as a holy mantra across different sites. We are told that diversity is good for us. It makes for an enriched multicultural society."[11] Ahmed chronicles that diversity discourse proliferates both in words and images: "the language of diversity certainly appears in official statements (from mission statements to equality policy statements, in brochures, as taglines) and as a repertoire of images (collages of smiling faces of different colors), which are easily recognizable as images of diversity."[12] While the language of equity and/or anti-racism can draw attention to systemic exclusion and the need for corrective measures, the discourse of diversity, in language or in images, might suggest that these goals have already been achieved: we are diverse, we are committed to diversity. In this way, Ahmed suggests that the language of diversity is both descriptive and normative: it both implicitly describes the workplace (we are diverse) and names norms (we are committed to diversity). Ahmed identifies that diversity discourse originated from U.S. managerial discourse, and as such, angles towards market and commercial goals rather than action or redistributive justice. A common management rationale is that diversity is good for business, and that diverse perspectives leads to creativity and innovation. However, challenges remain in creating organizational cultures that encourage difference or a clash of ideas and perspectives. Ahmed identifies that diversity discourse leverages "digestible" difference, and contrasts this celebratory circulation of "consumable" diversity with "conflicting heterogeneity," in the words of Himani Bannerji.[13]

As such, diversity discourse can be used *in place of* programs that seek to challenge inequalities within organizations. Ahmed traces scholarship that reveals that "'diversity' is a sign of the lack of commitment to change and might even allow organizations ... to conceal the operation of systematic inequalities."[14] Ahmed suggests that diversity discourse can be used as "a form of public relations ... diversity is mobilized in response or as a response to a problem."[15] "Diversity" can become a response that contains, avoids, minimizes, obscures, or obfuscates the problem of racial inequality. "Diversity" is a slippery word: using it can be a way for an organization to assert it is already diverse, rather than committing to the ongoing work of equity and inclusion. Nonetheless, using this word can also be a way for equity-deserving groups to accomplish their goals strategically: if the language of equity or anti-racism is seen as problematic, then "diversity" might allow for inroads to create change.

In opposition to diversity discourse or hollow celebrations of diversity, Cedric Herring and Loren Henderson forward the concept of "critical diversity" to not only celebrate demographic difference but also to register challenges of inequality. They write, "critical diversity must not only be about inclusion; it also requires an analysis of exclusion and discrimination. It therefore must challenge hegemonic notions of colorblindness and meritocracy."[16] Here, Herring and Henderson reference not only including people from equity-deserving groups, or moving beyond mere representation. A critical diversity framework examines systemic social exclusion while striving for change; meaningful critical diversity work continually names and reflects on exclusion, and does not assume that exclusion is readily solved or no longer needs attention with increased representation alone.

Critical creative industries scholarship has made some inroads in mobilizing a critical diversity framework, though the challenges of lack of representation and lack of inclusive working conditions require ongoing attention and strategies for change. In *Creative Justice*, Mark Banks forwards a holistic framing for social justice in the creative industries. Banks draws on the framework of "parity of participation," which Nancy Fraser defines as "social arrangements that permit all (adult) members of society to interact with one another as peers."[17] For Banks, strategies to strive towards parity of participation in the creative industries, or arrangements to work towards equity and inclusion, include quotas, blind auditions, and fair pay. While quotas and blind auditions might tackle hiring and lack of representation, fair pay can address inclusion and fairer working conditions within a working environment. Banks also suggests recuperating and giving worth to cultural forms of value, alongside a harm reduction framework, "reducing the physical and psychological harms and injuries inflicted by cultural work."[18] Banks' concept of creative justice acknowledges social inequality and biases and develops a range of measures to addresses these problems. This concept also allows for the development of questions that acknowledge but move beyond assessment of harmful working environments, including "what kinds of values or actions might underpin a fairer or more just cultural work? What kinds of better working lives do we want to imagine or help create?"[19]

In *Race and the Cultural Industries*, Anamik Saha provides a theoretical framework for understanding the potentials and challenges of moving towards both more diverse representation and more diverse content, including more diverse and nuanced stories being produced by the cultural industries. Focusing on Western news media, Saha provides clear evidence of negative representations of racialized minorities. Though Saha does not focus on film and television portrayals, these negative representations of racialized minorities in broader forms of media have also been well documented. Saha demonstrates a correlation between a lack of diversity in employees in organizations and negative representations of racialized people being produced by these organizations. Saha's work makes an important intervention in decoupling representation from structural change in the creative industries, balancing a political economy approach that recognizes concentrations of power, alongside individual contributions and capacities. Saha's approach suggests finding a balance between individual *agency* to create change and intervene in the lack of diversity and negative representations in the creative industries and broader *structures* (economic, social, and political) that constrain the ability to create change.[20] As such, celebrating diversity or that there is diverse representation within an organization does not, in itself, mean that these diverse individuals can enact organizational change themselves, and that the organizational culture supports change-making. In short, representation does not necessarily mean inclusion or transformation of a culture.

In her collection of essays entitled *Decolonizing Culture,* Anuradha Vikram speaks to the clash between the "political intention" of art work produced by "artists of color who refuse to conform to the externally dictated characteristics of their racial and national identities" and the "structural conditions" in the financing of this work.[21] Vikram's analysis again suggests this tension between individual agency and intention to create change, including working autonomously, and broader structural constraints, including economic considerations. Saha suggests recognizing tensions between change and continuity and macro- and micro-level interventions in creative industries contexts. This approach tempers easy celebration of introducing a limited number of individuals into key creative positions as necessarily ushering in change in the creative industries. Saha outlines the need for more attention to institutional contexts and professional practices in studies of race and creative industries, including ownership, regulation, policy, concentration, and industry lore, as these factors impact individual capacity to create change within their organizations. These considerations also suggest the importance of a critical diversity framework, so that questions of power and fairness can be accessed, beyond mere numeric reporting, celebration of diversity, and other forms of diversity discourse.

Diversity Discourse and the Creative Industries Context

The now widespread acknowledgement of exclusion, discrimination, harm, and abuse in the creative industries in critical creative industries scholarship challenges earlier celebratory accounts of the creative industries as open, talent-led, and meritocratic. These celebratory accounts were popularized through creative industries policy discourses, but also through earlier academic work, like that of Richard Florida. Critiques of Florida's work, in particular his 2002 book *The Rise of the Creative Class*, which named and celebrated a so-called "creative class," are now commonplace. In his 2017 book, *The New Urban Crisis*, Florida revises some of his earlier position, recognizing the negative impact on urban development and other categories of workers resulting from an enlarged policy emphasis on the creative industries. It is not worthwhile to retrace these critiques of Florida's notion of the "creative class" at length here as these critiques are well established.[22] Instead, I briefly retrace the promise of the creative industries celebrated by Florida with his positioning of the creative industries with regards to diversity and highlight how diversity discourse is evident in this positioning. In *The Rise of the Creative Class*, Florida identifies characteristics of the "creative class" and correlates these characteristics with economic growth. He terms these characteristics the 3Ts: technology, talent, and tolerance. This final T, tolerance, refers to "openness to diversity."[23] Due to Florida's influence on creative industries policy proliferation, I query how he defined diversity in *The Rise of the Creative Class*. To quantify the "tolerance" factor of a region, Florida developed a Composite Diversity Index (CDI) or Tolerance Index, which amalgamates three indicators he created: the Gay Index (% of residents who identify as gay or lesbian); the Bohemian Index (% of residents who work as artists); and the Melting Pox Index (% of residents who are foreign-born immigrants). In later editions of the text, Florida discusses how he updated these indexes in various editions of the book. In 2004, Florida added the Integration Index to the CDI, noting that "racial diversity is not associated with high-tech growth, innovation, or economic development."[24] The Integration Index measures the level of integration versus segregation of a metro area, or "the level to which a metro's given racial and ethnic groups are mixed together."[25] In the 2012 version of the book, the CDI includes: 1) the share of immigrants or foreign-born residents; 2) the Gay and Lesbian Index; and 3) the Integration Index. Florida gives cities a CDI score; for example, San Diego has the top "Tolerance Index" score of .751.

How diversity is measured and quantified shifts across iterations of Florida's text, variously touching on homosexuality, artistic practice, immigration, and integration as elements of "diversity," but it is beyond my scope and purpose to drill down into how and why Florida's diversity rubrics shift in various revisions and editions of his text, or to fully interrogate how he composed or quantified any of his Indexes. For Florida, diversity does not mean the proportion of the workforce that is a visible minority or from an underrepresented group. I forward two observations: 1) the drive to quantify diversity using set indicators or give a numeric diversity "score," such that different scores can be ranked and 2) the assumed correlation between "talent" and "tolerance." With the shifting CDI, "tolerance" is loosely if not bizarrely defined and yet it is assumed to be a characteristic of the creative class. "Diversity" is a floating signifier in Florida's book: he both acknowledges "long-standing divisions of race and gender"[26] in the creative class workforce (diversity as demographic difference) and refers to diversity as difference in creative styles (diversity as an array or mix). As such, diversity does and does not mean demographic difference in Florida's text. Nonetheless, diversity is celebrated as a positive and depoliticized value, and something that is an integral part of the creative class:

> Diversity has become a politically charged buzzword. To some it is an ideal that we should always be striving for; to others it is the Trojan-horse concept that introduced affirmative action and other liberal abominations to our society. The Creative Class people I study use the word a lot, but not to press any political hot buttons. Diversity is simply something they value, in all its manifestations. It is spoken of so often, and so matter-of-factly, that I take it to be a fundamental marker of Creative Class values. As my focus groups and interviews reveal, members of this class strongly favor organizations and environments in which they feel that anyone can fit in and get ahead."[27]

Diversity here is forwarded as a thing that is liked, that is commonsensical, and that is presumed to be associated with meritocratic advancement. However, valuing the idea of diversity, "feeling" that the environment is meritocratic, and having "tolerance" for diversity is different than the creative class workforce being demographically diverse. In fact, "feeling" that "anyone can fit in and get ahead" reinforces the supposed existence of a meritocracy and leaves systemic social inequality (a political hot button?) unexamined. In contrast, conversations about lack of representation and inclusion have surfaced other types of "tolerance" in the creative industries, connected to the celebration of talent: tolerance for discrimination and abuse and for harmful working conditions, which have proved to be more difficult to surface, quantify, or address.

Beyond "Just Add Women"

While the creative industries have been falsely framed around loose and imprecise notions of diversity in the past, "diversity" continues to be used in a pattern of problem/response as a containment strategy for news stories that surface problems of abuse and harm in these industries. In *Feminism for the 99%*, Cinzia Arruzza, Tithi Bhattacharya, and Nancy Fraser query the "diversity" response and forward that the work of feminism is not for the advancement of individual (white, middle class, straight, able bodied, cisgender) women, but is for broader systemic equity:

> Far from providing the solution, liberal feminism is part of the problem. Centered in the global North among the professional-managerial stratum, it is focused on 'leaning in' and 'cracking the glass ceiling.' Dedicated to enabling a smattering of privileged women to climb the corporate ladder and the ranks of the military, it propounds a market-centered view of equality that dovetails perfectly with the prevailing corporate enthusiasm for 'diversity.' Although it condemns 'discrimination' and advocates for 'freedom of choice,' liberal feminism steadfastly refuses to address the socio-economic constraints that make freedom and empowerment impossible for the large majority of women. Its real aim is not equality, but meritocracy.[28]

Christina Dunbar-Hester critiques the "diversity" response as the "just add women" approach; when women get "added" in as a diversity measure, this does not address the underlying problems of exclusion and discrimination.[29] For example, in 2016, former Fox news host Gretchen Carlson filed a sexual harassment lawsuit against Roger Ailes, head of Fox News, galvanizing many more women to come forward to share their stories of sexual violence spanning decades. Carlson's lawsuit alleged that she was fired from her television program, "The Real Story with Gretchen Carlson," after she turned down Ailes' sexual advances. After an internal review, Ailes was forced to resign, receiving a $40 million settlement package. After further allegations of sexual violence and settlements from Fox News host Bill O'Reilly surfaced, a Fox News shareholder filed a derivative lawsuit against the Fox Board and officers, which concluded in a

$90 million settlement to shareholders. Here, the creation of diversity programs becomes the response. Fox News announced the creation of a "Workplace Professionalism and Inclusion Council" on the same day as the $90 million derivative lawsuit settlement. Commenting on the creation of the Council, Fox deployed diversity discourse. CNBC reported that "Fox will enhance governance and said it created the Fox News Workplace Professionalism and Inclusion Council to ensure a proper workplace environment, bolster training and further the recruitment and advancement of women and minorities."[30] In this example, adding more women and "minorities" becomes a response to sexual violence. A further example of the "diversity" response emerged in 2018, when Netflix fired its communications spokesperson Jonathan Friedland, after news of his "insensitive" and racist remarks circulated, including "his descriptive use of the N-word on at least two occasions at work." After this firing, Netflix hired well-known Black diversity consultant Vernā Myers as vice president of "Inclusion Strategy" to infuse "cultural diversity, inclusion and equity" across Netflix's operations.[31] In these cases of Fox and Netflix, the words "diversity" and "inclusion" are used as remedial public relations strategies: councils get formed, consultants get hired.

In some companies, diversity as problem/response has been mediated by creating chief diversity officer (CDO) executive positions. In 2018, the executive search consultancy company Russell Reynolds Associates published a report titled *A Leader's Guide: Finding and Keeping Your Next Chief Diversity Officer*. The report opens with the business case for diversity, which commonly argues that diversifying internal workforce composition can attract more diverse audiences and customers, thereby increasing revenues. Here, this business case is extended to discuss damage control, and the damaging financial costs of "discrimination allegations," with decline in market capitalization following "incidents involving bad executive behavior."[32] Key findings in this report include the proliferation of CDO positions, profiling that 47% of companies included on the S&P 500 index (500 large companies listed on stock exchanges in the United States) have CDOs or equivalent. These CDOs are new in their roles, with two-thirds of individuals in CDO positions hired or promoted into their roles within the past three years at the time of the report in 2018. Other findings from this report include that many CDOs are not adequately resourced to fulfill their roles, or are performing other workplace roles alongside the CDO position. This report contrasts the rhetoric of supporting diversity and inclusion with (lack of) action and implementation, noting a disconnect between diversity and inclusion and overall business strategies: "among all leaders surveyed [1857 executives], D&I came in last on a list of eight potential business priorities."[33] A profile on this report from *Fortune* magazine boldly states in its headline that "Chief Diversity Officers are Set up to Fail."[34] Diversity departments and diversity staff may be a trend that is not sustained. In 2020, *Variety* magazine reported that "five members of CBS' nine-person corporate diversity team have been let go or have been told that their positions are likely to be eliminated. Among those affected are two high-ranking corporate diversity execs and three assistants, one of whom is a contract employee."[35] Given these challenges, how can the integration of diversity and inclusion as organizational priorities be sustained beyond a pattern of problem/ response, or beyond tokenized representation?

Another example of a top-down and individualized "diversity" response, emerging from the Annenberg Inclusion Initiative, is the development of the "inclusion rider." The concept of a rider is common in the entertainment industries, as musicians, actors, and other creative professionals often have preferred working conditions, including food and drink choices, in their employment contracts. An "inclusion rider" suggests that creative professionals advocate for the representation of people from underrepresented groups, including women, people of colour, queer, or disabled individuals, in their employment contracts. As such, this strategy might be better named a "diversity" rider; as previously mentioned, diversity and inclusion are often used as interchangeable and synonymous terms, and this imprecision and conflation can be a symptom of diversity discourse. At the 2018 Academy Awards, Frances McDormand brought the concept of the inclusion rider into mainstream conversation, as she concluded her acceptance speech for her Best Actress award by stating, "I have two words to leave with you tonight, ladies and gentlemen: inclusion rider!"[36] Prior to this speech in 2018, the Annenberg Inclusion Initiative had developed an inclusion rider template, to "strongly [encourage] hiring and casting of qualified individuals from under-represented backgrounds." This template is provided as a "flexible and adaptable framework," not "something to be cut and pasted into a contract." This template opens with a "statement of purpose" that suggests the importance of increasing the number of women and individuals from underrepresented groups but does not suggest quotas as benchmarks or other specific targets for increased diversity and representation in the creative industries. In the suggested inclusion rider template, the deliverable connected to this statement of purpose is auditioning "at least one female and one person from any other under-represented group for all supporting roles," and similarly interviewing "at least one female and one person from any other under-represented group for off-screen positions" such as editor, director of photography/cinematographer, composer, and so on.[37] Beyond interviewing, there is no suggested target for employment, or any discussion of what improved or more inclusive working conditions might look like if more women or people from underrepresented groups were to be employed. Assessing news stories about incremental improvement in diverse representation in film and television, Isabel Molina-Guzmán comments, "by framing stories around narratives of individual success and the branding of the entrepreneurial self, the news texts marginalize discussion of institutionalized racism and sexism.[38] Through these individualized "diversity" responses, there is an absence of discussion of institutionalized racism and sexism in the creative industries.

Diversity Report as Genre

With increased conversations about the negative repercussions of the lack of diversity in the creative industries, we can assess what strategies and responses are emerging from creative industries companies, alongside initiatives like the 4% challenge and the inclusion rider. Here, I turn to a genre of text I term the "diversity report," and note the lack of critical diversity and holistic framing around diversity and strategies for change in this genre. In my investigation, I look to the so-called "top six" media companies in 2020, based on market capitalization.[39] I examine diversity reports available online (either as downloadable documents or as tabs/section of websites) from AT&T, Comcast NBCUniversal, the Walt Disney Company, Netflix, Sony, and Charter Communications between 2018 and the first quarter of 2021 (the time of the writing of this book), assessing to what extent these companies acknowledged and strategized change around the challenges of underrepresentation and harmful working conditions in their companies. As an everyday consumer might be unlikely to consult a company's diversity report online, we can imagine that the audience for this genre is company investors and shareholders. Discussing how diversity circulates, Dunbar-Hester argues that cultivating diversity without a critique of power merely leads to furthering industry goals, suggesting the difference between diversity discourse and critical diversity.[40] In this light, it is not surprising that diversity reports from major industry stakeholders, these "top six" entertainment companies, celebrate diversity in order to reach industry goals, namely profit.

Below, I provide an overview of some common elements of the contents of the diversity report and characterize its overarching emphasis. As a genre, the diversity report is a platform for celebration, for pre-empting critique, and for marketing a product. The diversity report offers diversity as part of the company's brand, part of the company's products for sale: it is consumable. A common feature of the diversity report genre is lists of what the company offers with regards to diversity, sometimes presented without discussion. "Diversity" is committees and conferences; it is awards and employee resource groups; it is charts and graphs; it is partnerships and sponsorships. In this genre, diversity discourse proliferates and diffuses diversity, but problems are not named or acknowledged—though diversity is celebrated, there is very little or no mention of the challenges of systemic racism, exclusion, or sexual violence. Following Ahmed, I ask, what are we doing when we use the language of diversity in these reports?[41] If diversity is everyone and everywhere, announced as already incorporated into a company's core tenets and practices, it is also nowhere, not something that suggests change is needed.

Identifying the "D" and the "I" in the "D & I"

To begin this investigation of the genre of the diversity report, here I return to the distinction between diversity and inclusion. To simplify, if diversity is demographic difference, inclusion is the climate or qualities of a workplace. Climate or quality might be more difficult to quantify with a chart or graph, yet diversity and inclusion remain terms that are often used synonymously or in tandem, or are further neutralized through the common acronym "D & I" in these reports. This acronym can mask an unnamed problem, further abstracting away from "diversity" and "inclusion," which are already typically loosely and imprecisely defined, by using acronyms rather than naming the problem. This acronymization proliferates in diversity discourse. In the 2018 Diversity and Inclusion Report, *We Stand For ... Including Everyone* from Comcast NBCUniversal, Minority-led, Minority-serving organizations become "MLMS," Women-led, Women-serving organizations become "WLWS."[42] Underlying these terms is the experience of marginalization and the need for corrective measures to work towards equality; terms like "MLMS" further abstract these experiences. As Sara Ahmed states, "an equality regime *can be* an inequality regime given new form, a set of processes that maintain what is supposedly being redressed."[43] With various techniques such as acronymization, the diversity report as genre mobilizes a set of processes that maintains a status quo, while at the same time espousing a rhetoric of progressive social values. "Diversity" may not always be used to suggest demographic diversity in these reports, but can also mean an array or mix. For example, in its *Corporate Report 2020*, Sony suggests its "business portfolio is diverse." Demographic difference is not specifically highlighted, though there is a reference to "pursu[ing] the creation of the very best by harnessing diversity and varying viewpoints" in the company's stated core values.[44]

Inclusion is often named but remains at the periphery of the diversity report. As noted above, the challenges and problems of inclusion, in particular physical and psychological safety and wellbeing in creative industries workplaces, are now well known. Internal working practices might be confidential, but they could also be a source of pride; part of the "brand" on offer through these reports. These reports do not name or discuss the problems of harm, harassment, abuse, sexual violence, discrimination, exploitation, burnout, or any other type of internal workplace challenge. In the "top six" diversity reports, Charter Communications offers the most scant information about "Inclusion Programs," referencing employee resource groups and "Charter Inclusion Talks," a speaker series "built around cultural heritage and affinity—like Black History, Women's History, Asian Pacific American Heritage and LGBT Pride."[45] The *AT&T 2018 Diversity and Inclusion Report Annual Report* references being named "one of the Best Workplaces for Diversity" by the "Great Place to Work" award, which surveys employee experience, including trust, pride, and camaraderie. If diversity proliferates as a consumable or quantified outcome, so too do awards: Great Place to

Work is a corporate consultancy company that provides services to companies, and presumably then awards its clients its certification of workplace experience.[46] In 2020, the Walt Disney Company posted on its website that "for the 14th consecutive year, the Walt Disney Company has earned a perfect score of 100 on the 2020 Corporate Equality Index (CEI). The national benchmarking survey measures corporate policies and practices related to LGBTQ workplace equality and is administered by the Human Rights Campaign Foundation."[47] In this example of the proliferation of diversity awards, there is a "perfect score" for equality, which can suggest that there is no further work to be done, or that a problem does not exist or has been solved.

The Walt Disney Company's 2019 *Belong* report opens by referencing a "Diversity and Inclusion Journey." Here, "journey" does not suggest movement through problem and response, learning/unlearning bias, or establishing measures to work towards equality or inclusion; if anything, physical travel through a global marketplace might be the most appropriate framework for the movement that is evoked in this "journey." There is some initial rhetoric towards inclusion with the statement "we thrive when ideas and decisions from all people are valued and encouraged," but inclusive working practices that would promote this type of workplace climate are not named. Instead, the *Belong* report suggest a diffuse approach to diversity: across many platforms and many parts of the company. As Disney is an expansive parent company with a multitude of holdings, the report is able to profile an array of programs and initiatives from a variety of subsidiary companies. The report opens by positioning diversity as representation: "we are a better company when our people at all levels reflect the life experiences of our audiences." Though demographic diversity is not named here, "life experiences" would seem to reference the importance of diverse demographic representation through "all levels," presumably invoking senior management positions that are often noticeably less diverse.

Many of the "top six" diversity reports make similar gestures towards diversity in an expansive sense, both across audiences and employees, referencing women, people of colour, veterans (including their spouses), members of the LGBTQ+ community, and people with disabilities. In these diversity reports, many of these commitments to diversity are addressed numerically, celebrating that the company is purportedly already diverse. For example, after its opening rhetorical commitment to diversity and inclusion, the *Belong* report provides diversity data; mostly angling towards representation. Much of this diversity data lacks specificity: 72% of Disney's U.S. workforce are women and/or people of colour; 78% of new hires were women and/or people of colour; 50+ languages represented by Disney parks and resorts cast members around the world.[48] These statistics are presented to speak for themselves, or as evidence of the diversity journey, but we lack information about the type and quality of employment that is invoked. For example, if we consider Disney theme parks, many languages spoken by employees could suggest demographic diversity, but we do not learn anything about the position, quality of pay, or working conditions at these theme parks. Similarly, Comcast NBCUniversal's 2019 report *Our Values in Action* celebrates that "62% of our employees were women or people of color at YE [year end] 2018," but this number lacks information about type or quality of employment.[49] Discussing the technology sector, Dunbar-Hester illuminates that in globalized workforce, women of colour "actually abound,"[50] but this does not mean the advancement of women or racial inclusion, given the predominance of low-wage contract work. Given the expansiveness of the top-grossing entertainment companies, women and people of colour may work in a variety of positions: employment in itself does not necessarily indicate fairness, safety, or equality. In some diversity reports, there is added granularity about diverse representation (usually women or people of colour) in leadership or management positions, yet often the emphasis remains on what has been achieved rather than challenges or underlying problems.

Some of the commitment to diversity in diversity reports is signalled visually: there are many photographs of smiling multicultural employees in these "top six" diversity reports. The 2018 ComcastNBC Universal *We Stand For … Including Everyone* report cover has a central image of a smiling pregnant woman in a bright green dress: this composition and colour draws the viewer's attention to this pregnant belly as a focal point of the cover image of the report. But the report does not reference maternity or parental leaves, childcare, or any other accommodations for working mothers or parents. Dunbar-Hester suggests that "representation as a goal has limits as a project of empowerment, as noted by scholars of postfeminism and race. Representation as a producer or a consumer … is not necessarily indicative of a change in social power or social status."[51] In short, representation does not ensure social change, nor does diversity ensure inclusion. Ahmed suggests that "diversity" can mask ongoing inequalities; she cites Chandra Talpade Mohanty's analysis that diversity discourse "bypasses power as well as history to suggest a harmonious empty pluralism."[52] This harmonious empty pluralism is the presented picture in these "top six" diversity reports, often visually depicted with upbeat and smiling diverse faces.

Products and Programs

In the "top six" diversity reports, a product-and-program vision of diversity underlies the diffuse and celebratory approach to diversity—products and programs that are positioned to reveal diversity in action, though what these products and programs celebrate is often loosely defined. The Disney *Belong* report names products that are intended to signify the commitment and celebration of diversity. The film *Black Panther* is cited as a "game-changing phenomenon" (without reference to the Black-centric focus of the film). The film *Coco* is called "a culturally conscious, vibrant celebration of Mexican culture." Another product that is noted is "the landmark book, *WOMEN: The National Geographic*

Image Collection (October 22, 2019) [which] features 400 powerful photographs from the incomparable national geographic archives." The promotional copy of this book celebrates that "the future is female," but the book itself does not wholly celebrate female creators, as it also includes a number of photos of women (taken by male photographers). For example, the book includes the iconic photograph of the unnamed "Afghan girl," without consideration of the colonial history of *National Geographic* magazine, and its role in perpetuating a white and Western-centric gaze at "the other," including women, and in particular racialized women. Through these celebrations of "diverse" products in the diversity report, we learn little about employees and the working conditions that enabled or constrained the creation of these products.

Alongside products which are forwarded to signify diversity, diversity reports commonly provide an overview or list of programs to target representation, often based in a "foot-in-the-door" approach to creating opportunities and access. These programs point externally, to enable people from underrepresented communities to enter the creative industries workforce. While systemic barriers to accessing creative industries opportunities are important to note, this approach does little to dismantle discrimination or bias within the internal company culture. For example, the *Belong* report provides an overview of the Disney Launchpad Shorts Incubator program, designed to incubate "experienced directors from underrepresented backgrounds" through a seven-month program that includes mentorship, script development, and production of a live-action short film. In collaboration with littleBits, an educational technology company, Disney also has the "Snap the Gap" program for ten-year old girls, which aims to "close the gender gap in STEM." There are many similar programs across "top six" diversity reports, including "Creative Talent, "Access to Action," "Young Storytellers," and so on. Other programs in these diversity reports can gesture more broadly externally, moving towards corporate social responsibility and civic engagement. For example, the *2018 AT&T Diversity and Inclusion Annual Report*'s section on "Communities" opens by stating "AT&T has a long legacy of enriching and strengthening the diverse communities we serve. Through our philanthropy and our employees' volunteer efforts, we continue to support underserved populations and empower diverse members of our communities."[53] Philanthropy and engaging employees in volunteer efforts angles outwards, and does not necessarily have any relationship with internal workplace practices or fostering inclusion internally.

There are small moments across these reports where problems are acknowledged with a lack of diversity, rather than merely celebrating already existing diversity, moving beyond the product-and-program approach. Examples of these small moments include the 2019 *AT&T Diversity & Inclusion Annual Report*'s note about the commitment "to making the entertainment industry more equitable. In January of 2019, a challenge was issued by Time's Up and the Annenberg Inclusion Initiative in response to studies that show women directed only 4% of the decade's 1,000 highest-grossing movies. Along with other studios, Warner Bros. accepted the '4% Challenge' to hire one female director within the following 18 months." This "commitment" is presented with an accompanying image of a woman of colour, smiling, and there are no further references to the #MeToo movement or what makes the entertainment industries inequitable.[54] Comcast NBCUniversal's *Our Values in Action* 2019 report also notes that Universal Filmed Entertainment Group accepted the 4% challenge, discussed as having emerged from a study by the Annenberg Inclusion Initiative, without reference to Time's Up, further disacknowledging the problems of sexual violence in the creative industries.[55]

Across these "top six" reports, the clearest acknowledgement of problems in the creative industries comes from Netflix's 2021 *Inclusion Takes Root at Netflix: Our First Report.* This report replaces previous material on Netflix's website, that largely remained in the vague and celebratory vein of diversity discourse. In the 2021 *Inclusion Takes Root* report, Netflix opens by stating, "the company added inclusion as a cultural value in 2017, but here's what we found: we weren't as great as we thought we were, or aspired to be," later also commenting, "let's be clear, we're not where we want to be and we need to do better."[56] Some of the identified strategies for increasing inclusion at Netflix include hiring more inclusively, reaching outside of established networks, equitable pay, and inclusive benefits. Though Netflix also discusses creating access to the creative industries through programs in underrepresented communities and employee resource groups, the main emphasis is on changing the internal company culture to improve equity, rather than placing a burden to change or lack of qualifications on people from underrepresented groups. This changing tone may be suggestive of the post-2020 environment, after the murder of George Floyd and global uprisings protesting racial inequity. While the Walt Disney Company had yet to publish an updated 2020 diversity report at the time of the writing of this book, in May 2020 the company published an email sent out to employees on its website, titled "Resolve in a Time of Unrest: A Message to Fellow Employees." Posting this internal email to the company website makes it part of the company brand, and here the brand acknowledges problems, "the pandemic coupled with these recent injustices have pushed the issues of racial disparity into the open." This email continues, "while we don't have all the answers, we resolve to use our compassion, our creative ideas and our collective sense of humanity to ensure we are fostering a culture that acknowledges our people's feelings and their pain. We also realize that now more than ever is the time for us all to further strengthen our commitment to diversity and inclusion everywhere."[57] It remains to be seen what this tangible strengthened commitment will look like from Disney, but we can note here validating people's feelings and pain as one small initial step. Below, I turn to a genre I call the inclusion action plan, to assess strategies for more meaningful and broader culture shifts, beyond only increasing representation of people from underrepresented groups.

Inclusion Action Plan

In contrast to the overarching emphasis on diversity discourse in the "top six" diversity reports, here I forward an alternative, emerging genre, the inclusion action plan, developed by varied not-for-profit organizations, research labs, unions, and foundations. While industry "D & I" reports outline what is already being done through the "products and programs" approach, the inclusion action plan names problems and identifies guidelines to remedy or bring clarity to the problem. Instead of emphasizing representation through quantifying diversity, the inclusion action plan emphasizes identifying and valuing difference through creating supportive conditions (rather than tokenizing, stigmatizing, or homogenizing). The inclusion action plan often forwards pedagogical approaches, through bringing awareness and attention to challenges in the identified sector. This pedagogy often angles towards specificity rather than diffusion, for example identifying a specific creative sector or a specific problem to be discussed. Here, I examine three inclusion action plans: 1) *Think Before You Appropriate: Things to Know and Questions to Ask in Order to Avoid Misappropriating Indigenous Cultures—A Guide for Creators and Designers*, published by the Intellectual Property Issues in Cultural Heritage Project from Simon Fraser University in Canada; 2) *Clear Expectations: Guidelines for Institutions, Galleries and Curators Working with Trans, Non-Binary and Gender Diverse Artists in Australia*, researched by two artists, Spence Messih and Archie Barry for the National Association for the Visual Arts (NAVA) in Australia; and 3) *Agenda for Change Report*, published by Equity UK, a trade union for actors, singers, models, performers, directors, choreographers, designers, stage managers, and other creative workers in the United Kingdom. While these three reports may not be representative of all inclusion strategies across all creative sectors, these reports are illustrative of what I identify as a three-part typology of the inclusion action plan: naming, defining, and forward action.

Naming

The work of inclusion involves first acknowledging the problems that create a lack of inclusion, or simply naming that a lack of inclusion exists. For example, *Agenda for Change* opens by naming sexual violence in the performance industries: "this is a moment of change. A raft of allegations has shone a spotlight on sexual harassment in our industry—behaviour that was never acceptable and should never have been tolerated. It is now incumbent on all of us to create a culture shift."[58] In contrast, this type of language of acknowledgement is absent in the diversity report. *Agenda for Change* aims to bring clarity to what constitutes "unacceptable behaviour" in the performance industries. One step in identifying or naming a problem is suggesting that certain behaviours are "unacceptable" in themselves.[59] The *Think Before You Appropriate Guide*, targeting design work, first starts by naming "misappropriation" of Indigenous' peoples cultures, noting "systemic imbalances of power" and the context of colonialism: "due to the laws and policies that were imposed on them by non-Indigenous governments, [Indigenous peoples] have had little say over their own affairs, including over the practice and use of their cultural heritage. As a result, misappropriation of Indigenous forms of expression has been particularly widespread and harmful, hence the strong pushback as Indigenous peoples seek to regain some control."[60] This document emphasizes harm and imposition, though the terms "colonization" or "colonialism" are not explicitly used. The first section of the *Clear Expectations* report is titled "What is the Need for this Resource," and addresses the harm of misgendering trans, non-binary, and gender-diverse artists, calling attention to the "hateful history of trans erasure, tokenisation and disempowerment."[61] In naming this problem, this opening "What is the Need" section identifies power imbalances between institutions such as galleries and "minority groups." Further, *Clear Expectations* names negative consequences of this power imbalance, including "commodification of personal identity, the tokenisation of work, having the complexity of one's practice be reduced to a gender-centric reading and witnessing the erasure of gender diversity in broader gendered contexts. Other challenges include being excluded from dialogue, being misgendered in a public domain and having artwork censored" (Figures 3.1 and 3.2). In addition to specificity in its scope with regards to gender diversity and visual arts, *Clear Expectations* also opens by acknowledging its own scope and the limitations of this scope: "we acknowledge that this resource will be unable to address all situations, as the art world, gender and language are constantly changing constructs,"[62] again suggesting specificity rather than diffusion.

Defining

In addition to naming a problem, inclusion action plans often aim to clarify appropriate or inappropriate behaviour and practices through providing definitions. These definitions and glossaries are pedagogical, educating readers by providing explanation and context, rather than assuming prior familiarity or knowledge. These definitions can also operate as reference material and as a resource. For example, the *Think Before You Appropriate Guide* opens with definitions of cultural appropriation and misappropriation, using the latter term to acknowledge power, power imbalances, misuse of culture, and resulting harm, including but not limited to economic harm. *Think Before You Appropriate* differentiates misappropriation from cultural appropriation (sometimes discussed as "cultural appreciation" in other contexts), or ongoing exchange and flows of inspiration. *Clear Expectations* includes an opening glossary, called "Terms You May Have Heard," explaining terms like trans, cis, and genderqueer, and then explains the difference between physical sex, gender, and sexuality. In the *Agenda for Change* document, sexual harassment is not explicitly defined as a term; given the broad range of behaviours that might classify as sexual harassment, and different terms used in relation to this problem (misconduct, assault, abuse,

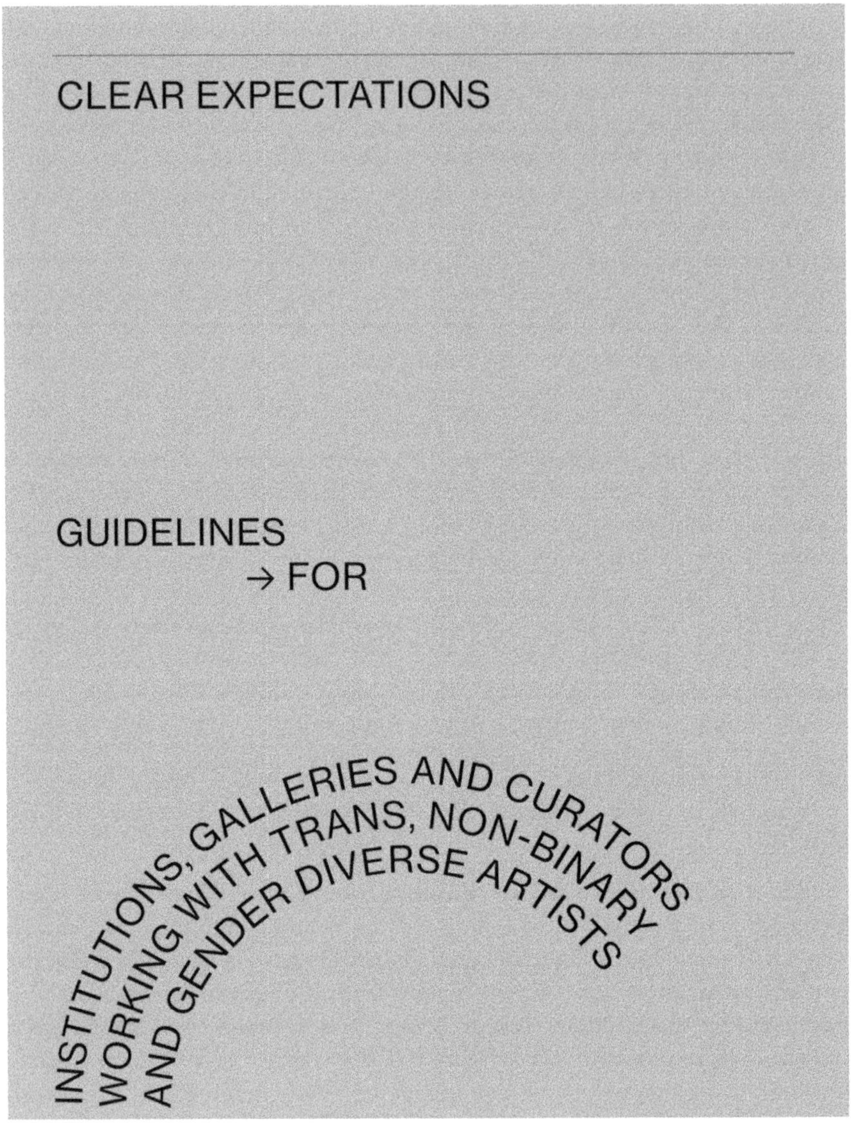

FIGURE 3.1 *Clear Expectations: Guidelines for Institutions, Galleries and Curators Working with Trans, Non-Binary and Gender Diverse Artists* cover image. © *Clear Expectations: Guidelines for Institutions, Galleries and Curators Working with Trans, Non-Binary and Gender Diverse Artists*, 2019, written by Archie Barry and Spence Messih. Commissioned and published by The Countess Report and supported by NAVA. Publication Design by Thought & Found

INTRODUCTION

What is the need for this Resource?

Visibility and representation is not always an inherently positive and beneficial experience for those being represented and should not be assumed as such. Being 'represented' often comes at a large personal cost where artistic exposure does not equal actual resources or access to influence, nor does it make the lives of trans, non-binary and gender diverse artists easier. Visibility often means having to respond on someone else's terms, speak only about one's gender identity and provide evidence of, and defend, one's own existence.

For trans, non-binary and gender diverse artists, representation can lead to various issues including the commodification of personal identity, the tokenisation of work, having the complexity of one's practice be reduced to a gender-centric reading and witnessing the erasure of gender diversity in broader gendered contexts. Other challenges include being excluded from dialogue, being misgendered in a public domain and having artwork censored.

Experiencing harm from the bureaucracy of institutional decision-making is a common experience for trans, non-binary and gender diverse people, even in the Australian arts sector. Institutions, galleries and curators often fail to respect and affirm the gender identities of trans, non-binary and gender diverse people — this is particularly alarming as institutions often engage with this community of people to represent their gender identities. Through lack of considered care and education, institutions, galleries and curators can commodify and profit off the representation of trans identities, bodies and experiences. In doing so, they perpetuate a hateful history of trans erasure, tokenisation and disempowerment. Acknowledging the power that institutions, galleries and curators hold, it is crucial that minority groups are treated with informed and nuanced care and respect. This is a responsibility that institutions, galleries and curators must accept.

This resource aims to provide institutions, galleries and curators with tools and strategies for working with and supporting trans, non-binary and gender diverse people.

FIGURE 3.2 "What Is the Need for This Resource" from *Clear Expectations*. © *Clear Expectations: Guidelines for Institutions, Galleries and Curators Working with Trans, Non-Binary and Gender Diverse Artists*, 2019, written by Archie Barry and Spence Messih. Commissioned and published by The Countess Report and supported by NAVA. Publication Design by Thought & Found

harassment), further clarity and definition about what is or is not sexual harassment could be useful. The document suggests that a step-by-step guide offering clarity on unacceptable behaviour is forthcoming from Equity. However, the document does acknowledge that "sexual harassment is on a spectrum of bad behaviour that also includes bullying and harassment,"[63] noting that sexual banter can contribute to culture of tolerance for harassment, and asks that companies (called "engagers" in the report, or those who are hiring), set their own clear policies and protocols, including examples of inappropriate and illegal behaviour

FIGURE 3.3 *Agenda for Change* cover image from Equity UK © Equity UK, 2018

(Figures 3.3 and 3.4). Furthermore, the *Agenda for Change* document identifies sectors of the performance industries that can inflict or condone and perpetuate harassment, including agents, casting directors, Boards, educators and training

Introduction

This is a moment of change. A raft of allegations has shone a spotlight on sexual harassment in our industry – behaviour that was never acceptable and should never have been tolerated. It is now incumbent on all of us to create a culture shift.

Contents

p 5 **The Union**
> Internal procedures
> Contracts, industrial agreements and non-disclosure agreements (NDAs)
> Awareness-raising campaign
> Equity helpline
> No more bystanders
> Intimacy direction
> The law

p9 **The industry**
> Engagers
> Agents
> Casting directors
> Boards
> Educators and training providers

p13 **The workplace**
> Castings and auditions
> Workplaces and venues

Equity has always championed the rights of our members. We are, and will remain, a safe space for workers from across the entertainment industries. We are the first line of defence against bad behaviour and the go-to source of advice whenever our members face problems of any kind. We want to empower members affected by bullying, harassment or sexual harassment to come forward with their experiences and we will support them when they do.

We strive to be more effective still. In response to the testimonies on sexual harassment last autumn, we conducted a members' survey and established a working group which took evidence from a wide range of interested parties including other unions, trade bodies and vocational training providers. This work produced nearly 200 ideas and forms the basis of this report.

The report focuses on sexual harassment but recognises sexual harassment is on a spectrum of bad behaviour that also includes bullying and harassment. It offers a string of action points, for Equity and for the people, organisations and venues with whom our members work.

There is often a sexual element - sometimes obvious, sometimes subtle - in the work our members do. Clear boundaries that should be always present in these situations are not always recognised and at worst are ignored. This is a problem that can extend to audiences who sometimes fail to differentiate between a performer and the fictional character they are portraying. ▶

www.equity.org.uk 3

FIGURE 3.4 "Introduction" from *Agenda for Change* © Equity UK, 2018

providers, and workplaces and venues. These elements of the *Agenda for Change* report are collectively part of defining the problem of sexual violence in the performance industries, by identifying some of its varied sources.

Moving Forward

The final element of the typology of the inclusion action plan identified here is action and strategies to move forward towards greater inclusion. In these documents, the naming-defining-moving forward typology of the inclusion action plan is largely sequential. Though problems and definitions might emerge at various points throughout these documents, these documents do not suggest forward action without first clearly stating the nature of the problem (e.g. impacts of colonialism; trans erasure; sexual harassment). That said, the emphasis of these documents is on what to do (alongside recognizing why action is needed). The guidelines that are outlined suggest that structure is a foundation for inclusion. Discussing inclusive cultures, Dunbar-Hester states that "diversity advocates imagine and create social foundations, rules, and norms that form the basis for association within their communities" as "democratic social relations and loose structure are certainly not equivalent."[64] Inclusion action plans outline norms and guidelines in an easy-to-grasp, educational manner, bringing clarity to problems. In contrast to the diversity report, the inclusion action plan suggests strategies for moving forward, rather than outlining or celebrating what has already been done in the past. The diversity report also places the burden of change in affected individuals, suggesting that underrepresented individuals need programs or resource groups, rather than the culture needing to change to create more inclusive conditions. In identifying actions to move forward, the inclusion action plan does not mobilize an individual deficit model, which remains in a meritocratic paradigm, but instead suggests collective action. *Clear Expectations* suggests that "one way to directly demonstrate that your program and organisation is inclusive of trans, non-binary and gender diverse artists is to turn your words into actions."[65] This document emphasizes the organization (not the individual) as the unit of analysis and the locus where change needs to happen; there is also emphasis on forward action. Identified action items in *Clear Expectations* include asking about preferred gender pronouns; respecting privacy around identity; addressing audiences in gender inclusive ways; paid consultation; inclusive labelling of bathrooms, and so on. Holistically, the document also suggests supporting career development of gender diverse artists, moving past tokenism and towards inclusion, and creating safer and more supportive environments.

Similarly, *Think Before You Appropriate* outlines norms to move beyond misappropriation in design work, outlining five elements of responsible creative collaborations, including free prior and informed consent; shared control over process and product; acknowledgement and attribution; respect for cultural differences; and reciprocity and benefit-sharing (Figures 3.5 and 3.6). The document concludes with case studies to enable readers to evaluate particular design scenarios and how they do or do not align with the criteria provided for responsible creative collaboration, offering fictional but true-to-life scenarios of the design of housewares, logos, jewellery, garments, and board games that depict Indigenous cultures. The *Agenda for Change* document outlines a multi-pronged awareness raising campaign, that includes those entering the field, "prepar[ing] students for the world of work, including an understanding of personal space and boundaries, consent, acceptable behaviour and dealing with unacceptable behaviour."[66] However, the burden of change is not placed on students, as the need for education and awareness is distributed across the performance industries in this

What makes for a responsible creative collaboration?

In order to avoid misappropriation, it is necessary to engage in creative collaborations with Indigenous partners that go beyond "cultural advising" and do much more than merely asking for advice from an Indigenous person. Adhering to the following core principles can help ensure that you are engaging with Indigenous partners in a respectful and responsible manner.

Free prior and informed consent
When initiating a collaboration, present your goals clearly. Make sure that those giving consent do so freely, without feeling pressured and with full understanding of the consequences. Ensure that they are truly in a position to make decisions, and are recognized in their community as having the necessary knowledge and authority on the matter at hand.

Shared control over process and product
Build a relationship in which your partners are comfortable with how much input and control they have over the goals, approach, and final outcomes. Recognize that, due to others' appropriative behaviours in the past, you may have to work long and hard to build a trusting and balanced relationship.

FIGURE 3.5 Elements of "What Makes for a Responsible Creative Collaboration" from *Think Before You Appropriate: Things to Know and Questions to Ask in Order to Avoid Misappropriating Indigenous Cultures—A Guide for Creators and Designers* © Intellectual Property Issues in Cultural Heritage Project from Simon Fraser University, 2015

document. Further, for students to be educated, there need to be standards and norms to adhere to, in the identified areas of consent, boundaries, and acceptable behaviour, and there need to be clear structures and recourse for "unacceptable behaviour." Much of the suggested forward action in the *Agenda for Change* document suggests the need for formal codes of conduct and professional standards, such as "casting directors should actively discourage one-to-one meetings in non-professional environments."[67]

We can see this work of the inclusion action plan as care work. Following Ahmed, I suggest that this care work is reattachment labour: naming, defining, and suggesting remediation for legacies of harm. Given that diversity discourse lacks context and historical/structural analysis with empty celebrations of diversity, care is needed to reattach these considerations in a critical diversity framework. Ahmed suggests that diversity practitioners are often trying to do vital work through a "politics of reattachment." She writes, "practitioners aim to reattach diversity to the meanings it may lose on or in its travels. If the success of

Acknowledgement and attribution

Make sure you identify those you work with, and describe the nature of your collaboration clearly to your consumers. Even the most responsible collaboration can seem suspicious if its nature is not communicated clearly. Using ambiguous wording that misrepresents practices in order to avoid negative attention is a sure way to breach consumer trust, and can even constitute false advertising under the law.

Respect for cultural differences

Take into consideration that the worldview and experiences of the people whose cultural heritage inspires you may differ from yours. Ensure that your approach isn't at odds with or, worse, threatening to their values and practices, and take steps to adapt your process and objectives accordingly.

Reciprocity and benefit-sharing

Work with your partners to find an appropriate balance between what you are receiving and what you are giving in the exchange. This includes negotiating monetary compensation for all parties involved, as well as discussing and sharing other benefits that may come out of the collaboration.

FIGURE 3.6 Further Elements of "What Makes for a Responsible Creative Collaboration" *Think Before You Appropriate* © Intellectual Property Issues in Cultural Heritage Project from Simon Fraser University, 2015

diversity is partly that it becomes detached from histories of struggle over inequality, then the success of diversity work might require reattaching the word to those same histories."[68] In Chapter 4, I continue the exploration of meaningful inclusion work and turn to the care work of centring difference, profiling individuals and collectives seeking to create space within the creative industries for underrepresented forms of creative practice, moving beyond a deficit model and towards communities of care.

Notes

1 Dino-Ray Ramos, "Tessa Thompson and Kerry Washington Join Colleagues in TimesUp 4% Director Challenge to Work With Female Directors – Update," *Deadline*, January 25, 2019, accessed October 26, 2020, https://deadline.com/2019/01/female-filmmakers-sundance-usc-annenberg-inclusion-initiative-paul-feig-nina-jacobson-angela-robinson-stacy-smith-diversity-inclusion-1202542025/

2 Stacy Smith et al., *Inequality in 1,200 Popular Films: Examining Portrayals of Gender, Race/Ethnicity, LGBTQ & Disability from 2007 to 2018* (Los Angeles, CA: Annenberg Inclusion Initiative, 2019), http://assets.uscannenberg.org/docs/aii-inequality-report-2019-09-03.pdf
3 Time's Up, "About," *Time's Up*, n.d., https://timesupnow.org/about/
4 Rachel Montpelier, "Women Directing 40 Percent of Upcoming Disney Films, CEO Announces," *Women and Hollywood*, January 31, 2019, accessed December 14, 2020, https://womenandhollywood.com/women-directing-40-percent-of-upcoming-disney-films-ceo-announces/
5 Alexis Reliford, "Mamma Mia and Pitch Perfect's Studio Just Took the 4% Challenge & Threw Down a Gauntlet to Hollywood," *Refinery29*, January 29, 2019, accessed December 14, 2020, https://www.refinery29.com/amp/en-us/2019/01/222693/annenberg-inclusion-intitative-announces-4-percent-challenge
6 Lynn Shore et al., "Inclusion and Diversity in Work Groups: A Review and Model for Future Research," *Journal of Management* 37, no. 4 (2010): 1262–1289; Lynn Shore, Jeanette N. Cleveland, and Diana Sanchez, "Inclusive Workplaces: A Review and Model," *Human Resource Management Review* 28, no. 2 (2018): 176–189.
7 Alexandra Kalev, Frank Dobbin, and Erin Kelly, "Best Practices or Best Guesses? Assessing the Efficacy of Corporate Affirmative Action and Diversity Policies," *American Sociological Review* 71, no. 4 (2006): 589–617.
8 Amy Edmondson, *The Fearless Organization: Creating Psychological Safety in the Workplace for Learning, Innovation, and Growth* (Hoboken, NJ: John Wiley & Sons, 2018), 22, 69.
9 Ibid., 201–202.
10 Mark Banks, *Creative Justice: Cultural Industries Work and Inequality* (London: Rowman & Littlefield, 2017), 155.
11 Cited in Sara Ahmed, *On Being Included: Racism and Diversity in Institutional Life* (Durham, NC: Duke University Press, 2012), 51.
12 Ibid., 51–52.
13 Ibid., 69, 53.
14 Ibid., 53.
15 Ibid., 143.
16 Cedric Herring and Loren Henderson, *Diversity in Organizations: A Critical Examination* (New York: Routledge, 2015), 24.
17 Cited in Banks, *Creative Justice*, 149.
18 Ibid., 155.
19 Ibid., 4.
20 Anamik Saha, *Race and the Cultural Industries* (London: Polity Press, 2018).
21 Anuradha Vikram, *Decolonizing Culture: Essays on the Intersection of Art and Politics* (San Francisco, CA: Art Practical Books & Sming Sming Books, 2017), 13.
22 For critiques of Richard Florida's work, see for example Mark Banks, "Creative Economies of Tomorrow? Limits to Growth and the Uncertain Future," *Cultural Trends* 2, no. 5 (2018): 367–380; Angela McRobbie, *Be Creative: Making a Living in the New Culture Industries* (London: Polity Press, 2016); Oli Mould, *Against Creativity* (London: Verso, 2018).
23 Richard Florida, *The Rise of the Creative Class, Revisited* (10th Anniversary Edition) (New York: Basic Books, 2012), 232.
24 Ibid., 246.
25 Ibid., 403.
26 Ibid., 58–59.
27 Ibid., 57.
28 Cinzia Arruzza, Tithi Bhattacharya, and Nancy Fraser, *Feminism for the 99%: A Manifesto* (London: Verso, 2019), 11.

29 Christina Dunbar-Hester, *Hacking Diversity: The Politics of Inclusion in Open Technology Cultures* (Princeton, NJ: Princeton University Press, 2020).
30 "21st Century Fox in $90 Million Settlement Tied to Sexual Harassment Scandal," *CNBC.com*, November 21, 2017, accessed October 26, 2020, https://www.cnbc.com/2017/11/21/21st-century-fox-in-90-million-settlement-tied-to-sexual-harassment-scandal.html
31 Etan Vessling, "Netflix Hires Verna Myers as Head of 'Inclusion Strategy,'" *The Hollywood Reporter*, August 29, 2018, accessed October 26, 2020, https://www.hollywoodreporter.com/news/netflix-hires-verna-myers-as-inclusion-strategy-head-1138225
32 Tina Shah Paikeday, Harsonal Sachar, and Alix Stuart, *A Leader's Guide: Finding and Keeping Your Next Diversity Officer* (New York City: Russell Reynolds Associates, 2019), 2.
33 Ibid., 6.
34 Ellen McGirt, "Chief Diversity Officers Are Set Up to Fail," *Fortune*, March 4, 2019, accessed October 26, 2019, https://fortune.com/2019/03/04/chief-diversity-officers-are-set-up-to-fail/
35 Joe Otterson and Daniel Holloway, "ViacomCBS Cuts Diversity Staff Amid Consolidation," *Variety*, February 5, 2020, accessed October 25, 2020, https://variety.com/2020/tv/news/cbs-diversity-1203493784/
36 Rachel Paula Abrahamson, "Frances McDormand Explains the Meaning of 'Inclusion Rider' After Her Oscars Win," *UsMagazine*, March 5, 2018, accessed October 26, 2020, https://www.usmagazine.com/celebrity-news/news/frances-mcdormand-explains-meaning-of-inclusion-rider/
37 Inclusion Rider Template, *USC Annenberg Inclusion Initiative*, accessed March 18, 2021, available at http://assets.uscannenberg.org.s3.amazonaws.com/docs/inclusion-rider-template.pdf
38 Isabel Molina-Guzmán, "#OscarsSoWhite: How Stuart Hall Explains Why Nothing Changes in Hollywood and Everything is Changing," *Critical Studies in Communication* 33, no. 5 (2016): 444.
39 Shobit Seth, "The World's Top Media Companies," *Investopedia,* October 7, 2020, accessed October 27, 2020, https://www.investopedia.com/stock-analysis/021815/worlds-top-ten-media-companies-dis-cmcsa-fox.aspx
40 Dunbar-Hester, *Hacking Diversity*, 16.
41 Ahmed, *On Being Included*, 1.
42 Comcast NBCUniversal, *We Stand for Including Everyone: Diversity and Inclusion Report 2018* (Philadelphia, PA: Comcast NBCUniversal, 2018), 31, https://update.comcast.com/wpcontent/uploads/sites/33/2018/07/Comcast_DI_Report_2018_final2.pdf
43 Ahmed, *On Being Included*, 8.
44 Sony Corporation, *Corporate Report 2020* (Tokyo: Sony, 2020), 2, 4, https://www.sony.net/SonyInfo/IR/library/corporatereport/CorporateReport2020_E.pdf
45 "Fostering an Inclusive Environment," *Charter Communications*, February 7, 2020, accessed October 30, 2020, https://corporate.charter.com/newsroom/fostering-an-inclusive-environment
46 AT&T, *2018* AT &T *Diversity and Inclusion Annual Report* (Dallas, TX: AT&T, 2018), https://about.att.com/ecms/dam/pages/Diversity/Annual_Report/ATT_DI_Report_DIGITAL_5.pdf
47 "The Walt Disney Company Earns Top Marks for LGBTQ Workplace Equality," *The Walt Disney Company*, January 21, 2020, accessed March 26, 2021, https://thewaltdisneycompany.com/the-walt-disney-company-earns-top-marks-for-lgbtq-workplace-equality/

48 The Walt Disney Company, *Belong: Our Diversity and Inclusion Journey* (Burbank, CA: The Walt Disney Company, 2019), 2, https://thewaltdisneycompany.com/app/uploads/2019/09/DiversityAndInclusionCommitment.pdf
49 Comcast NBCUniversal, *Our Values in Action: 2019 Comcast NBC Universal Values Report* (Philadelphia, PA: Comcast NBC Universal, 2019), 17, https://update.comcast.com/wp-content/uploads/sites/33/dlm_uploads/2019/05/ComcastNBCU_print_0730-web.pdf
50 Ibid., 20.
51 Dunbar-Hester, *Hacking Diversity*, 189.
52 Ibid., 13–14.
53 AT&T, *2018* AT&T *Diversity and Inclusion Annual Report*, 43.
54 AT&T, *2019 AT &T Diversity and Inclusion Annual Report* (Dallas, TX: AT&T, 2019), 7, https://about.att.com/ecms/dam/pages/Diversity/Annual_Report/ATT_DI_2019_Annual_Report.pdf
55 Comcast NBCUniversal, *Our Values in Action*, 21.
56 Netflix, *Inclusion Takes Root at Netflix: Our First Report* (Los Gatos, CA: Netflix, 2021), https://about.netflix.com/en/news/netflix-inclusion-report-2021
57 Bob Chapek, Bob Iger, and Latondra Newton, "Resolve in a Time of Unrest: A Message to Fellow Employees," *The Walt Disney Company*, May 30, 2020, accessed March 26, 2021, https://thewaltdisneycompany.com/resolve-in-a-time-of-unrest-a-message-to-fellow-employees/
58 Equity UK, *Agenda for Change Report* (London, Equity UK, 2018), 3, https://www.equity.org.uk/media/1263/agenda-for-change.pdf
59 Ibid., 11.
60 Intellectual Property Issues in Cultural Heritage Project, *Think Before You Appropriate. Things to Know and Questions to Ask in Order to Avoid Misappropriating Indigenous Cultural Heritage* (Vancouver: Simon Fraser University, 2015), 3, https://www.sfu.ca/ipinch/sites/default/files/resources/teaching_resources/think_before_you_appropriate_jan_2016.pdf
61 Spence Messih and Archie Barry for the National Association for the Visual Arts (NAVA), *Clear Expectations: Guidelines for Institutions, Galleries and Curators Working with Trans, Non-Binary and Gender Diverse Artists* (Woolloomooloo, NSW: NAVA, 2019), 2, https://visualarts.net.au/media/uploads/files/Clear_Expectations_Guidlines_FA_Digital.pdf
62 Ibid., 1.
63 Equity UK, *Agenda for Change*, 3.
64 Dunbar-Hester, *Hacking Diversity*, 50–51.
65 Spence Messih and Archie Barry for the National Association for the Visual Arts (NAVA), *Clear Expectations*, 8.
66 Equity UK, *Agenda for Change*, 11.
67 Ibid., 13.
68 Ahmed, *On Being Included*, 80.

4

FROM MARGINS TO CENTRE: BUILDING INCLUSION THROUGH PEDAGOGICAL ENCOUNTER

In 2017, controversy emerged when Columbian–Canadian, Afro-Indigenous musician Lido Pimienta invited "brown girls to the front" of the audience at her concert in Halifax, Canada during the Halifax Pop Explosion (HPX) music festival. This call echoed and extended a long-standing tradition of inviting "girls to the front" that was popularized during the riot grrrrl movement, originating in Olympia, Washington, in the 1990s, inviting women fans to move to the front of the stage. This "girls to the front" invitation intended to create physical safety for fans who are girls in punk and hardcore scenes, not only because these fandoms can often be expressed through physical aggression but also because of the problems of sexual violence at music events. Beyond physical safety, the "girls to the front" call also invites "girls" to take up material and non-material space, to assert their belonging and importance in fandom spaces that otherwise can diminish their worth and visibility as fans.[1] Pimienta's call of "brown girls to the front" extends the "girls to the front" call and draws attention to the existence of racialized inequalities, centring women fans of colour in the "indie" music space, which otherwise can be white dominated.

After Pimienta's call at this 2017 event, a white woman volunteer, present at the front of the stage to take photographs of the concert, was unable to understand herself to be implicated in Pimienta's request, or otherwise was unwilling to comply, and would not move away from the front of the stage. In media interviews about this incident, another musician who was present explained, "finally after saying it about 10 times—and the woman refused to move—[Pimienta] said, 'You're cutting into my set time and you're disrespecting these women, and I don't have time for this.'"[2] In its comment on the incident, HPX acknowledged the "overt racism" of the incident and reported that "this volunteer was removed by Lido herself." In *Billboard Magazine*, Pimienta commented more fully on her

DOI: 10.4324/9781003031338-4

rationale for her call and for removing this volunteer, based in her experience at music shows:

> I noticed how white women were usually at the front and brown girls would be behind the white girls, a bit more shy, a bit more restrained. Even at HPX, I had to call out a few black girls who were 'too shocked' and felt I was 'putting them on the spot' by saying, 'Girl come to the front! This is for you!'[3]

Commenting on her social location as an "immigrant, as an Afro-Indigenous person, as an intersectional feminist, as a mother," Pimienta explains, "I understand what it is like to not see yourself in the media, to not see yourself in institutions and to not see yourself represented or reflected" in music. This incident reveals the dynamics of race and representation in the creative industries, spanning both cultural production and cultural participation, raising questions of who is visible and valorized as artists and fans. These racial politics of visibility are shaped by power and resources: who is "seen" also manifests in who is championed and supported, and in what ways.

This 2017 "brown girls to the front" incident demonstrates a desire for interruption, to centre difference and those on the margins, and to complicate a binary of mainstream and marginalized. In this specific incident, Pimienta made use of her literal platform, in this case her stage, to redirect this flow, and these conversations are increasingly happening in popular discourses, through social media and the press, where the language of "centring" has entered the vernacular. With Bernice Fisher and Joan Tronto's definition of care-as-process, discussed in Chapter 2, centring is a form of "caring about," or paying attention, redirecting attention to people, processes, and forms of cultural production that have been marginalized by dominant norms.

This "brown girls to the front" incident is also a (failed) pedagogical encounter, where a white woman failed to self-assess and modify her behaviour—a potential moment of learning and unlearning the dominant norms of white supremacy that shape the creative industries. In this discussion of learning and unlearning, I return to the distinction between diversity and inclusion discussed in Chapter 3, and focus on the complexity of building inclusive cultures that centre forms of difference. A dominant neoliberal creative industries environment can create a toxic environment, lacking in trust, co-operation, and teaching and learning because of an overarching focus on competition and individual advancement. Adding "diversity" into this environment does not necessarily result in more inclusion. Centring difference can also suggest centring different working processes, including teaching and learning, mutual support, relationality, and a sense of collaboration rather than competition.

This chapter has several goals. First, I note this rise of the discourse of "centring," and locate this discourse in Black intellectual thought, including cultural studies, critical race, and feminist work by Stuart Hall and bell hooks. This chapter also seeks to explore what the framework of centring the margins can look like in practice, and what potentials and challenges emerge through inclusive modes of social relations and working processes. I profile the work of centring from practice-led perspectives, turning to two case studies of grassroots collectives and initiatives that work pedagogically to centre difference and foster inclusion.

The Discourse of Centring

Early cultural studies work introduced popular culture into the academic arena, forwarding critical questions about class, taste, value, and cultural production. Raymond Williams' essay "Culture is Ordinary," discussed in the Introduction, highlighted "everyday" culture, and the culture of the working class, validating these forms of culture as *culture*, in opposition to a definition of culture as high culture, or elite forms of culture. More than 60 years after Williams' essay, these conversations have shifted, with popular culture largely deemed both a worthy object of study and a worthy pursuit of time in academic and popular discourses. Nonetheless, questions of whose forms of cultural production are valued and centred remain salient, particularly from an intersectional approach that highlights continued disparities in power and privilege with regards to race, gender, class, sexuality, disability, and other structural factors.

The Dialectic of Margin and Centre

In his 1981 essay "Notes on Deconstructing the Popular," Stuart Hall discusses how divides are constructed between the "central domain of elite or dominant culture, and the culture of the 'periphery,'" identifying a "key opposition: the people/not of the people." According to Hall, the "popular" is not static but is instead "a sort of constant battlefield."[4] Hall's argument is that it is not the content of cultural products that deem or shift their societal valuation, or cause them to "go up the cultural escalator;" rather, power is a "process by which the relations of dominance and subordination are articulated," including through cultural products.[5] Wary of positioning "ordinary people" as "cultural dopes," Hall asserts that representations exert power, but people have the capacity to analyze these popular culture representations. Nonetheless, Hall identifies the cultural industries as a key vehicle, a constitutive site for power relations: "the cultural industries do have the power to constantly rework and reshape what they represent; and, by repetitions and selection, to impose and implant such definitions of ourselves as fit more easily the descriptions of the dominant or preferred culture."[6] As such, Hall notes tensions and contradictions in what is central and what is peripheral, which invites attention to the shifting movement of these boundaries. The cultural/creative industries maintain distinctions between centre/margins, even though these divides are shifting. Hall's invocation of the "cultural escalator" suggests vertical movement: devalued cultural products being recuperated and re-evaluated with "enhanced" value, yet this escalator is still an enactment of power, "a continuous and necessarily uneven and unequal struggle, by the dominant culture, constantly to disorganize and reorganize popular culture." In Hall's analysis, this vertical movement is an extractive process, where the dominant elite selectively elevates forms of cultural production from the margins while maintaining hierarchy and power.

What other types of movement are possible, and what does cultural value look like from the margins, beyond extraction by the dominant culture? These questions of cultural value are impacted by structures of power and privilege that are not only economic but are also racialized and gendered. Eleonora Belfiore identifies the relational nature of how forms of value, including cultural value, are expressed and shaped by power relations. Drawing on Pierre Bourdieu, Belfiore highlights the "symbolic violence" of misrepresentations through a case study of Roma people's negative responses to the reality television show *My Big Fat Gypsy Wedding*, highlighting "different access to the power to bestow value and legitimise aesthetic and cultural practices."[7] Acknowledging the systemic nature of unequal access to power, and the power to represent and legitimize, below I also explore what value in cultural production looks like from marginalized and underrepresented social locations. While barriers to accessing and disseminating cultural production in a creative industries context exist, marginalized social locations can offer alternative and expanded forms of value. Beyond the symbolic violence of misrepresentation, what values emerge when we centre the margins?

For bell hooks, these questions of margins and centre mean foregrounding the value in the margins, from her social location as a Black woman. In her essay "Choosing the Margin as a Space of Radical Openness," she asserts that the margins enable "a different mode of articulation."[8] In *Feminist Theory: From Margin to Center*, hooks queries feminist theory from this position, asserting that "much theory emerges from privileged women who live at the center, whose perspectives on reality rarely include knowledge and awareness of the lives of women and men who live on the margin. As a consequence, feminist theory lacks wholeness, lacks the broad analysis that could encompass a variety of human experiences."[9] hooks' reflections emerge from her experience growing up in segregated Kentucky, and she opens her book as follows: "to be on the margin is to be part of the whole but outside the main body." hooks outlines that racial segregation meant physical separation, her small Kentucky town being divided by railway tracks and "stores we could not enter, restaurants we could not eat in, and people who we could not directly look in the face." This physical separation through racial segregation required and enabled a mode of seeing, focusing attention, and understanding, providing an "oppositional world view."[10] This world view opens a dialectic between margin and centre by asserting the existence of the margin outside of and in relation to the centre: "our survival depended on an ongoing public awareness of the separation between margin and centre and an ongoing private acknowledgment that we were a necessary, vital part of that whole." hooks' analysis suggests that centring as an action and a process means shifting attention away from dominant, normative centres, and paying attention to and valuing the margins.

Much of the discussion and valorization of the creative industries has emerged from privilege at the centre, resulting in a lack of wholeness and lack of broad analysis; by attuning our attention elsewhere we can investigate what modes of creating on the margins look like. In her essay "Postmodern Blackness," hooks notes that as the "'politics of difference" began to circulate through postmodern theory in the 1990s, these discussions of difference became detached from an examination of "the politics of racism."[11] hooks' intervention asserts the continued importance of structural analysis when assessing difference. As discussed in Chapter 3, Sara Ahmed's analysis of the "politics of reattachment" highlights the care labour and care thinking needed to sustain historical and structural analysis when centring difference. In "Postmodern Blackness," hooks references art critic Robert Storr's comments on "the absence of any sustained research into what artists of color and others outside the mainstream might be up to."[12] Thirty years after hooks' initial publication date, these comments about the absence of sustained research about underrepresented artists and cultural producers remain, unfortunately, apt. However, with shifting public discourses, the absence of this sustained attention and research is increasingly discussed, catalyzing new work and visions for the creative industries.

Design Justice and Disability Justice

This dialectic of margin and centre has also been theorized from the perspectives of design justice and disability justice. These frameworks enable a critical appraisal of hegemonic norms, assessing who these norms exclude while highlighting modes of value and resistance on the margins. In *Design Justice: Community-Led Practices to Build the Worlds We Need*, Sasha Costanza-Chock analyzes this process of centring value in the margins from the framework of design justice, raising social justice concerns of equity and inclusion. Though the field of design might be most commonly associated with technology and aesthetics, Costanza-Chock foregrounds design as a process of how problems are defined and what approaches are brought to attempt to solve these problems. She opens by referencing the work of the Design Justice Network, which originated at the Allied Media Conference, citing its published principles. These principles outline and define a design justice framework: "design justice rethinks design processes, centers people who are normally marginalized by design, and uses collaborative, creative practices to address the deepest challenges our communities face."[13] Costanza-Chock outlines that this perspective of centring is "ethical" and can lead to better outcomes: "the tacit and experiential knowledge of those marginalized within the matrix of domination is sure to produce ideas, approaches, and innovations that a nonmember of the community would be very unlikely to come up with."[14] This framework for inclusion does not attempt to integrate marginalized peoples into dominant and unchanged norms, but instead values difference and differing perspectives as a source of innovation. Discussing different "paradigms" of diversity work, David A. Thomas and Robin J. Ely highlight the paradigm of "integration and learning," which moves beyond mere compliance with policies and laws, and beyond the so-called "business case" for diversity, which is that people from underrepresented communities can make inroads into diverse markets and thereby increase revenues. The value of diversity in the "business case" is limited to market-based motivation, which "can leave some employees feeling exploited." In contrast, the integration and learning perspective on diversity highlights that people from underrepresented communities "bring different, important, and competitively relevant knowledge and perspectives about how to actually *do work*—how to design processes, reach goals, frame tasks, create effective teams, communicate ideas, and lead"(emphasis in original).[15] The integration and learning perspective affirms the importance of pedagogical encounters that enlarge modes of working in the creative industries.

Similarly, a disability justice framework questions and recasts a deficit model of disability, suggesting that disability can enable creativity and ways of knowing, doing, and being that can be adaptive and brilliant. Rather than attempt to integrate or "normalize" disability into the mainstream, a disability justice framework centres different forms of values in the margins.[16] In *Care Work: Dreaming Disability Justice*, Leah Lakshmi Piepzna-Samarasinha writes, "in the deficiency model of disability, there's nothing good about disability, no skills or brilliance. We are just a fault to be cured. The only good crip is a cured crip, one who has ceased to exist. Cure is healing is elimination." Piepzna-Samarasinha suggests that changing this script, from the deficit model to a disability justice model, "is a giant paradigm shift. Our crip bodies aren't seen as liabilities, something that limits us and brings pity, or something to nobly transcend, 'cause I'm just like you. Our crip bodies are gifts, brilliant, fierce, skilled, valuable. Assets that teach us things that are relevant and vital to ourselves, our communities, our movements, the whole goddamn planet."[17] Moving beyond the deficit model for disability means seeing value in knowledge and existence on the margins, rather than seeing disability as a problem to be rehabilitated. Applying the perspective from this framework in a creative industries context suggests both acknowledging structural barriers in accessing to power and resources while also moving beyond a deficit model that suggests that people from underrepresented and marginalized communities are lacking in entrepreneurial knowledge or are lacking the means of self-expression or self-representation. Given that the mainstream creative industries environment is rife with labour problems and exclusion, a critical creative industries perspective might explore not how to ensure more representation within this system (though representation is and remains an important priority), but more broadly, how to centre different systems and different modes of articulation in cultural production from the margins.

The Politics and Practice of Centring

Moving beyond increasing representation in harmful, flawed, and exclusionary systems and towards different, more inclusive systems necessitates enlarged perspectives but also necessitates practical tools and resources. In *Centering Marginalized Communities: A Framework for Intersectional Money in Politics Events*, Jasmine Gomez and Allie Boldt of Free Speech for People and Demos develop a framework for diversifying the "money in politics" movement. Though these authors name a specific type of event, their guiding principles have broader applicability beyond their particular context, in terms of what the work of centring can look like in practice. Gomez and Boldt open their *Centring Marginalized Communities* document by noting the "systems of oppression" that create marginalization "including structural racism and white supremacy, heteronormativity, transphobia, misogyny, xenophobia, and ableism."[18] Centring difference begins by acknowledging that these systems of oppression create marginalization and devalue forms of difference. At the same time, centring difference recuperates value in the margins rather than angling towards homogeneity. Gomez and Boldt's recommendations include:

1. A focus on personal narratives provided by grassroots activists;
2. Education about why big money in politics and claims of corporate rights are harmful to democracy, using class and race analyses, and;
3. Space to discuss forward-thinking solutions to empower the community to act.[19]

These recommendations emphasize opportunities and spaces to learn and create, informed by structural analysis, alongside valorizing personal experiences as valid forms of knowledge. In their document, Gomez and Boldt follow these three guiding principles with practical tips and resources about how to centre marginalized communities by reflecting on the structure of community consultations, including logistics of coordination and organization (including who will be reached by events based on where and when they are held); advertising (what communities will be reached by different forms of advertising); payment (to compensate for work vs. expecting volunteer labour); art (representative of communities addressed); panelists and co-sponsors (that are representative); and afterlife (where and how the event will live on to ensure information is available). These recommendations demonstrate a reflexivity on access needs, and demonstrate a shift in how access and resources (i.e. power) are configured, in the interest of social change.

Disrupting the dominant margin/centre binary requires shifting attention away from dominant and hegemonic norms and centring people and perspectives that have been marginalized by these dominant systems In 2020, CBC Arts columnist and award-winning playwright Amanda Parris debuted a new column on the CBC online (the CBC is Canada's national broadcaster), profiling the creative work of Black artists. She describes the focus of this column as follows:

> Black Light is a weekly column that will spotlight, champion and challenge art and popular culture that is created by Black people and/or centres Black people. Why is this column important? Because from Mathieu da Costa to Aubrey Drake Graham, Black folks have long been translating, transforming and transgressing the Canadian landscape. Black Light will shine a focused and consistent light on those that do so through their art and examine them in conversation with the work being created by Black artists around the world. The work created by Black artists often goes undocumented. It's a consistent and systemic problem in Canada—one that's created a cultural amnesia that renders Black art and Black artists invisible. Black Light is a small attempt to rectify this issue."[20]

Here, Parris asserts that Black people have long contributed to Canadian society, starting with Mathieu da Costa, the first recorded Black person to arrive on the territory that is now known as Canada in the early 17th century.[21] Citing this early example of Black history in Canada puts Drake, who is also named, and his explosive fame in context. While Drake's success is sometimes credited as putting his hometown of Toronto and Canada more broadly on the hip hop and by extension global creative industries map, Parris cites a more than 300-year history of Black contribution in Canada. What has been lacking is documentation, critical appraisal, support and celebration, not creativity or contribution. In her Instagram Stories previewing her "31 Black Canadian Female Playwrights You Need to Know" article, published in the Black Light column on March 6, 2019, Parris writes, "I couldn't find a list of Black Canadian female playwrights anywhere on the Internet so I decided to make one. Here are 31 names (one for every day in March). Collectively these 31 names have written 92 productions. Read them. Teach them. Remount them."[22] These imperative sentences serve a pedagogical function, operating as a call-to-action to followers and readers, to centre underrepresented Black artists in the creative industries landscape.

Parris' column demonstrates a dual focus on and balance between centring underrepresented and underacknowledged Black cultural production and critiquing the systemic racism that devalues Black art. Her column gathers and shares information with her audience about Black artists and cultural producers who have individually and collectively not received sustained attention in Canada and beyond. 2020 also saw increased awareness and conversation about systemic anti-Black racism and increased attention to the Black Lives Matter movement after the murder of George Floyd in May 2020. In his 1993 essay "What is this 'Black' in Black Popular Culture," Stuart Hall opens with "a question: What sort of moment is this to pose the question of black popular culture? These moments are always conjunctural. They have their historical specificity; and although they always exhibit similarities and continuities with the other moments in which we pose a question like this, they are never the same moment."[23] Through the explosive uprisings of summer 2020, a summer which was a particular historical moment based in long-standing dynamics of racism, conversations about racism and racial inequity in the creative industries more forcefully came to the fore. Though these conversations have long cycled through public consciousness, led by artists and scholars of colour, after the summer of 2020 there was an increased urgency around these conversations, in part bolstered by social media and the hypervisibility of anti-Black racism.

This historical moment also brought renewed attention to anti-Black racism in Canadian creative industries. In "Canadian Cultural Institutions Have Silenced Black Voices for Years. Can We Write a New Chapter?" from June 8, 2020, Parris writes, "Black artists and activists in Canada have a long history of speaking truth to power and calling out anti-Black racism, from its most overt forms to its most passive micro-aggressions. But their acts of bravery reveal a history of institutionally enforced silencing, erasure, defamation and suppression."[24] Here, Parris places the heightened awareness and discussions of systemic racism in summer 2020 in a longer trajectory of advocacy, critique, and activism from Black artists and cultural workers that predates this moment. Parris' historical focus on the long-standing nature of systemic anti-Black racism contextualizes the centring of Black forms of cultural production as not only celebration but also critical intervention. It is not a matter of circumstantial factors, lack of means, or mere lack of visibility that has caused marginalized forms of cultural production to be devalued and ignored. The relationship of centre to margins has been enforced through the enactment of power; marginalization has been created by systems of oppression, including anti-Black racism, that manifests in racists acts and backlash alongside an ongoing imbalance in cultural valuation. Parris concludes by suggesting that the rise of social media has contributed to a shift in the balance of power, where systemic injustice is no longer safely buried or invisible, noting a "moment of reckoning." How might we understand this moment as an opportunity for learning how to do differently in the creative industries? What alternative models of more inclusive social relations exist, and how do these alternatives enable unlearning of harmful dominant norms? Below, I turn to an analysis of pedagogical models and discuss their relevance to inclusion in creative industries contexts.

From Public Pedagogy to Critical Pedagogy

Education scholars increasingly recognize the importance of learning in out-of-school settings, identifying that formal education in schools is not the main or key site for young people's learning.[25] Nonetheless, pedagogy has continued salience both as a concept and as a youth and lifelong experience. Michael Hoechsmann and Stuart Poyntz suggest pedagogy is a "bridging concept" between structure and agency, as pedagogy mediates the formative impact of institutional contexts and the empowering potential of learning.[26] Highlighting pedagogy outside of school settings, Henry A. Giroux foregrounds the role of popular culture in informal or out-of-school learning as one of "public pedagogy," suggesting that popular culture is a site where "identities are being constantly transformed and power enacted."[27] Popular culture can offer both affirmation and resistance to hegemonic norms: various forms of media can both reflect and offer alternatives to dominant cultural norms through the representations that these media provide.[28] For example, Robin Redmon Wright and Jennifer Sandlin's study of the 1960s television program *The Avengers* argues that television forms a site of adult learning, and viewers of *The Avengers* both learned and incorporated the feminist example of the character Cathy Gale into their own lives.[29] The flip side of this equation, that forms of media may enable expansion—that forms of media can be reductive and communicate harmful and limited tropes—can also be true. In *Teaching Community: A Pedagogy of Hope*, hooks comments that "since much of the pedagogy of domination is brought to us in the United States by mass media, particularly via television, I rarely watch TV."[30]

This framework of public pedagogy that highlights the pedagogical function of popular culture and other forms of media draws attention to the role of the creative industries. As discussed in the Introduction, cultural industries theorists like David Hesmondhalgh assert the importance of studying creative industries products, such as television programs or other forms of art and media, because they inform our view of ourselves, others, and the world. In short, representation matters. Critical pedagogy offers further inroads for an expanded pedagogical analysis, beyond the function of the content of cultural production (i.e. What is this cultural product teaching you?), to also consider forms of teaching and learning through relational social practices (i.e. How are we learning through our interactions together?). Here, we can return to hooks, in particular her book *Yearning: Race, Gender, and Cultural Politics*, for further discussion of the space of marginality in cultural production and the capacity of this space to foster alternative and inclusive social practices through teaching and learning. In her essay "Choosing the Margin as Space of Radical Openness" from this collection, hooks reinforces that the "margins have been both sites of repression and sites of resistance" and outlines a "definite distinction between that marginality which is imposed by oppressive structures and that marginality one chooses as a site of resistance—as location of radical openness and possibility."[31] This "politics of location" identifies "the spaces where we begin the process of re-vision."[32] Above, I cited hooks' comment on the role of mass media as a pedagogical vehicle for dominator culture. But hooks also acknowledges the complexity of representation, asserting a desire to move past a focus on "good and bad images," outlining that this kind of focus "may be more fundamentally connected to the western metaphysical dualism that is the philosophical underpinning of racist and sexist domination than with radical efforts to reconceptualize 'black cultural identities.'"[33] She identifies cultural production as a key site for liberation, "the location for possible transformative thinking about the nature of black experience."[34] As such, "counter-hegemonic cultural production" is a space of complexity, a "place of confrontation and encounter," but also of pleasure.[35]

For hooks, the margins are a space of pedagogical encounter, a site for collective engagement and critique, alongside fostering enjoyment and connection with others. Identifying the importance of critical pedagogy contributions from Paulo Freire, hooks suggests that "education for critical consciousness is the most important task before us."[36] In the landmark critical pedagogy text *Pedagogy of the Oppressed*, Freire articulates a vision of education that is emancipatory, that strives towards empowerment of oppressed and marginalized peoples in the goals of liberation and humanization. For Freire, liberation is "the process of humanization" in light of the historical reality of ongoing dehumanization, in particular of marginalized peoples. Liberation through this process of humanization is "a praxis: the action and reflection of men and women upon their world in order to transform it."[37] Critical pedagogy enables this process of humanization so that praxis becomes possible. This view of the potentials and role of education differs from what Freire identifies as a "banking model," where an expert teacher "deposits" knowledge into the passive pupil to be learnt by rote. Critical pedagogy strives to open dialogic space for encounter through "problem posing" and critical inquiry, "forged *with*, not *for* the oppressed" (emphasis in original).[38] Freire writes, "education as the practice of freedom—as opposed to education as the practice of domination—denies that man is abstract, isolated, independent, and unattached to the world; it also denies that the world exists as a reality apart from people. Authentic reflection considers neither abstract man nor the world without people, but people in their relations with the world."[39] It is important to acknowledge that formal education remains a site of domination, not freedom, for many people and in particular marginalized peoples; this framework of critical pedagogy outlines alternative possibilities and sites for liberation.

In Freire's comments, learning is outlined as the development of an understanding of a relational self, that self and world are co-constituted; learning itself is also articulated as relational (and not transactional). Cultural production can be a site of pedagogical encounter through creating space for openness and possibility, not through didactic transaction, but through relational exchange. We can overlay this critical pedagogy emphasis on relationality with care ethics, a framework that allows for an assessment of the kinds of interactions and relations that become possible through care. Discussing care in teaching work, Nel Noddings asserts that "a caring teacher is not someone who should be 'willing to do almost anything to bring my students to mastery of the basic skills.'" Instead, a caring teacher is someone who valorizes the student as a person and develops relationship and rapport accordingly. Noddings writes, "among the intangibles that I would have my students carry away is the feeling that the subject we have struggled with is both fascinating and boring, significant and silly, fraught with meaning and nonsense, challenging and tedious, and that whatever attitude we take toward it, it will not diminish our regard for each other. The student is infinitely more important than the subject."[40] Liberation, humanization, and freedom may appear as idealized goals, and we can also underscore friction, discomfort, and difficulty in the process of praxis, made possible through practices of care.

Below, I explore pedagogical modes of centring the margins, teaching and learning for doing differently through building inclusion in the creative industries. In *Freedom Dreams: The Black Radical Imagination*, Robin D. G. Kelley asks "what are today's young activists dreaming about? We know what they are fighting against, but what are they fighting for?"[41] I profile two grassroots organizations dedicated to education within the creative industries context: PEERS program, an incubator program for underrepresented emerging artists, and the Dandelion Initiative, an education and training program for gender-based and sexual violence prevention and survivor supports in and beyond the creative industries. In these profiles, I spotlight what these grassroots forms of education are fighting for or imagining by returning to the characteristics of relational autonomy and widening access, which are enabled by care thinking for the creative industries, and move beyond a goal of mere representation.

Navigating Relational Autonomy and the Politics of Inclusion: Supporting Critical Conversations with PEERS

What Was PEERS?

PEERS was a paid three-month long peer mentorship program organized by Whippersnapper Gallery in Toronto, Ontario, incubating groups of emerging artists, curators, arts organizers, or other cultural producers, that ran from 2015 to 2017. Whippersnapper Gallery is an artist-run centre "committed to the cultivation of inclusive spaces for emerging visual and media arts, community arts, and experimental forms of exhibition making."[42] As such, Whippersnapper centres the perspectives of underrepresented artists and provides access to a professional and accommodating platform that enables artists to take risks, experiment, and incubate their professional development. The PEERS program was founded in 2015 by Mohammad Rezaei and Maggie Flynn, supported by a three-year grant from the Ontario Trillium Foundation.

I sat on the Board of Directors at Whippersnapper Gallery from 2015 to 2020. Some of the time when PEERS was running was when I was on maternity leave and away from active duties in 2016–2017, so I welcomed the opportunity to reach out to Joshua Vettivelu through the course of writing this book to learn more about the operations of PEERS. Josh is an artist working with the mediums of sculpture, installation, performance, video, and drawing. They were the director of programming at Whippersnapper from 2016–2018, and ran three iterations of PEERS (PEERS 2, PEERS 3, and PEERS Projects, akin to a PEERS alumni cohort). Josh describes their art practice as being "about examining how desire, language, and power build the world. Specifically, how languages of resistance have to be developed socially, but before they can be developed socially they have to be developed internally."[43] PEERS also fostered some of these languages of resistance, internally and socially, by carving out resistance in the form of some relief or space away from a productivity narrative that mandates output as a benchmark and metric for success. Instead, pedagogical spaces can build inclusion through working to foster horizontal exchanges and co-learning without competition. The call for applications for PEERS participants in 2016 describes the program as follows: "the PEERS program leverages collectively-accumulated knowledge and ideas to support participants in developing the skills and relationships needed to build artistic infrastructure that has a lasting impact on the communities in which we coexist. Rather than a hierarchy of mentor to mentee, this program will be an opportunity for participants to learn from the diverse experiences of their peers. Equal parts shared learning, and 'do-your-own-thing,' participants will be able to focus on the development of practice, discourse, and ideas, without pressure to produce anything."[44]

How Was PEERS Run?

Commenting on PEERS' organizational structure, Josh says, "it sounds very simple, but the way that it was done became very important." Josh cites ongoing friendships with all of the PEERS participants as a lasting impact of this program, rather than emphasizing the further career development of individual artists, even if many of the artists have continued on with impactful professional careers. The "way it was done" began with reflexivity on applicants and structural factors that impact how participants do or do not gain access to art world institutions and supports. Importantly, PEERS offered participants an honorarium payment for participation, mindful that time away from paid work to participate in programs is a privilege not available to many emerging artists. The 2016 Call for Applications states, "forming a practice is hard when you're juggling day jobs and night jobs. The participation of all participants will be recognized with a $500 honoraria meant to offset some of the costs of your time contribution towards the development of the program and your own practice."[45] As director of programming reviewing applications to the PEERS program, Josh noticed that they had mostly shortlisted BIPOC artists, so they decided to prioritize BIPOC applicants for the group. More broadly, reflecting on race and representation in art institutions, Josh comments on an administrative strategy of setting "maximum capacity for historically overrepresented artists" instead of the inverse, where many institutions often work to meet "a minimum requirement of diversity." Commenting on the language of "historical overrepresentation," Josh also suggests this strategy "address[es] what's really happening," which is the pervasiveness of white supremacy, rather than a lack of artistic talent or merit from historically underrepresented artists. Josh further reflected on selecting PEERS applicants by aiming to find a balance between applicants affiliated with the local art university (Ontario College of Art and Design University or OCAD University) and local community members from the neighbourhoods where Whippersnapper is situated in Toronto: Chinatown and Alexandra Park. Josh describes a reflexive balancing act, identifying that OCAD is a "well resourced" environment, but at the same time, "there are students who are not well-resourced." Access to resources can be financial, but also can be access to support systems, and PEERS attempted to provide this type of support system, "shar[ing] resources laterally" amongst participants.

PEERS was structured around weekly meetings, with participants getting together to talk. Josh says PEERS entailed "people who came together and rallied each other, while pooling resources and having discussions that were difficult and intense. Having a residency that wasn't materially productive. We were there, what do we need, let's find a way to get it." Josh characterizes this type of environment as providing some "relief" through having a space to talk through collective and differing experiences, "create [ing] language around what is happening ... We would talk about contract negotiations, or why did we all have the same experience in school. Or to the people that didn't go to art school ...What is the art school/non-art school hierarchy? When it's just people sitting around a table and the point is to talk to each other, all of these things became really interesting." This sense of relief and these critical conversations can be both joyful and difficult. After Josh opened a few PEERS meetings, different participants took turns leading meetings, and Josh remembers, "one PEER, Rekha Ramachandran, led a session that was very tactile. [She] brought squishy things, it was just fun. Fun with really smart people who would also deep-dive into the experience. One of those beautiful generative moments. It was freeing." At the same time, holding space for these difficult and intense conversations can also bring forth a number of challenges. Josh comments, "the reality of it is that the care of bringing people together is actually so difficult. You have to anticipate and find polite ways of asking and gauging. People bring a lot of stuff. When you are being as vulnerable as we were, people were bringing all their stuff. It went in ways that we did not expect."

Can We Make It Last?: Survival, Refusal, and Recognition

One component of PEERS was also bringing in guest speakers, with PEERS participants collaboratively deciding who they wanted to invite to speak. One guest speaker was artist Deanna Bowen, passing on "survival strategies, her own personal [experience], what has happened, not advice. That's a lot of how PEERS was framed, the lateral peers-ness." This internal conversation format with guest speakers led to PEERS putting on a Conversation Series of events, similarly focusing on critical conversations about artist experiences and arts institutions. For example, Deanna Bowen also participated in a PEERS event with fellow artist Abbas Akhavan called "Damned If You Do: A Conversation on the Politics of Refusal," an event developed through the PEERS group's questions of "How do you refuse? What if they don't let you refuse? What if you don't want to refuse?" and addressing "often tricky negotiations that 'marginalized' artists must make when navigating neoliberal art and funding systems—where inclusion is often based on a mandated disclosure and performance of identity politics" (Figure 4.1). In the "Damned If You Do" event, Abbas commented that inclusion can sometimes manifest as "hospitality that can become ambivalent. It's whether or not when you're invited into a space being understood for who you are or [whether you are] serving as a placeholder."[46]

Josh also reflected on these politics of inclusion and refusal in an article for *C Magazine* after the "Damned If You Do" event, titled "When We are Welcomed into the Fold, Where Do We Keep What is Left Behind," commenting on the financial implications of navigating and refusing problematic art world dynamics:

> When faced with precarity, outright refusal is not always an option for everyone. However, the reality of precarity is often overlooked when artists are forced to make ethically uneasy decisions about when to accept money and opportunity. The accusation of 'selling out' seems deeply invested in upholding artists to a utopian politic of liberal purity that disregards sustainability; it is a fantasy that absolves the accuser of the reality that, under capitalism, we are all always selling pieces of ourselves."[47]

Here, Josh comments on navigating the balance of artistic and economic goals in racial capitalism: sustainability and survival in this system entails strategies to mitigate the at-times conflicting demands of art and making a living.[48]

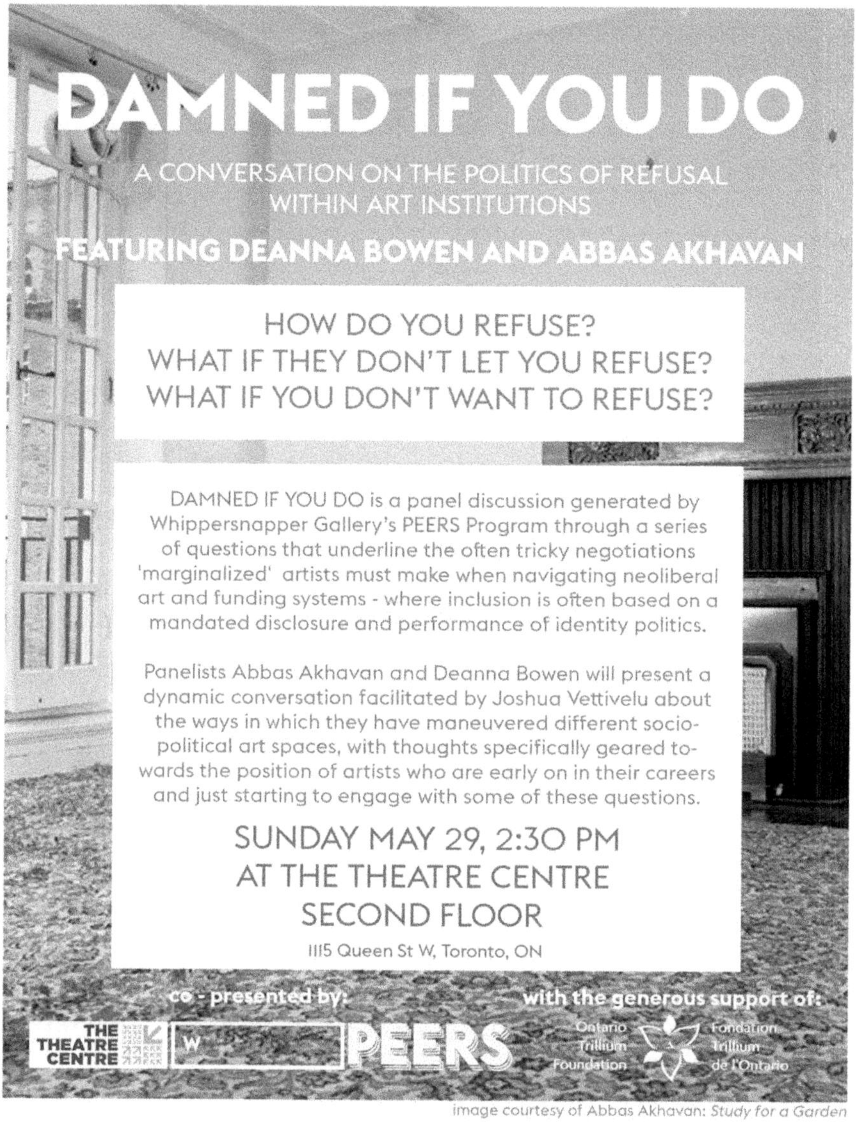

FIGURE 4.1 "Damned If You Do" Event Flyer from PEERS Program © Image by Joshua Vettivelu, art work by Abbas Akhavan

Highlighting these survival strategies, Josh comments on how to attune the attention, where the gaze is directed for recognition, contrasting institutional recognition (which also can entail financial support and economic survival) with community recognition:

> I have often felt that the starting stages of my career, when there were no eyes on me, was when I was able to experiment and make mistakes with few repercussions. In retrospect, I realize that during this period I may have been invisible to the institutions from which I sought recognition, but I was far from being neglected. Instead, I was being fostered by a community that understood my intentions—and this was an incredibly fertile source of recognition.[49]

This space that Josh sketches here, the space of the community that understands, nurtures, and incubates artistic practice, can be understood as the relational marginal space that hooks outlines: space of openness and possibility. In contrast to Abbas' comments about inclusion in art institutions as a racialized artist as a tokenized "placeholder," these spaces, as hooks writes, the spaces "where we begin the process of re-vision," can be foregrounded for their inclusive and pedagogical capacities. But developing, nurturing, and maintaining these spaces and the care labour this entails also comes with other costs. Commenting on the burnout of the role of the director of programming at Whippersnapper, Josh highlights the low pay but high volume of curatorial output of the role. These conflicts of "time, money, exhaustion," as Josh puts it, are not sustainable. Josh comments, "everyone was treading water and we had to call it on the ambition and the level we were putting out. We had excavated the bottom and we all fell through." While Josh remains proud of the work that was done through their time at Whippersnapper, they also highlight that this was achieved at "the cost of the body," raising important questions about the material impact of care labour that exists within overarching capitalistic systems.

Accessing Safe Workplaces Through Education and Training: The Dandelion Initiative

Origins

The Dandelion Initiative (DI) is a not-for-profit organization dedicated to gender-based and sexual violence prevention and survivor supports. DI was founded by Viktoria Belle, who is an educator and survivor. After her assault in 2015, Viktoria filed a police report and went through a legal process for over a year, before charges against her rapist were dropped. Viktoria comments, the "process failed me, as it does so many survivors, which is why only 5% of survivors report."[50] In 2016, when Viktoria found out that these charges had been dropped, a trial was underway for sexual assault charges against Jian Ghomeshi, a CBC radio host, who had sexual harassment complaints both in the workplace at CBC and in his personal life for many years. An independent investigation into the CBC concluded that Ghomeshi's behaviour can be "considered to create an intimidating, humiliating, hostile or offensive work environment" and that "CBC management condoned this behaviour."[51] The criminal charges brought against Ghomeshi stemmed from his personal life, including four counts of sexual assault and one count of choking.

The Ghomeshi trial galvanized survivors, who protested in front of Toronto Old City Hall, where the trial was taking place, holding signs and chanting, "we believe survivors." Ghomeshi was eventually acquitted on all charges.[52] Ghomeshi later had the audacity to publish an article in the *New York Review of Books* referring to himself as "a #MeToo pioneer," in that his charges and trial led to a heated conversation in Canada about the pervasiveness of sexual violence and the capacity for the creative industries to enabler abusers, before a global conversation exploded with the #MeToo movement 2017.[53] Under the mantle of a group named the Sexual Assault Action Coalition, Viktoria participated in these protests at City Hall, alongside organizing supports for survivors, via the vehicle of a Facebook group. In 2016, further grave incidents emerged in Toronto in the nightlife industry at a bar called College Street Bar, where a young woman was forcibly confined and assaulted by the bar manager and owner. Both the bar owner and the manager, Gavin MacMillan and Enzo De Jesus Carrasco, were convicted of gang sexual assault and drugging the victim, and they were sentenced to nine years in prison in 2020. At the time of the writing of this book, MacMillan was out on bail after appealing his conviction.[54]

In 2016, Viktoria says, "everything felt like it was on fire" and this College Street Bar incident was a "defining turning point." Viktoria received a message through her Sexual Assault Action Coalition Facebook group from the family of the College Street Bar survivor, who didn't know who else to reach out to for support and action. Viktoria has a background in early childhood education and was working in the public policy sector during this time, but quit her job to devote her attention to sexual violence prevention work full-time. "I did this with everything," she says. The DI started by protesting outside of College Street Bar. Viktoria says, "it was started by a group of survivors, women and non-binary folks, predominantly queer and BIPOC survivors" who "saw such a real need for survivor-centric training and education that was led by survivors," suggesting the importance of centring the needs, views, and expertise of those who have been impacted by sexual violence. The DI's first training program, Safer Bars and Spaces, directed to sexual violence prevention in the nightlife industry, was born out of the College Street Bar assault (Figure 4.2). Viktoria describes this program as the

FIGURE 4.2 "Safer Bars and Spaces" Program Flyer from the Dandelion Initiative © The Dandelion Initiative

genesis of the DI, from which other programs, like Safer Artistic Spaces, have grown like branches. Safer Artistic Spaces addresses arts spaces and sectors, including live music, live performance, venues, and film, and addresses workers like performers, artists, and contract workers. These types of spaces are often not formal workplaces, and as such, may not be governed by formal employment standards. "But you still have rights," Viktoria says, and this program addresses violence and safety in this context.

Programming

> *"We fundamentally believe in the power of education as a resistance to gender-based violence."*[55]

Informed by Viktoria's policy background, the DI's programming takes a multi-faceted approach to sexual and gender-based violence prevention and support. The DI's report, *Don't Rebuild on Our Backs: Report on Gender-Based Violence Before, During, and After COVID-19* notes: "our program uses a socio-ecological model for gender-based violence prevention that focuses on connecting primary (policies), secondary (training), and tertiary (direct support) practices which have been proven to provide the best long-term outcomes for preventing and responding to gender-based violence."[56] Much of the DI's programming connects to the middle point of what Viktoria calls this "sandwich," alongside the organization supporting policy development within organizations and providing direct supports to survivors at no cost, including group sessions, supporting individuals to get counselling, and giving survivors small sums of emergency money.

Viktoria notes the context of adapted legislation in the province of Ontario in Canada, where the DI is active; in 2016, Bill 132 was passed, called the Sexual Violence and Harassment Action Plan, an amendment to the Occupational Health and Safety Act, which includes provisions to require employers to develop workplace harassment prevention programs and policies. Speaking to this context and to the training that the DI offers, Viktoria says, "let us help you do this instead of downloading a template from the Government of Ontario's website, because it's not going to help you." Viktoria emphasizes moving beyond lip-service compliance and instead towards holistic and sustainable safety and health, beginning with "working to repair a culture." Viktoria speaks to the DI's socio-ecological approach to creating "a web of accountability between legislation provincially, regulation municipally, and policies and practices in workplaces, especially in precarious workplaces, in feminized workplaces."[57] A precariously employed and feminized staff base cannot be expected to shoulder the burden of changing a culture. The DI's three-pronged approach recognizes that training is important, but in isolation cannot change pervasive problems of widespread normalization, acceptance, or dismissal of sexual and gender-based violence. She says, "we use this model to reinforce the reality that individuals alone, cannot be responsible for culture change. The skills and value-building we foster with teams needs to be reinforced through policy, environment, and ongoing learning."[58]

Pedagogy

How can pedagogy work towards repairing a culture, given the pervasiveness of sexual violence? Viktoria says, "after every single session I have taught, every single time, a survivor has disclosed they have experienced gender based-violence either at that workplace, another workplace, or in their life." She emphasizes that repairing culture is "not punitive, not a penal process that you're doing." When a company books the DI's Safer Bars and Spaces training, the organization mandates that owners and managers attend trainings alongside staff, working towards stabilizing "unequal dynamics between back of house and front of house." Front of house staff (largely comprised of women) are more likely to witness sexual violence take place, and face a greater possibility of experiencing it directly in their workplace environments, whereas back of house or managerial staff (positions dominated by men) often hold decision-making power. Having both of these groups participate in training aims to open a pedagogical space with both groups involved in repairing a culture.

The DI's trainings are delivered through a flipped format, with participants receiving an eight-chapter handbook before the training session begins, covering definitions of topics like sexual violence, consent, power and privilege, toxic masculinity, and rape culture, putting this information in the context of particular industries, like the nightlife industry. Viktoria says the DI offers specific services, geared towards specific industries rather than attempting to be diffuse or cover all equity topics: "we are not here to teach you anti-racism; we are not here to teach you everything in three hours so that nothing is meaningful. We want to connect you to the incredible community leaders that you can and should learn from beyond the Dandelion. We want to teach you sexual and gender-based violence prevention and response practices, policies, and survivor-centred supports." Providing this material before the first training session allows the time in the session with the facilitator and participants to be interactive and dialogic. Viktoria says, "the goal is to feel and make meaning from the teachings, rather than bombard you with stats." When facilitating training sessions, the DI creates an online and in-person space that aims to foster equity, empathy and learning through good boundaries, humility, and community care, telling participants, "if you are going to be racist or transphobic or sexist, we will determine our threshold for that, and we'll tell that to you, we'll communicate that to you in way that is respectful." A second session in the two-part flipped format covers drug-facilitated sexual assault, industry-specific bystander intervention techniques, verbal and non-verbal tools, de-escalation tactics, and how to support survivors, again with an eight-chapter workbook providing information about these topics, sent before the second session. The time spent in the session "allows folks to develop norms and activities with each other" so that the training is "part learning, part doing."

Viktoria speaks to the satisfaction and joys of the DI's work in multi-faceted ways, from continuous learning ("at every single session we do, someone teaches us something") to engaged participants ("every single workshop, when we read the feedback, it's a win, because even people who are challenging in the session, typically are really positive" [Figure 4.3]); to being able to work with peers and developing community with volunteers,

FIGURE 4.3 "Now Serving: Education in 2020" Flyer from the Dandelion Initiative © The Dandelion Initiative

members of the board of directors, committees, and long-term supporters; building policies and programs for organizations through sustained collaborative work ("it feels like a win each time that happens, even if the relationship is challenging"); alongside the challenging and vital work of supporting survivors, to "see them through all the way" with filing criminal or informal charges, if that is what they choose to pursueFigure 4.3. "I can't express what that experience is like to be able to support someone through that. It's hard, but it has to happen," says Viktoria. At the same time, "vicarious trauma is really real," says Viktoria, and staff can and do burn out from this work. With this in mind, the DI has developed mechanisms to ensure a supportive environment internally, with monthly care sessions, focusing on emotional, mental, physical, and spiritual safety. Every two months, the DI also has externally facilitated debriefs. Viktoria says, "debriefing is a really powerful tool to manage compassion fatigue and to manage trauma." She talks about keeping her friends and family close, "lots of laughing and lots of playing and being human and nice to each other."

For next steps, the DI hopes to move to a next stage of hiring and training facilitators, furthering this work by training the trainers, or as Viktoria says, "start training all different types of people to do this [work] in their own unique ways for their own unique communities and workplaces," such that this ongoing work of eliminating gender-based and sexual violence can continue to develop and grow.

These profiles of the PEERS program and the DI highlight the role of informal and out-of-school, community-based pedagogies in centring difference through developing more caring and inclusive models to foster learning, beyond dominant norms that are exclusionary and harmful. In Chapter 5, I continue this exploration of pedagogical spaces through highlighting the role of community youth arts program in incubating creative careers and in developing inclusive working practices.

Notes

1 For fuller discussion of the riot grrrl movement and the history of the "girls to the front" call, see Sara Marcus, *Girls to the Front: The True Story of the Riot Grrrl Revolution* (New York: Harper Perennial, 2010).

2 David Friend, "Halifax Music Fest Apologizes for 'Overt Racism' at Polaris Winner's Concert," *CTV News*, October 27, 2017, accessed December 3, 2020, https://www.ctvnews.ca/entertainment/halifax-music-fest-apologizes-for-overt-racism-at-polaris-winner-s-concert-1.3651940

3 Calum Slingerland, "Lido Pimienta Speaks Out About 'Overt Racism' at Halifax Pop Explosion, *Exclaim*, October 31, 2017, accessed December 3, 2020, http://exclaim.ca/music/article/lido_pimienta_speaks_out_following_overt_racism_at_halifax_pop_explosion

4 Stuart Hall, "Notes on Deconstructing the Popular," in *Cultural Resistance Reader*, ed. Stephen Dunmore (London: Verso, 2002), 185–192, 188, 187.
5 Ibid., 188, 189.
6 Ibid., 187.
7 Eleonora Belfiore, "Whose Cultural Value? Representation, Power and Creative Industries," *International Journal of Cultural Policy* 26, no. 3 (2018): 383–397, 384.
8 bell hooks, "Choosing the Margin as a Space of Radical Openness," in *Yearning: Race, Gender, and Cultural Politics* (Toronto: Between the Lines, 1990), 145–155, 147.
9 bell hooks, *Feminist Theory: From Margin to Center* (New York: Routledge, 2015), xviii.
10 Ibid., xvii.
11 bell hooks, "Postmodern Blackness," in *Yearning: Race, Gender, and Cultural Politics* (Toronto: Between the Lines, 1990), 26.
12 Ibid.
13 Cited in Sasha Costanza-Chock, *Design Justice: Community-Led Practices to Build the Worlds We Need* (Cambridge, MA: MIT Press, 2020), 6.
14 Ibid., 26.
15 David A. Thomas and Robin J. Ely, "Making Differences Matter: A New Paradigm for Managing Diversity," *Harvard Business Review*, September–October 1996, accessed March 17, 2021, https://hbr.org/1996/09/making-differences-matter-a-new-paradigm-for-managing-diversity
16 It is beyond the scope of this chapter to provide a full exploration of the field of disability justice. For further reading, see for example Aimi Haimraie, *Building Access: Universal Design and the Politics of Disability* (Minneapolis: University of Minnesota Press, 2017); Eli Clare, *Brilliant Imperfection: Grappling with the Cure* (Durham, NC: Duke University Press, 2017).
17 Leah Lakshmi Piepzna-Samarasinha, *Care Work: Dreaming Disability Justice* (Vancouver, BC: Arsenal Pulp Press, 2018), 232, 75.
18 Jasmine Gomez and Allie Boldt, *Centering Marginalized Communities: A Framework for Intersectional Money in Politics Events* (New York City: Demos, 2017), 1, https://www.demos.org/research/centering-marginalized-communities-framework-intersectional-money-politics-events
19 Ibid.
20 Amanda Parris, "2020's Must-See Projects by Black Artists," *CBC Arts*, January 10, 2020, accessed December 3, 2020, https://www.cbc.ca/arts/2020-s-must-see-projects-by-black-artists-1.5421164
21 "Mathieu da Costa," *Wikipedia*, accessed December 7, 2020, https://en.wikipedia.org/wiki/Mathieu_da_Costa
22 Amanda Parris, "31 Black Canadian Female Playwrights You Need to Know," *CBC Arts*, March 6, 2020, accessed March 17, 2021, https://www.cbc.ca/arts/31-black-canadian-female-playwrights-you-need-to-know-1.5487368
23 Stuart Hall, "What Is This 'Black' in Black Popular Culture," *Social Justice: A Journal of Crime, Conflict and World Order* 20, no. 1 (1993): 104–114, 104.
24 Amanda Parris, "Canadian Cultural Institutions Have Silenced Black Voices for Years. Can We Write a New Chapter?," *CBC Arts*, June 8, 2020, accessed March 17, 2021, https://www.cbc.ca/arts/canadian-cultural-institutions-have-silenced-black-voices-for-years-can-we-write-a-new-chapter-1.5600064
25 For discussion of out-of-school learning, see for example Glynda Hull and Katherine Schultz, eds., *School's Out!: Bridging Out-of-School Literacies with Classroom Practice* (New York, NY: Teachers College Press, 2002); Henry Jenkins, *Convergence Culture: Where Old and New Media Collide* (New York, NY: New York University Press, 2006); Henry Jenkins, Mizuko Ito, and danah boyd, *Participatory Culture in a Networked Era: A Conversation on Youth, Learning, Commerce, and Politics* (Cambridge, UK: Polity Press, 2015); Julian Sefton-Green, *Learning at Not-School: A Review of Study, Theory, and*

Advocacy for Education in Non-Formal Settings (Cambridge, MA: The MIT Press), 2013. For discussions on the limits of out-of-school learning and digital spaces to foster diversity and inclusion in learning, see for example Kim Andreasson, ed., *Digital Divides: The New Challenges and Opportunities of e-Inclusion* (New York: Routledge, 2015).

26 Michael Hoechsmann and Stuart Poyntz, *Media Literacies: A Critical Introduction* (Hoboken, NJ: Wiley Blackwell, 2012), 41.

27 Henry A. Giroux, "Public Pedagogy as Cultural Politics: Stuart Hall and the Crisis of Culture," *Cultural Studies* 14, no. 2 (2000): 341–360, 355.

28 For further discussion of public pedagogies, see for example, Henry A. Giroux, "Public Pedagogy and the Politics of Resistance: Notes on a Critical Theory of Educational Struggle," *Educational Philosophy and Theory* 35, no. 1 (2000): 5–16; Jennifer A. Sandlin, Brian D. Schultz, and Jake Burdick, eds., *Handbook of Public Pedagogy: Education and Learning Beyond Schooling* (New York: Routledge, 2009).

29 Robin Redmon Wright and Jennifer A. Sandlin, "Popular Culture, Public Pedagogy and Perspective Transformation: *The Avengers* and Adult Learning in Living Rooms," *International Journal of Lifelong Education* 28, no. 4 (2000): 533–551.

30 bell hooks, *Teaching Community: A Pedagogy of Hope* (New York: Routledge, 2003), 11.

31 bell hooks, *Yearning: Race, Gender, and Cultural Politics* (Toronto: Between the Lines, 1990), 151, 153.

32 Ibid., 145.

33 Ibid., 19.

34 Ibid., 18.

35 Ibid., 1, 4.

36 Ibid., 5.

37 Paulo Freire, *Pedagogy of the Oppressed* (50th Anniversary Edition), trans. Myra Bergman Ramos (New York: Bloomsbury Academic, 2000), 79.

38 Ibid., 48.

39 Ibid., 81.

40 Nel Noddings, *Caring: A Relational Approach to Ethics and Moral Education* (2nd ed., Updated) (Berkeley: University of California Press, 2013), 20.

41 Robin D. G. Kelley, *Freedom Dreams: The Black Radical Imagination* (Boston: Beacon Press, 2002), 8.

42 "About," *Whippersnapper Gallery*, accessed March 16, 2021, https://whippersnapper.ca/about

43 Joshua Vettivellu, personal interview, November 27, 2020.

44 Whippersnapper Gallery, "Call for Applications: Whippersnapper PEERS," *Whippersnapper Gallery*, January 11, 2016, accessed March 17, 2021, https://www.facebook.com/events/whippersnapper-gallery/call-for-applications-whippersnapper-peers/149632632063317/

45 Ibid.

46 Quoted in Joshua Vettivelu, "When We Are Welcomed into the Fold, Where Do Keep What Is Left Behind," *C Magazine*, Issue 133, Spring 2017, accessed December 10, 2020, https://cmagazine.com/issues/133/when-we-are-welcomed-into-the-fold-where-do-we-keep-what-is-left

47 Ibid.

48 For the origin and discussion of the term racial capitalism, or the extraction of economic and social value from racialized people in capitalistic systems, see Cedric J. Robinson, *Black Marxism: The Making of the Black Radical Tradition* (London: Zed Press, 1983).

49 Ibid.

50 Viktoria Belle, personal interview, December 2, 2020.

51 CBC News, "CBC Inquiry Concludes Management Mishandled Jian Ghomeshi," *CBC News*, April 16, 2015, accessed December 8, 2020, https://www.cbc.ca/news/cbc-inquiry-concludes-management-mishandled-jian-ghomeshi-1.3035574
52 Karolyn Coorsh, "Protests Outside Toronto Courthouse Following Ghomeshi Acquittal," *CTV News*, March 24, 2016, accessed December 8, 2020, https://www.ctvnews.ca/canada/protests-outside-toronto-courthouse-following-ghomeshi-acquittal-1.2831313
53 The Canadian Press, "Jian Ghomeshi's Essay in the New York Review of Books Draws Fire," *CBC News*, September 14, 2018, accessed December 8, 2020, https://www.cbc.ca/news/canada/toronto/jian-ghomeshi-new-york-review-books-1.4823955
54 The Canadian Press, "Men Convicted in College Street Bar Sexual Assault Saw Women as 'Disposable,' Judge Writes," CBC News, June 4, 2020, accessed August 8, 2021, https://www.cbc.ca/news/canada/toronto/college-bar-gang-rape-judge-decision-sentencing-1.5597971
55 The Dandelion Initiative, *Don't Rebuild on Our Backs: Report on Gender-Based Violence Before, During, and After COVID-19* (Toronto: The Dandelion Initiative, 2020), 1.
56 Ibid., 19.
57 Viktoria Belle, personal interview, December 2, 2020.
58 The Dandelion Initiative, *Don't Rebuild on Our Backs*, 19.

5

YOUTH CREATIVE WORK AND COMMUNITY ARTS

Through my "Community Youth Arts as Creative Industries Incubators" research project, I attended a "social justice mixer" event hosted by VIBE Arts, a community arts program in Toronto, Canada. This event was designed as an opportunity for youth involved and employed at VIBE to network with one another, spanning professional development and social elements. A representative from a partnering organization was present, giving a presentation to youth on how to get involved, and inviting them to offer input about the direction of the organization's activities. A nice spread of food was laid out, and an announcement to see one of the program staff for transit tokens if they were needed was made. The mixer featured a musician performing and speaking about the themes of their social-justice oriented music as well as the pleasures and challenges of working towards social-justice goals through cultural production. I was surprised by the level of engagement at this event, with the youth attendees readily engaging in requests for audience participation; some youth also started dancing at the front. I was struck by the differences between my experience of engaging youth in my own university classroom, where such spontaneous expressions of enthusiasm are rare. Though attendance at this mixer might lead to further professional development opportunities, this did not appear to be the exclusive or main draw of the event; social and professional elements seemed to be intertwined. Over the course of the research project, I sought to gain understanding of this intertwining of social and professional, both in terms of how community arts programs can offer meaningful supports, and how the creative industries might learn from these more inclusive practices, given the challenges of exclusion in this sector.

Community programs are increasingly using art and media as tools to engage youth, especially those from marginalized backgrounds.[1] Through the pedagogies and programming that are offered and through the support networks that youth

DOI: 10.4324/9781003031338-5

create amongst themselves at these sites, these programs act as spaces of knowledge transfer, skill sharing, teaching, and learning in novel ways. The role of these programs in fostering social cohesion with marginalized youth has been noted, but little research has evaluated the pedagogical innovations of these programs as they encourage youth to continue on with the creative projects and skills they learn and forge creative careers. Beyond learning the skill or content of art making or entrepreneurship, community youth arts programs can enact transformative pedagogies through enabling critique, empowerment, and connection with others.[2]

In the "Community Youth Arts Programs as Creative Industries Incubators" research project, I assessed the working practices of engaging youth in the community youth arts sector, and interrogated how these practices might inform the mainstreaming of inclusion in the creative industries, recognizing that inclusion needs to be actively fostered. I aimed to document what an inclusive culture can look like and feel like, while also registering the challenges of creating these types of environments. As such, this chapter addresses the intersection of creative industries employment and pedagogical innovation, asking how the latter can inform the former. I work from the assumption that these two spheres of creative industries employment and community arts pedagogies can and do overlap: the creative industries can be spaces of teaching and learning, and the community arts can scaffold entrepreneurship and employment. I recognize that structural barriers restrict access to creative industries employment and investigate how community youth arts can provide supports, while also recognizing that the creative industries are exclusionary and need to change to become more inclusive.

Community Arts as Site of Inquiry

Funded through the Social Sciences and Humanities Research Council (SSHRC) in Canada, the "Community Youth Arts Programs as Creative Industries Incubators" research project examined mechanisms through which community youth arts organizations incubate creativity and assist youth in navigating the entry-level phase of creative work in Toronto, Canada. While I contrast working practices in the community arts sector and the mainstream creative industries, I seek to bring these sectors into alignment and into conversation with one another, moving past a binary model that pits one against the other, through a case study of three particular programs. Rather than suggesting that these best practices could be incorporated into the creative industries wholesale, the community arts can offer inroads to recuperate and reimagine the social realm through reflexivity on inclusive working practices in the creative industries.

Structure and Purpose of Community Arts

Some research contrasts the transformative social space of the community arts sector in opposition to mainstream creative industries working practices, especially with regards to diversity and inclusion in entry-level creative industries work. In light of continued challenges of participation, representation, and cultural diversity in the creative industries, Sarita Malik, Caroline Chapain, and Roberta Comunian highlight the role of the community filmmaking sector in the U.K. in engaging with diversity from a "bottom-up" approach and offering a more inclusive model of engagement, supported by alternative business models, including self-distribution and crowdfunding.[3] While the authors raise concerns about the sustainability of these financing methods, they also privilege community filmmaking as a site of widening access to cultural production.

Much of the academic literature on community arts angles towards a U.K. context and discussion of this milieu; comprehensive histories of Canadian community arts remain to be written. Nonetheless, Toronto offers a key locale for attention to community youth arts programming. 2005 became known as the "summer of the gun" in Toronto in the media, a period marked by an upswing in youth gang-related violence and deaths. This period also saw an upswing in funding for youth arts programming, with attention turned to existing initiatives and organizations in the youth arts sector alongside funding new programs to work with so-called "at-risk" youth.[4] However, this funding and attention were not evenly sustained, and larger, systemic roots of social exclusion remained unaddressed.[5]

Working from the U.K. context, Kate Oakley, Mark Ball, and Malaika Cunningham provide an overview of the historically politicized nature of the community arts as a form of art practice that is participatory and socially engaged.[6] The authors draw on François Matarasso's work and definition of community arts as "a complex, unstable and contested practice, developed by young artists and theatre makers seeking to reinvigorate an art world they saw as bourgeois at best and repressive at worst."[7] Following Matarasso, Oakley, Ball and Cunningham argue that in recent decades, this form of art practice has been instrumentalized, angling towards remediation and personal change rather than social change. The community youth arts sector in Canada has similarly felt these pressures, increasingly pushed towards quantifiable outcomes of participation for the youth who are involved. However, this sector can still offer supports and alternatives, despite increased pressure and instrumentalization. Jan Cohen-Cruz suggests that "community-based art is as much about the process of involving people in the making of the work as the finished object itself."[8] A relational focus on people and process in working practices enables the community arts sector, both formal and informal, to act as an inclusive space for capacity development and wellbeing for young people, and this affirmation of the self can further enable entrepreneurial development and economic self-advancement.

While Oakley, Ball, and Cunningham suggest that the community arts sector has moved towards personal change rather than social change, this binary model relies on distinctions between the private and the public that may be blurred in contemporary community arts practice, where personal change through an emphasis on wellbeing and economic empowerment is a part of social transformation. This articulation of the personal and the social has particular salience in the context of diversity and creative industries participation. Community arts programs, often mandated to work with marginalized youth and engage these youth in cultural/economic activity, can enable a widening of access and who is involved in cultural production, alongside a widening of how cultural production is defined and what it looks like. As such, the personal change of seeing oneself as an artist, and feeling validated and equipped to undertake creative industries work can move towards social change. Social justice facilitator and author adrienne maree brown highlights the role of "personal practice" in developing social change:

> The invitation here is to 'transform yourself to transform the world' inside your collective or group work. Name your personal practices to each other within your group. This may include practices around decolonizing your life; studying Black feminist thinkers; living a zero-waste existence; practices around mindfulness and spirit, body health, and exercise; focusing; organizing life, or practices around being present with friends, family.[9]

Being socially engaged also includes affirmation, support, kindness, respect, friendship, fun, caring for others, and intentionally fostering inclusive spaces where teaching and learning are prioritized and valued. When a dominant framework suggests neoliberal self-management and competition, these practices offer an alternative register of contestation. The community arts sector can act as a platform for this type of social change, through an emphasis on people and process in inclusive working practices.

Research Sites and Methodologies

In the "Community Youth Arts" research project, research took place with three community youth arts programs in Toronto, Canada over a year and a half: SKETCH Working Arts, VIBE Arts, and ArtReach. Each of these programs has a mandate to work with marginalized youth. Founded in 1996, SKETCH Working Arts engages "diverse young people, ages 16–29, from across Canada, who are navigating poverty, living homeless or otherwise on the margins."[10] This definition of "margins" is expansive at the program; a program coordinator told me that they invite participants to see themselves in this definition rather than monitoring who may attend. Current programming at SKETCH emphasizes LGBTQ2S+, racialized, and Indigenous youth. VIBE Arts offers arts programming to children and youth in "under-resourced" communities in Toronto and employs youth arts assistants to help facilitate these programs, alongside professional artists.[11] Operating as a microfunder, supported by funding from the Toronto Arts Council, ArtReach is "designed to support community-based arts initiatives that engage youth from under served populations who have experienced exclusion in Toronto."[12] Many ArtReach-funded projects engage racialized youth with the arts in community-based settings. For example, funded projects in 2017 included Black Artists for Black Lives, which conducted arts-based workshops with Black queer and trans youth aged 18 to 29 to encourage social and political engagement; Made in Exile, a theatre program for Tibetan youth to explore stories of living in exile; and Anishinaabe Community Spirit Dancers, which works with Indigenous children to teach traditional Pow Wow dancing.[13] Through this chapter I use the term "marginalized" to discuss youth who make use of the programs in the research study, as these programs aim to reach youth on the margins, who are under resourced, and who are under served, but I also highlight the structural conditions that create this marginalization.

In the "Community Youth Arts" research project, methodologies included participant observation, site visits, conducting focus groups, conducting professional development workshops, and semi-structured interviews (n=30). Research assistants in the research team, Calla Evans and Johannes Valdes, participated in the programming, events, and workshops put on by youth arts organizations in the study; Johannes also served in a volunteer role at SKETCH. Importantly, these three community youth arts programs in the research study all offer paid entry-level creative industries work, either offering employment/residencies for young artists to facilitate arts programs with other participants or offering microfunding for youth to develop and run their own arts-based programs in their communities. The research project investigated the ways that this employment/microfunding and the supports available at community youth arts programs enable personal development and career mobility for youth participants.[14] While the research project assessed the working practices, environments, and characteristics of community arts programs, an overarching focus was on the experience of paid employment in these programs. Though youth may access or participate in these programs in a variety of ways, research interviews were conducted with youth who were employed or who had been employed/funded as artists or arts facilitators by the programs in the study. As a sector of the creative industries, the community arts can model best practices in inclusion, but this sector also faces its own challenges, as presented in the discussion of best practices below.

Through the course of the research project, central research questions expanded from career mobilization and pedagogical innovation to also assess the characteristics of inclusive spaces that enable this career mobilization. Surveying best practices and challenges in these working practices in the community arts programs in the study, I documented how intentionality and reflexivity on program structure can enable an inclusive environment for teaching and learning in the pathway towards entry-level creative industries work. Here, I provide an overview of different models and rationales for working with youth in community settings, including *youth engagement* and *social justice*, ultimately forwarding an *incubator* model for working with youth. These models differ in their positioning of youth and in their projected outcomes of youth involvement with the arts. As discussed below, these models may overlap or share linkages in practice; nonetheless, I analyze these models of working with youth in community arts settings as a heuristic for assessing challenges and best practices in supporting youth life pathways through the arts in the community sector. I illustrate the typology of the *youth engagement*, *social justice*, and *incubator* models of working with youth in the community arts through examples of research projects that assess community youth arts programs in each of these three frameworks.

Models of Working With Youth in Community Youth Arts Programs

Youth Engagement Model

The rise of community youth arts programs has largely stemmed from a youth engagement model. This model emphasizes individual identity work, such as personal and social development of children and youth through gaining access and exposure to art-making in community programs. Anna Hickey-Moody's study of youth arts programs engages with youth creativity from a theoretical standpoint, mobilizing Gilles Deleuze's concept of creativity as the differential becoming of the world, investigating how "technologies of the self" can be developed through the arts.[15] Focusing on two U.K.-based and one Australian-based youth arts programs, Hickey-Moody argues that youth experiences in one program in particular, based in theatre, amplify the "irreducible humanness" that emerges from creating.[16] The author argues that youth arts are a form of public pedagogy that allow participants to "speak back to dominant discourses of place and creativity" but ultimately concludes that these programs "involve many young people who can become imaginatively captured, skilled, and inspired."[17]

The turn towards community youth arts programs stems from a broader interest in the formative role of out-of-school learning for youth. In *School's Out: Bridging Out-of-School Literacies with Classroom Practice*, Glynda Hull and Katherine Shultz highlight the role of community settings, such as community organizations and after-school programs, in shaping young people's worldviews, and suggest "the importance of building bridges between school, home, and community."[18] Early landmark work focusing on community-based education for youth includes Milbrey W. McLaughlin, Merita A. Irby, and Juliet Langman's book *Urban Sanctuaries: Neighborhood Organizations in the Lives and Futures of Inner-City Youth.*[19] While not focusing on arts programming in particular, this five-year ethnographic study established the often-vital role that community organizations play in the lives of marginalized youth; the authors call neighbourhood organizations "places of hope" that offer inner-city youth "support and optimism, fun and friendship."[20]

Academic studies of youth arts programs most commonly assess and evaluate the impact and outcomes of participation in these programs, in particular for marginalized youth, at the interpersonal level. For example, the Youth Public Arts Program (YPAP) in North Carolina engages "at-risk" youth with expression through the arts while building connections to their communities through mentorship. Paige Averett, Allison Crowe, and Christina Hall's study of YPAP found that participants in the program had improvements in their relationships with their families, peers, and community interactions.[21] Other benefits of participation in this program highlighted in this study include confidence, self-awareness, emotional regulation, and tangible skills in art-making. In the youth engagement model, the value of the arts is often instrumentalized, and psychological and vocational values of the arts are in particular emphasized. The arts are seen to "help in the successful transition to adulthood and the development of in-demand job skills."[22] These in-demand job skills are not necessarily skills of artistic production; rather, they are more generic work-related skills, such as the ability "to complete tasks" and "teamwork skills."[23]

This model is also sometimes used with so-called "at-risk" youth, including youth entangled with the criminal justice system; here, the arts can be seen as a tool to remediate harmful behaviour and reduce youth crime. Funding for these programs may come from government agencies that view these programs as a cost-effective strategy towards youth crime prevention. Elsewhere, I tracked how this funding might enable important and meaningful programs that do good work to exist, but this funding is ultimately unsustained.[24] The arts are also seen to promote social cohesion in a more holistic manner beyond reducing crime in the youth engagement model, as "research shows the enormous benefits to the health and well-being of children and youth when they have access to arts and creative activities. The results show increased learning and community involvement, a reduction in crime and high school drop-out rates, reduced psycho-social behavior and improved health and social skills."[25]

Rhetoric in the youth engagement model often focuses on "re-engaging" at-risk and marginalized youth through the arts, and studies focus on varying methods and impacts of this re-engagement process. Andy Brader and Allan Luke's study, titled "Re-Engaging Marginalized Youth through Digital Music Production" focuses on "flexible education" for marginalized youth who have left formal education systems.[26] The study highlights the importance of the digital space and digital tools, suggesting that online modes of cultural production and evaluation should be integrated into educational institutions (as opposed to traditional modes of evaluation in formal education systems). The authors suggest "digital arts production combined with social networking tools are effective 'hooks' for disengaged youth."[27] Similarly, Robert Brown and Neryl Jeanneret's study, titled "Re-Engaging At-Risk Youth through Art," assessed the impact of the "Evolution" program in Melbourne, Australia.[28] Run by artists, this program seeks to re-engage youth who are out of school and who identify as being unemployed. The authors assess the success of the program in reaching its target population in its focus on individualized programming that validates participants' identities as artists. Positive youth engagement through this program is also attributed to focusing on confidence-building, community-building, emotional support, and personalized relationships. On the whole, the title of Robin Wright et al.'s study, "Do Community Arts Programs Promote Positive Youth Development" is indicative of the strain and emphasis of both these programs and the research that assesses and evaluates the outcomes of these programs in the youth engagement model.[29] There is now a body of work that answers the question of the title of the aforementioned study in the affirmative: community arts programs are indeed documented to promote positive youth development on the whole.[30]

Community programs based in the youth engagement model often use art and media as the "hook" to gain youth interest and participation, but this mobilization of art neither fully does justice to youths' interests in cultural production, including as an employment avenue, nor to the art form itself.[31] While the youth engagement model attempts to reach and "re-engage" at-risk and marginalized youth, broader structural and systemic forces leading to social exclusion and leading to some youth being labelled "at-risk" often remain unexamined and interrogated in these programs. This mobilization of art with youth who are seen to need remediation or re-engagement may offer temporary or topical solutions to deeper systemic injustice; the individual identity work that is targeted may not envision youth as changemakers responding to these broader issues.

Social Justice Model

While similar in the interpersonal and skill development aspects of the youth engagement model, some community youth arts programs make use of a broader social justice model, oriented towards an outcome of enabling youth to understand themselves to be embedded in broader systems of power. This model might also target individual identity work through the arts, but this work is further contextualized by positioning individuals relationally to others and to communities. Working in this model, youth are enabled to respond to community issues through the arts. Shawn Ginwright and Julio Cammarota argue for a more nuanced understanding between youth arts programs and youth engagement, suggesting the need to move past a focus on the most egregious activities among youth.[32] Mobilizing the concept of "critical civic praxis," the authors explore the ways that organizations can provide opportunities for youth to critically engage in their communities, with but not limited to the arts, including activities like spoken word, volunteering, and participation in civic affairs; critical civic praxis is developed through engagement with ideas, social networks, and experiences that build individual and collective capacity to work towards social justice. This model of critical civic praxis acknowledges structural constraints in young people's lives, but also views young people as active participants in changing debilitative social conditions.

Mindi Rhoades makes use of Ginwright and Cammarota's concept, alongside Chela Sandoval and Guisela Latorre's concept of "artivism" to investigate Youth Video OUTreach (YVO), a program developed to engage LGBTQ youth through film production in Columbus, Ohio.[33] Rhoades' assessment of the program focuses on YVO's youth-driven mandate, engaging youth in community, collectivity, and social justice through arts programming, and building critical consciousness and creative expression through "transformational pedagogy."[34] As such, this model encourages marginalized youth to engage with wider socio-political issues and cultural critique and emphasizes community youth arts programs as key sites for these investigations, as these programs are outside of mainstream education which can often be oppressive for marginalized youth.[35]

A social justice model also forwards youth-led learning and critical engagement. Many community youth arts programs often remain adult-led, but sustainability of the programs has been shown to depend in part on peer learning and mentorship, practices which remain largely undeveloped in this sector.[36] Interestingly, Sophie Gartner-Manzon and Audrey R. Giles' study of the Alberta's Future Leaders Program (AFL) for Aboriginal youth assesses the lasting impacts of this program, not for the youth involved, but for former employees, youth workers, volunteers, and mentors.[37] The authors identify four common impacts that former AFL employees experienced: 1) increased awareness of colonialism and Aboriginal experience; 2) the ability to question stereotypes; 3) positive employment trajectories; and 4) a greater benefit from AFL "than the intended youth beneficiaries." Similarly, McLaughlin, Irby, and Langman locate part of the success of neighbourhood organizations in staff members' capacity to "locate 'the problem' of inner-cycle youth and the dysfunctional behaviors and attitudes associated with them primarily in the larger society and the general failure of social institutions to understand, support, or care for these teenagers."[38] It is unclear if this understanding translates into youth-led programming offered by the neighbourhood organizations in this study; the main emphasis seems to be on "loving agendas and positive missions" in a seemingly top-down manner rather than on critical praxis.

Methodologically, academic investigation of community youth arts programs often now moves towards participatory action research (PAR). Rather than documenting and assessing youth in community programs, PAR suggests a movement towards co-creating knowledge and researching with participants; in this spirit, researchers might run their own programs or partner with community organizations to do new programming, rather than assessing existing programs.[39] Working collaboratively with PAR has also been identified as a mechanism to enhance youths' social capital through engaging them as co-creators in the research process.[40] Art-based research methods (ABR) are often used in tandem with youth PAR towards social justice goals. For example, the "Taking Action! Building Indigenous Leadership in HIV Prevention using Arts-Based Methods" research project used art-marking workshops in six different Indigenous communities to explore the relationships between community, culture, colonization, and HIV. The researchers conclude that arts-based methods are an effective tool to work towards decolonization.[41]

Jangmin Kim states that visual and arts-based research methods are often seen as "youth-friendly" methods of working collaboratively with youth.[42] He provides the examples of Jill Chonody, Barbara Ferman, Jill Amitrani-Welsh, and Travis Martin's research project, which used photovoice to document young people's understandings of their experiences of the intersection between race, poverty, and violence.[43] Through their participation in a summer program in a community setting, participants analyzed representations of violence, causes of violence, and ways to addresses violence by recording their own experiences with photographs. In part due to the relative ease of the use of the method, photovoice is a common tool of engaging with youth to do research in community settings.[44] Nonetheless, engaging and researching with youth towards social justice goals takes place with a variety of artistic methods. Kim also provides the example of Diane Conrad's project using theatre with youth as tool to raise awareness and take collective action about community issues affecting their lives.[45] Through her research work and in her exploration of youths' perceptions of their own realities, Conrad came to problematize the designation of some youth as "at-risk," a term that her youth participants found offensive.[46]

Incubator Model

Extending and combining the youth engagement and social justice models of community youth arts programs, my research on community youth arts forwards an incubator model. Missing from both the youth engagement and the social justice models is the recognition that youth engage in art-making not only for interpersonal growth or for civic engagement but also for career development. Economic development can be understood not only as individual interpersonal work, but also part of a broader social justice mandate of self-determination and economic self-realization, in particular for marginalized youth. Many youth access community-based youth arts programs as part of an employment pathway to develop creative industries skills.[47] Community youth arts programs are able to offer on-site skill development, not only for interpersonal development but also for economic advancement through arts entrepreneurship. For example, at SKETCH Working Arts, scaffolded support for creative entrepreneurship stems from their "discover–develop–launch" model of social change (Figure 5.1). The "discover" phase of engaging with the arts at SKETCH includes creativity, affirmation of identity, and support. The "develop" phase of developing one's artistic practice includes developing skills, the self, ideas, and community. The

FIGURE 5.1 SKETCH Working Arts' Theory of Change © SKETCH Working Arts, 2015. SKETCH's Theory of Change has been updated since this research project

"launch" phase prepares youth to develop a new initiative or new phase of their artistic practice or self-discovery, including education, enterprise, leadership, and activism. Though this model may appear to linearly scaffold from one stage to the next, in practice these phases may co-exist or not lead to a next or further stage. As such, an incubator model does not need to assume that involvement with the arts necessarily means economic advancement or correlate with a neoliberal employability agenda.

SKETCH offers a range of programming, from easy-to-engage art activities when participants walk in the door, to registered weekly arts programs focusing on different disciplines, to "indie studio" and grant-writing clinics, focusing on the development of artistic/entrepreneurial practice. These opportunities for networking and exchange also exist at SKETCH through the "open studio" events at the end of each of their seasons/sessions. These open studio events are an opportunity for vending, exhibiting, and performing one's work, and have a celebratory, festive tone. A volunteer "vibes" crew monitors the space to maintain "good vibes," checking in with people to see how they are doing. The final open studio of the year, entitled "rad grad," short for "radical gratitude," operates as a sort of graduation for the community artists who have been doing year-long residencies to spotlight and exhibit the work they have developed through the year. An incubator model bridges a youth engagement model with a social justice/anti-oppressive practice framework that recognizes barriers for economic advancement and in society more broadly for marginalized youth. Beyond "engaging" youth or directing them towards civic praxis, an incubator model assists youth in developing their own life pathways and projects, in and beyond the space of community youth arts, as a model of social change. Key here is to enable youth-led learning or space for youth to develop their own projects and trajectories that may or may not linearly angle towards economic imperatives.

Geraldine Bloustein and Margaret Peters' overview of community-based organizations (CBOs) positions these sites as "alternative learning spaces" in the lives of young people who make use of the programs offered at these organizations.[48] Indeed, an incubator model demonstrates awareness that scaffolded support is needed to incubate creative projects, particularly for marginalized youth who may not have pre-existing access to resources or social networks that are often necessary in the creative industries. Bloustein and Peters' study notes the importance of informal and formal mentoring, skill development, accessibility, "ideologies and styles of pedagogies," trust, networks, and collaboration in working toward employment or entrepreneurship goals in CBOs.[49] The authors note the entrepreneurial aspirations of many youth who frequent these organizations, highlighting these youths' desire to "engage with and improve their own communities through music and art," melding entrepreneurial and social justice goals in social entrepreneurship. Lori Hager states "community youth arts are, as yet, uncomfortably situated in the nexus of prevention, reform, enrichment, the arts and social economic development."[50] This uncomfortable nexus, and these competing goals, is occupied by youth participants themselves, who enter and mobilize their participation at community youth arts programs with at times complex and multifaceted goals. Here, I turn to youth lived experience through an ethnographic study of three youth arts programs to more fully explore some of these contradictions between the personal, the cultural, the social, and the economic, and investigate how these programs offer supports for youth-led learning and creative career incubation. I identify best practices and challenges in the areas of AOP; providing funding and employment; fostering relationships; and attention to pedagogical practice as community youth arts programs endeavour to incubate youth creativity. In my discussion, I also consider these four identified principles as inclusive working practices for the creative industries.

Best Practices and Challenges from the Community Arts Sector

Anti-Oppressive Practice (AOP)

Through my analysis of three community youth arts programs, I highlight the important role of AOP in the organization or program structure, with identified sub-elements of conflict prevention, accessibility, and affirmation. Originating from social work, AOP recognizes that structural factors, like race, gender, sexual orientation, disability, age, class, etc., can result in systemic inequality. Helen Wong and June Ying Yee define an anti-oppressive framework as "the lens through which one understands how race, gender, sexual orientation and identity, ability, age, class, occupation and social service usage can result in systemic inequalities for particular groups."[51] As a relational lens, AOP foregrounds an understanding of how power dynamics and structural forces affect lived realities, and works intentionally to foster inclusion. AOP can also mean an emphasis on humanization and attempting to include the whole person.[52] This integrative approach to human identity and experience differs greatly from an neoliberal model which foregrounds financial gain and individual self-advancement outside of contextual factors. Karen Morgaine and Moshoula Capous-Desyllas highlight that AOP acknowledges the social-political context of lived experience, "shifting the focus from individual failure to structural issues and inequalities" while working towards empowerment through mutual support, collective efforts, education, opportunities for participation, and capacity building.[53] As such, this relational model that underscores social location and power dynamics can inform a care ethics framework for the creative industries to similarly target mutual support, opportunities, and capacity building in this field of work. Below, I discuss examples of what the identified AOP sub-elements of conflict prevention, accessibility, and affirmation look like in the community arts programs in the research study.

Conflict Prevention

In community arts settings, conflict prevention can emerge from attention to structural forces and barriers that impact lived experiences and individuals' capacities to participate in programming and create artistic work. Working on conflict prevention can mean creating conditions for diverse participants to work together and critically assessing what factors enable or prevent participants from engaging in community arts programming. At SKETCH Working Arts, conflict prevention means attempting to structure the space to meet physical, emotional, and cultural needs while also recognizing power imbalances and colonial legacies. The entrance to SKETCH has roles, responsibilities, and norms for being in that space posted, as well as a land acknowledgement, addressing the legacy of colonialism. Inclusion mechanisms take on a variety of means at SKETCH, including providing a lunch and dinner (self-serve style) during programming, and having tokens for transit available. Childcare is not provided and children are not officially invited into programming, but participants may bring their children and their dogs into the space. At SKETCH, one volunteer position is that of "host," who greets participants at the door, welcomes them into the space, provides tours and helps integrate newcomers into activities. Research assistant Johannes Valdes volunteered in this role at SKETCH through the tenure of the research project. These mechanisms can foster inclusion while also reducing conflict amongst participants.

At best, this attention and reflexivity on how people access the space creates an environment where critical conversations can occur about power dynamics and how they affect culture, creativity, and artistic practice. This can create a space for learning through dialogue. One research participant states, "[This event] turned into a conversation around [cultural] appropriation and it was really good to like talk about things like that because it's not really something that's discussed" (Participant 1). SKETCH also works with a model of transformative justice, working first to create conditions for mutual engagement, and seeking to remediate harm through conflict resolution rather than relying on punishment or stigmatization.[54] Because of the movement away from a punishment model, and because of an awareness of how marginalized youth are overrepresented in the criminal justice system, police are rarely contacted and participants are rarely banned from the space outright when conflict emerges. Instead, a transformative justice framework suggests working with both parties experiencing a conflict towards productive resolutions. At SKETCH, when the research project observed one participant referring to a past conflict with another participant, the facilitator who was present guided this participant away from name calling in front of others, while also directing this participant to key staff people they could talk to if they wished to further debrief on the past conflict. These facilitated conditions and framework around conflict prevention can result not only in reduced conditions of conflict, but also in increased capacities for mutual aid, trust, and sharing: elements of an inclusive culture that creative industries work environments could also consider further facilitating. As SKETCH is a registered charity, the organization receives financial and other donations. In one instance at SKETCH when several boxes of art supplies were donated, participants dealt with these donations by looking through the materials and setting aside supplies that they recognized that other participants who were not present might use or incorporate into their creative practices rather than only taking things for themselves, highlighting a caring desire for co-operation and sharing rather than competition or individual gain.

Accessibility

These elements of conflict prevention also angle towards larger questions of access, including who can and who cannot access a space, and what structural factors and barriers impact participants' capacities to mutually engage. Several community arts programs in the research project demonstrated an ongoing reflection on which populations their programs were reaching and which populations were excluded or not being reached. The programs themselves were designed with these concerns in mind, working to serve marginalized and under-resourced communities. As mentioned, mechanisms to foster inclusion include material resources, like providing food and tokens for transit. Other conditions for inclusion were facilitated, including inviting participants to state their preferred gender pronouns and striving to ensure information is accessible and available. For example, ArtReach offers funding to work with youth in under-resourced communities in Toronto, and the organization reflects on where and how they hold their workshops, choosing to operate in central locations that are accessible by transit. At some workshops, volunteers provide childcare so that participants who have children can engage in the workshops.

In interviews and focus groups that the research project held, many research participants voiced alienation from mainstream arts granting bodies and grant writing in general, but programs that specifically offered funding and opportunities to youth and emerging artists were perceived as more accessible: "the reason I think I applied [to this program] … is that it was focused for youth. I felt like the competition would be at my level" (Participant 15). In addition to programs and funding being specifically targeted to youth, there was also a perception of assistance and dissemination of information in an-easy-to-grasp manner: "a lot of the stuff [at this program] is super accessible, and even on the website. They really set you up to succeed" (Participant 17). In broader, creative industries contexts, we might also investigate how people can be set up to succeed and what these conditions of cultivating inclusive access for success can look like.

Affirmation

Many research participants cited their experiences in community arts programs to be positive and to affirm their sense of self through the arts. Interviewees often foregrounded the role of staff people in providing this affirmation, highlighting key staff people who played a role in their personal development by name. One participant states, "a lot of people encourag[ed] me to keep going which I really needed at that time of my life. They're there to support and help you in whatever situation you're in … they meet you where you're at" (Participant 8). This environment of "meeting people where they are at" allows for multiple entry points and skill levels and continued learning and capacity development from these multiple, affirmed starting points. Another participant states, "[the staff at this program] never gave up on me" (Participant 30), which suggests continuing to support and work with participants who may struggle or experience challenges, rather than suggesting these people are unworthy or undeserving of support. This continued affirmation and support allows for personal growth and expansion of the self: "the more I had been around [this program], I was like, 'oh crap, I've actually been suppressing a lot of who I actually am.' And I was only able to bring it out in this type of environment [by] being encouraged to just be who you are" (Participant 1). Research participants spoke to community arts programs centring lived experience and emotions and caring about individuals.

Many research participants were also employed or funded to run their own programs, and interviewees commented on trying to foster an inclusive or anti-oppressive environment with their own participants, and observed the impact that this environment had on others. One research participant stated, "[the program provided] a safe space where people can be heard. Once people feel heard or respected, then things happen organically. A lot of times to my surprise it's very positive and meaningful to them. To the individual themselves" (Participant 22). On the whole, a spirit of support and positive encouragement is infused through these community arts spaces, often through emphasizing positivity. In a grant-writing clinic I attended and volunteered with at SKETCH, called Art Hustle, instructions and guidelines were written on a white board at weekly sessions to help shape participants' focus for the time spent during the session. One week's set of guidelines concluded with the affirming message, "you/we got this!!!", not only encouraging individual efforts but also suggesting a relational model of mutual support with the invocation of "we," even when grant applications remain individually drafted and submitted. At ArtReach, program coordinators conduct site visits to check in with the youth grantees who were running their own programs with the funding they had received from the organization. Staff doing these site visits modelled affirmation in an authentic way through body language and verbal and non-verbal cues, indicating their engagement with the programming they were witnessing. The atmosphere created during these site visits was one of support rather than surveillance or monitoring. These characteristics of targeting conflict prevention, accessibility, and affirmation highlight the work of social reproduction to foster inclusion in and through the community arts.

Employing and Funding Emerging Artists to Support Skill and Goal Development

The predominance of unpaid work in the creative industries is increasingly well documented. In particular, the normalization of unpaid work and unpaid internships in the entry years (and beyond) in creative industries employment has raised questions about equity and access to employment in these fields, as normalized unpaid work can act as an exclusionary practice.[55] Given these labour dynamics, appropriately financially compensating youth who are working, training, and developing their artistic practices at community youth arts programs takes on particular importance. Community youth arts programs can offer employment and training to emerging artists to facilitate arts programs, or award youth funding to do their own projects and programs. This payment and funding, even if small, can act as a meaningful platform for youth to continue with their artistic practices, offering validation and career development.

Participants in the research project indicated positive and affirming qualities of being employed or funded by community youth arts programs. This affirmation was two-fold: it affirmed the sense of self as an artist at the level of identity but also at the level of vocational choice. Participants indicated that if they had not been employed by the community youth arts program, they would have pursued other paths or would be pursuing other forms of paid work. In a focus group, one participant contrasted employment as an arts facilitator (alongside their own artistic development) with work in the retail sector, which they would have stayed with if not employed by the community youth arts program. One interview participant spoke to the life-altering nature of their experience with community youth arts employment: "it was my first time ever acting … It was such a wonderful experience. I had never done anything like that before. And it was the first time anyone ever told me that I might be good at something like that. Or that I could excel at it …. It changed my life" (Participant 2).

In interviews, research participants spoke to this affirming impact of receiving funding both at the levels of identity and of career validation. One participant expressed, "[receiving funding] was a moment of like, 'Oh my god, I *am* capable of doing something'" (Participant 30), and another expressed, "[receiving funding meant] they are willing to take me seriously" (Participant 13). Some research participants explicitly connected this validation to their social location and the validation of their identities and projects in this regard:

> And I always had [desire] to take on a leadership role. But I was always afraid to. I think, again, it has a lot to do with the fact that I'm a woman and a woman of colour … I was like, 'Oh no, I can't do this.' But the fact that someone was like, 'Hey I think you have the potential to do something like that,' and the fact that I did it, and I was granted the grant, was like, 'wow people actually care about what I want to do' (Participant 14).

Beyond the interpersonal, research participants also voiced the importance of being paid to do their projects, as being paid to do the program or project meant being able to undertake the endeavour. One participant commented on the non-economic and economic elements of support from the community youth arts program as follows: "[The program gave] the structure you needed in order to understand the fundamental needs of your practice … The financial support was also great" (Participant 4).

This emphasis on the incubation of the arts or creative industries career differs from the youth engagement model, which envisions engagement and personal development from a broader and often remedial perspective. Instead, an incubator model can recognize barriers to advancement and target development from a youth-led perspective. One participant commented on receiving micro-funding as an important "stepping stone" to continue on with their project as a career: "It was good to be like, I can get paid for this ... It's been a good stepping stone to figuring out what I want to do. And I've started a non-profit organization, which is a year old now. Getting funding …. really made me feel more confident about this turning into full-time work" (Participant 15). Another participant commented on youth-led learning through the vehicle of developing their own project: "it was as if someone was recognizing a project that I had envisioned. I wasn't really sure what was going to come out of it, but … it made me realize that it was going to create something concrete. So, that was very helpful as a starting point … Having my own project, and then learning through my own project [was] … beneficial as a tool for advancing my own curiosities and learning and developing as a person" (Participant 20). When community youth arts programs enable project-based youth-led learning, this positions youth as changemakers and as entrepreneurial rather than latently "at risk." One participant commented on the positive external perspective of having received micro-funding for their own project: "[Having received funding] definitely helps … when I'm applying for jobs now. People see the initiative of … I'm not just working in the field, but I actually … saw a gap and tried to change things" (Participant 21).

Fostering Relationships Through Participation in Community Youth Arts Programs

Given the informal nature of pathways into the creative industries, social capital and access to networks can be a meaningful contributor to successful employment in this field; people from underrepresented communities can be at disadvantage in the creative industries due the exclusionary nature of networks.[56] In the "Community Youth Arts Programs as Creative Industries Incubators" research project, I highlight structural barriers and hegemonic patterns of exclusion that lead to lack of access to networks and limited social capital. I also understand community youth arts as an alternative mechanism to foster social capital as a feature of the social practices embedded in these programs. In focus groups and interviews, research participants spoke to building their own networks through mutual support and through arts facilitation. Some research participants saw employment as an arts facilitator as part of their overall portfolio and career development as a community artist, while other participants did not. Nonetheless, arts facilitation in community settings was seen to offer an opportunity to expand one's network and develop rapport with other artists and community members and stakeholders. As one research participant commented about their experience being funded by a community youth arts program, "now I'm in a place where I have a network, I know people" (Participant 18). One research participant commented favourably on an environment of reciprocity as it relates to professional development through community engagement and developing a network: "it's like the snowball effect, where I see you doing something so I'm going to do something to give back to you … so people want to give you opportunities. Actually doing that program ... helped me find a place in the community" (Participant 14).

In interviews, many participants consciously connected the relationships they were able to develop through the community youth arts programs with further professional opportunities. One participant first commented on the affirmation of being in a room with likeminded youth, "it was just helpful to be in a room with other artists. Obviously, people are in different stages in their understanding and that sort of thing, but it's just nice to feel a sense of community and support and also hear inquiries from your peers and see what they're thinking about" (Participant 19). This participant also commented on expansion of their network through expanded connections and the visibility brought by the funding from the community youth arts program: "what ends up happening with these funds is your … networks expand, you meet different people … [being funded] piques the interests of people [who] don't actually personally know me" (Participant 19). Another participant commented on consciously fostering relationships as a mechanism to expand their social capital: "my resume has kept growing ... I have to update it. It's essentially been like one person I meet, and then that person introduces me to one person, and I feel like that's why I've slowly become successful, because I run after finding, creating, and maintaining those relationships … I'm slowly finding that my name is being spread around through the communities" (Participant 30). For many research participants, mutual support and expanded professional capacity are intertwined as positive outcomes of participation in community youth arts programs: "my first … opportunity barrel-rolled into the next one the next year … so all of the organizations that I've worked with have led to each other … The best things that I've gained [from attending workshops] are just sharing our experiences. Like, you get to talk to other artists that work at [the organization]" (Participant 26).

This supportive and caring environment can act as platform for expansion of social capital, and the contact and involvement with community youth arts organizations can also incubate further career opportunities for youth participants, as some participants were able to mobilize their involvement through springboarding from participation in one program to further opportunities. One participant commented that "the first time I actually got a paid gig as [an artist], in Toronto, was from a relationship that [the community youth arts program] facilitated between me and [an outside organization]. And it kind of spiraled from there—in a good way … I know that getting my foot in the door isn't always the easiest thing if I'm not under the umbrella of this arts organization … [I] always have to use that foot first" (Participant 28). As such, the community youth arts organization can act as an alternative "foot in the door" in an industry where these types of connection often assume vital importance.

The connection with the community youth arts organizations in the research study, whose names are well known in Toronto, can lead to further connections and also other paid work, leading to further affirmation of the self as an artist: "Pride allowed us to perform on stage because of that. And got paid for that! And got exposure and got everything else! Personally, I didn't think I could perform at Pride this early in my career. So, that's a big thing that [the organization] provided" (Participant 11). One participant characterized their community youth arts program as a "connection hub," fostering connections between youth at the organization but also through "constantly pairing up with various organizations and other artists" (Participant 2). Another participant commented on the longevity of the connections made at the community youth arts program leading to further paid work beyond and after the time spent in the community youth arts program: "I still get contracted out to do workshops that aren't related to [the program] from other organizations that I've built through my relationships with [the program]" (Participant 4).

Attention to Pedagogical Practice

Given the challenges of entering into creative industries work, lessons might be learned from the specific attention to teaching, learning, and mentorship in the community arts sector. This research project highlights reflexivity on pedagogical practice when striving to create inclusive environments, which includes the sub-elements of open exploration, scaffolded support, and mentorship. A more inclusive and equitable environment might be fostered in the creative industries through reflection on pedagogical practice in the community arts sector. Fostering inclusion in this way offers an alternative inroad for change, beyond bolstering supports to get a "foot in the door." Here, the emphasis is on changing the organizational culture rather than correcting a perceived deficit or lack in the individual. Community youth arts programs can deliver a more personal, hands-on, human-centered and caring pedagogy than what can take place in formal education systems. One research participant commented favourably on this caring environment in the community arts sector, with a particular focus on diversity and inclusion: "I think the biggest difference is that I don't know if a school cares about you while you're there, you know. It is the good of the many and I doubt that a school would ever, you know, take a shot in the leg for, you know, a minority. Whether it be one person or a minority group or whichever. And that's really, I think, the big difference" (Participant 2). Below, I explore examples of what caring pedagogy can look like in practice and its implications for the creative industries.

Open Exploration

Many research participants commented on the openness of the learning environment in community arts organizations and the positive impact and empowerment of the freedom to explore and create. Research participants credited this environment with having a positive impact on wellbeing and on personal, artistic, and career development. At SKETCH, open exploration is facilitated through an intentional attempt to provide easy-to-engage with art activities. The organization offers programs and training in specific artistic mediums (ceramics, silk-screening, etc.) and professional development workshops, and tables are also set up in the space covered with butcher paper with markers and other art materials laid out, encouraging participants to come in and sit and draw, without having to enroll or join any specific programming. When research assistant Johannes once arrived for one of his volunteering shifts, he was told he had just missed a session of dancing on bubble wrap. In particular programming, like the live music jam, skill sharing is encouraged through the program facilitator encouraging participants to switch instruments with other participants and learning what they don't know how to play from one another. At ArtReach, the first level of funding offered, $5000, is meant to fund pilot projects, or programs that applicants haven't yet run but would like try: applicants do not necessarily have to have a track record of success or prior experience to be able to receive this funding to run a new program.

Commenting on this type of open environment, one research participant stated, "[before this] I've never really worked in environments that necessarily give freedom to explore and create. [It's] really awesome that the organization allows ... emerging artists to ... create and explore and figure things out" (Participant 23). Given this environment of open exploration, some research participants commented on the challenges of navigating a seeming lack of structure: "when I went to [the program], it was like, 'have fun! Just go for it!' I, at first, didn't really know how to use the space because there's just so much freedom. So it was a little overwhelming at first to be like, 'just go for it'" (Participant 10). Another research participant commented that a seeming lack of structure had its own logics through a self-charted pathway: "there's no traditional learning environment at [the program]. There is structure, like a really good structure where you know kind of what's happening—and even when you don't know what's happening, you can figure out easily what you want to do. But it's also a structure where you have more liberation as in you get to choose what you want to do and you get to focus specifically on what interests you more" (Participant 11). Open exploration encourages independence, and it can also be understood to foster inclusion through offering expansive pathways and opportunities to take risks or experiment.

Scaffolded Support

Beyond a freedom to explore or try out new projects, community arts programs also can enable inclusion through making tasks accessible to diverse learners through an environment of scaffolded support. In constructive learning theory, Lev Vygotsky forwards the "zone of proximal learning," a supported space where learners are able to develop skills they do not already possess through the guidance and support of a "more knowledgeable other."[57] David Wood, Jerome S. Bruner, and Gail Ross use the term "scaffolding" to describe the activities of this more knowledgeable other with the learner in the zone of proximal development.[58] In the community arts sector, scaffolded support for learning can come from facilitators but also from participants helping other participants with an environment of mutual support and valourizing existing skills and knowledge.

Accessibility can be targeted through scaffolded support to try to ensure that participants can access and engage in programming and funding that organizations offer. ArtReach both provides funding to youth to run their own programs with youth participants in their communities, and provides support to access this funding and to run these programs. In a workshop run by ArtReach about applying for the ArtReach grant, a facilitator described an approach to working on an application as "chunking," or breaking large pieces of work into more manageable segments of work, rather than conceptualizing the project or application as one large whole. In addition to providing terms or tools to scaffold participants' work, this approach was observed in the facilitation style of the workshop itself, providing reassurance and accommodating participants at differing points of development. Alongside offering grants, ArtReach also offers a pitch competition, where applicants are shortlisted as finalists to pitch their idea for a youth arts program or business. ArtReach also offers workshops for finalists leading up to the pitch competition, including practice and trial runs of the timed pitch. When a participant stumbled over their words repeatedly or appeared very nervous, facilitators would soften their tone of voice, turn off the timer, and invite the participant to sit down at the table with them, creating a less intimidating space.

In interviews, research participants commented favourably about this scaffolded approach to work tasks and the support it provides. One research participant states, "After I failed the first [grant application], I went to a lot of the [organization's] workshops, which I really … appreciated. I think they were really useful because they do outline the process and they help you through it, and it made the people more accessible so that [I] knew it was a person and wasn't just a number or an email. So, I actually went, and I approached them, and asked for feedback on my grant proposals" (Participant 20). Another participant commented in positive ways on check-in points, as the knowledge of having to do this check-in ahead of time enabled more organization and planning: "the midway point for checking in to see how our programs are going, the reports we have to do—I found that really helpful because it kept you focused and [made] sure things go as planned" (Participant 28). These forms of scaffolded support can be understood as tending to space of social reproduction: care work to create structures to affirm and enable success.

Mentorship

Many community arts programs have formal or informal mentorship structures, enabling participants to form supportive relationships with staff or more experienced participants. Many research participants commented positively and named particular staff people in interviews, particularly in the context of mentorship: "this mentor is a really big part of [the program] for me. The fact that they're at [the organization]? Like I feel most grounded because they're there as well. They give me like direction in [the program] as well" (Participant 11). Some research participants commented on the unevenness of mentorship structures and the benefits of guidance from an active and present mentor: "I feel like I probably got more guidance than other people because I would meet regularly with [a staff person at the program]. It was every week in the beginning. Then it was every other week and then once a month towards the end of the year. But some people would only meet with their mentors like once a month. Once a quarter. And they weren't really around that much" (Participant 3). Beyond this pairing of youth participants with staff, some community arts programs enable participants to move into mentorship positions as they become more experienced through their participation in programs, creating movement towards a youth-led structure. One research participant comments, "now the youth, who ... took the program [before], the first cohort, [were] actually the facilitators for the next cohort. So that was really cool and interesting to see" (Participant 22). Mentorship may empower participants to continue with their creative practices, such that they may be able to access leadership positions, enabling some mobility within personal/career development. Alongside open exploration and scaffolded support, effective mentorship can be an inclusive practice that moves beyond noting or targeting diversity. Pedagogical practice offers opportunities for teaching and learning, alongside a supportive environment to enable growth.

Challenges of Working with Youth in the Community Arts Sector

Community youth arts programs often target wellbeing, skill development, and relationship building through fostering inclusion and offering supports, but challenges remain in transitioning to employment beyond community youth arts programs. Moreover, systemic barriers to advancement for marginalized youth can be more pervasive than the supports that community youth arts programs can offer. Many of the challenges voiced by research participants in the "Community Youth Arts" research project stemmed from the unevenness of the structures and supports offered by these programs. For example, mentorship is identified as a best practice, but it is not always readily available at all programs. Some research participants have actively sought out these supports and networks, but this relies on individual navigation and self-advancement, in the absence of available and accessible structures. Further challenges arose with a perception of lack of accountability and intervention into problematic dynamics that emerged in community youth arts programs. For example, one research participant spoke to their paid position at a community youth arts program and observing others underperforming or simply not showing up for work and continuing to be paid; this participant spoke to calibrating and dialing back their own performance when witnessing a lack of intervention into this dynamic. These experiences speak to a tension between inclusion and intervention in anti-oppressive spaces and a need for further structure or policy development into clear protocols and definitions for problematic behaviour.

Another type of challenge in the community arts sector emerged from tensions between caring for others through community arts and caring for the self. Many research participants spoke positively about the work of facilitation and engaging their participants' personal development. One interviewee stated "facilitation is not just about teaching people about what you do but it is also about 'holding' people. Like holding people where they are and having the capacity to understand what their capacities are, you know? Emotionally, physically and then artistically. And having these things expressed through the creative medium that you're facilitating" (Participant 5). But some research participants commented on the exhaustion and burnout of this work, raising tensions between community arts as an employment avenue, a source of work for emerging artists alongside their individual artistic practice, and the larger purpose of community arts to facilitate wellbeing and empowerment. One participant commented, "I think that after I did the program I fell into an awful place. I think it just had to do with a lot of stress and pressure. I went from this high, and as soon as it was done, it was like, I don't think I'm ok. I just took care of everyone else and I'm not okay" (Participant 14). Another participant voiced the need and the challenge of creating boundaries around the facilitation work: "within community arts, there needs to be a level of disconnect. You need to be able to remove yourself, and develop a career that supports other human beings … It's not about you … That's really hard to do … In community arts, we have to learn when to let go" (Participant 30). These comments suggest the limits of a relational model of self and relational forms of caring work, and highlight the need to centre and care for the self, alongside caring for others. Moreover, when dominant frameworks devalue care, caring labour is often poorly compensated, and is often performed by women, racialized, LGBTQ2S+, and other marginalized people. Though there may be an awareness of these challenges in the organizations doing this work with diverse youth participants, these tensions between creating a broad and inclusive space for diverse participants, taking care of oneself, and creating a structure for accountability remain.

Through the funding and the employment that they offer to youth and in particular to marginalized youth, community youth arts programs can offer meaningful supports to youth who aspire to creative careers. Making funding available for youth to run their own programs and projects is a vital way for youth to develop skills and experiences to incubate their careers. Positioning community youth arts as pathway for youth to incubate their own projects, rather than as a means to engage "at-risk" youth, can enable youth-led learning that often angles towards community and civic engagement, alongside social justice goals. It is important for community youth arts programs to financial compensate youth for work and for participation in programs in order to create access to these programs and inclusive employment opportunities. In research projects, it is also important to financial compensate community youth arts program participants for their time and work. Compensation and reciprocity from researchers are expected in the community youth arts sector, and research projects should be designed with these objectives in mind.

At community youth arts programs, opportunities for youth to collaborate and expand their networks beyond the community youth arts program can be further developed. These programs can further develop feedback mechanisms for youth to share their experiences being employed and facilitating programs in this sector; feedback should be incorporated into improved working practices on an ongoing basis. Community youth arts programs often have a mandate to enable art making and art experiences in community-based settings, and may not always have an awareness of themselves as employment routes for entry-level creative work. Not all youth at community youth arts programs aspire to creative careers; nonetheless, developing greater awareness of how youth access and mobilize participation in community youth arts programs as part of their larger career trajectories could allow for reflection on employment policies and practice. Community arts programs may also lack awareness of themselves as an employer, and proper employment practices, including fair pay and clear policies for raises and promotion, alongside structured supports for workers, can be underdeveloped in this sector. Many research participants indicated they heard about these programs by word of mouth and targeted outreach from staff members. More knowledge and support for the important and often transformative role these programs play in the lives of aspiring and emerging artists could allow for greater access to participation in these programs. The community arts sector should not be regarded as a quick fix or a magical solution to the problems of lack of diversity and inclusion in the creative industries, but this sector can nonetheless offer inroads to reflect on and rethink working practices, to strive towards reimagining this sector in a more inclusive, sustainable, and equitable manner.

Notes

1 William Charlan, "The Youth Arts Apprenticeship Movement: A New Twist on an Historical practice," *Art Education* 58, no. 5 (2005): 39–47; S. Fuller, *Youth Participation in Arts, Heritage, Culture and Community: A National Conversation* (Ottawa, ON: Government of Canada, Department of Canadian Heritage, Citizen Participation Branch and Atlantic Evaluation Group, 2009); Kathleen Gallagher, *Why Theatre Matters: Urban Youth, Engagement, and a Pedagogy of the Real* (Toronto, ON: University of Toronto Press, 2014); Heather E. McLean, "Cracks in the Creative City: The Contradictions of Community Arts Practice," *International Journal of Urban and Regional Research* 38, no. 6 (2014): 2156–2173; Anita Sinner and Diane Conrad, eds., *Creating Together: Participatory, Community-based, and Collaborative Arts Practices and Scholarship across Canada* (Waterloo, Ontario: Wilfrid Laurier University Press, 2015).

2 Patrick Farren, "'Transformative Pedagogy' in Context: Being and Becoming," *World Journal on Educational Technology: Current Issues* 8, no. 3 (2016): 190–204.

3 Sarita Malik, Caroline Chapain, and Roberta Comunian, "Rethinking Cultural Diversity in the UK Film Sector: Practices in Community Filmmaking," *Organization* 24, no. 3 (2017): 308–329.
4 Miranda Campbell, *Out of the Basement: Youth Cultural Production in Practice and in Policy* (Montreal: McGill Queen's University Press, 2013); Elizabeth Fix and Nadine Sivak, "The Growing Case for Youth Engagement through Culture," *Ontario: Our Diverse Cities No. 4.* (Ottawa, ON: Department of Canadian Heritage, 2007), 145–151.
5 Amanda Parris, "I Spent My 20s Working with Toronto Youth, and Today's Gun Violence Conversations Feel Like Déja Vu," *CBC Arts,* July 24, 2018, accessed January 7, 2020, https://www.cbc.ca/arts/i-spent-my-20s-working-with-toronto-youth-and-today-s-gun-violence-conversations-feel-like-deja-vu-1.4759224
6 Kate Oakley, Mark Ball, and Malaika Cunningham, *Everyday Culture and the Good Life* (CUSP Working Paper Series No 9) (Guildford: Centre for the Understanding of Sustainable Prosperity, 2018), https://www.cusp.ac.uk/wp-content/uploads/WP09-Everyday-Culture-and-the-good-life.pdf
7 François Matarasso, "'All in This Together': The Depoliticisation of Community Art in Britain," *Community, Art, Power: Essays from ICAF Rotterdam: International Community Arts Festival* (2013): 215, cited in Oakley, Ball, and Cunningham, *Everyday Culture*, 7.
8 Jan Cohen-Cruz, "An Introduction to Community Art and Activism," *Upei*, 2002, accessed March 17, 2021, https://library.upei.ca/sites/default/files/an_introduction_to_community_art_and_activism_cohen_cruz.pdf
9 adrienne maree brown, *Emergent Strategy: Shaping Change, Changing Worlds* (Chico, CA: AK Press, 2017), 256.
10 Sketch, "About: Who We Are," *Sketch*, n.d., https://sketch.ca/about/
11 Ibid.
12 Ibid.
13 ArtReach, "Funded Projects," *ArtReach.org,* n.d., https://www.artreach.org/fundedprojects
14 The experiences of youth accessing these programs as part of an employment pathway forms my main understanding of the community arts as a sector of creative industries employment. These programs are staffed by facilitators / program coordinators, but the experience of these staff people is beyond the scope of this research.
15 Anna Hickey-Moody, "Youth Arts and the Differential Becoming of the World," *Journal of Media & Cultural Studies* 24, no. 2 (2010): 203–214.
16 Ibid., 213.
17 Ibid.
18 Glynda Hull and Katherine Schultz, eds., *School's Out!: Bridging Out-of-School Literacies with Classroom Practice* (New York, NY: Teachers College Press, 2001), 3.
19 Milbrey W. McLaughlin, Merita A. Irby, and Juliet Langman, *Urban Sanctuaries: Neighborhood Organizations in the Lives and Futures of Inner-City Youth* (San Francisco, CA: Jossey-Bass, 1994).
20 Ibid., 8.
21 Paige Averett, Allison Crowe, and Christina Hall, "The Youth Public Arts Program: Interpersonal and Intrapersonal Outcomes for At-Risk Youth," *Journal of Creativity in Mental Health* 10, no. 3 (2015): 306–323.
22 Creative City Network of Canada, *Making the Case for Culture: Arts and Positive Change in Communities* (Canada: Creative City Network, 2005), 2.
23 Ibid., 6–7.
24 Campbell, *Out of the Basement.*
25 Linda Albright, *Creative Spaces of Children and Youth* (Toronto, ON: Arts Network for Children and Youth, Submission to the Government of Canada's Ministry of Finance 2009 Federal Budget, 2009), 2.

26 Andy Brader and Allan Luke, "Re-Engaging Marginalized Youth through Digital Music Production: Performance, Audience and Evaluation," *Pedagogies: An International Journal* 8, no. 3 (2013): 197–214.
27 Ibid., 213.
28 Robert Brown and Neryl Jeanneret, "Re-Engaging At-Risk Youth through Art—The Evolution Program," *International Journal of Education & the Arts* 16, no. 14 (2015): 1–18.
29 Robin Wright, Lindsay John, Ramona Alaggia, Eric Duku, and Tanya Morton, "Do Community Arts Programs Promote Positive Youth Development?" *Critical Social Work* 9, no. 1 (2008).
30 Anne Bamford, "Croydon Local Cultural Education Partnerships (LCEP): Impact Evaluation Report," *Croydon Action Research Report* (2018): 1–47; Alison Rhodes and Rachel Schechter, "Fostering Resilience Among Youth in Inner City Community Arts Centers: The Case of the Artists Collective," *Education and Urban Society* 46, no. 7 (2014): 826–848; Toya Northington, "ArtThrust Teen Empowerment Program: Teaching Youth to Fly Against Resistance," *Social Work with Groups* 41 (2017): 139–150; Anne Wallace-DiGarbo and David C. Hill, "Art as Agency: Exploring Empowerment of At-Risk Youth," *Art Therapy: Journal of the American Art Therapy Association* 23, no. 3 (2006): 119–125.
31 Here I am drawing on Mark Banks' concept of "creative justice" from *Creative Justice: Cultural Industries, Work and Inequality* (London, UK: Rowman & Littlefield International, 2017).
32 Shawn Ginwright and Julio Cammarota, "Youth Activism in the Urban Community: Learning Critical Civic Praxis Within Community Organization," *International Journal of Qualitative Studies in Education* 20, no. 6 (2007): 693–710.
33 Chela Sandoval and Guisela Latorre, "Chicana/o Artivism: Judy Baca's Digital Work with Youth of Color. Learning Race and Ethnicity: Youth and Digital Media," in *The John D. And Catherine T. MacArthur Foundation Series on Digital Media and Learning,* ed. Anna Everett (Cambridge, MA: The MIT Press, 2008), 81–108.
34 Mindi Rhoades, "LGBTQ Youth + Video Artivism: Arts-Based Critical Civic Praxis," *Studies in Art Education* 53, no. 4 (2012): 317–329.
35 Bic Ngo, Cynthia Lewis, and Betsy Maloney Leaf, "Fostering Sociopolitical Consciousness with Minoritized Youth: Insights from Community-Based Arts Programs," *Review of Research in Education* 41 (2017): 358–380.
36 Karen Strobel, Ben Kirschner, Jennifer O'Donoghue, and Milbrey Laughlin, "Qualities That Attract Urban Youth to After-School Settings and Promote Continued Participation," *Teachers College Record* 110, no. 8 (2008): 1677–1705; Remi Warner and Grassroots Youth Collaborative, *Youth on Youth: Grassroots Youth Collaborative on Youth Led Organizing in the City of Toronto* (Toronto, ON: Ontario Region of the Department of Canadian Heritage, 2005).
37 Sophie Gartner-Manzon and Audrey R. Giles, "A Case Study of the Lasting Impacts of Employment in a Development through Sport, Recreation and the Arts Programme for Aboriginal Youth," *Sport in Society* 19, no. 2 (2015): 159–173.
38 McLaughlin, Irby, and Langman, *Urban Sanctuaries*, 97.
39 Moshoula Capous-Desyllas and Karen Morgaine, eds., *Creating Social Change Through Creativity: Anti-Oppressive Art-Based Research Methodologies* (London, UK: Palgrave Macmillan, 2018); Alice McIntyre, *Participatory Action Research* (London, UK: Sage, 2008); Rachel Pain, Geoff Whitman, and David Milledge, *Participatory Action Research Toolkit: An Introduction to Using PAR as an Approach to Learning, Research and Action* (Durham, UK: Durham University, 2011).
40 S. Nombuso Dlamini, Cynthia Kwakyewah, and Yvette Daniel, "Promoting Youth Community Engagement Through Active Youth Participation in Research:

Possibilities and Limitations," *Journal of Teacher Education & Educational Leadership* (2016): 88–100.

41 Sarah Flicker et al., "'Because We Have Really Unique Art': Decolonizing Research with Indigenous Youth Using the Arts," *International Journal of Indigenous Health* 10, no. 1 (2014): 16–34.

42 Jangmin Kim, "Youth Involvement in Participatory Action Research (PAR): Challenges and Barriers," *Critical Social Work* 17, no. 1 (2016): 38–53.

43 Jill Chonody, Barbara Ferman, Jill Amitrani-Welsh, and Travis Martin, "Violence Through the Eyes of Youth: A Photovoice Exploration," *Journal of Community Psychology* 41, no. 1 (2013): 84–101.

44 Melvin Delgado, *Urban Youth and Photovoice: Visual Ethnography in Action* (New York, NY: Oxford University Press, 2015).

45 Diane Conrad, "Popular Theatre: Empowering Pedagogy for Youth," *Youth Theatre Journal* 18, no. 1 (2004): 87–106.

46 Kim, "Youth Involvement in Participatory Action Research."

47 Geraldine Bloustein and Margaret Peters, *Youth, Music, and Creative Cultures: Playing for Life* (London, UK: Palgrave Macmillan, 2011); Amanda Coles, *Focus on Youth: Canadian Youth Arts Programming and Policy* (Ottawa, ON: Department of Canadian Heritage, 2007); Robin Wright, Lindsay John, and Julia Sheel, *Edmonton Arts and Youth Feasibility Study: Final Report* (Ottawa, ON: Research Report, Department of Justice Canada - Youth Justice Policy, 2005).

48 Bloustein and Peters, *Youth, Music, and Creative Cultures,* 23.

49 Ibid., 39.

50 Lori Hager, *Reform or Enrichment: Policy Mandates and Program Goals in Community Youth Arts* (New York, NY: Community Arts Network, 2008), cited in Bloustein and Peters, *Youth, Music, and Creative Cultures,* 4.

51 Helen Wong and June Ying Yee, *An Anti-Oppression Framework for Child Welfare in Ontario* (Toronto, ON: Ontario Association of Children's Aid Societies, 2010), 6.

52 Jeff Karabanow and Ted Naylor, "Using Art to Tell Stories and Build Safe Spaces: Transforming Academic Research into Action," *Canadian Journal of Community Mental Health* 34, no. 3 (2015): 67–85.

53 Karen Morgaine and Moshoula Capous-Desyllas, *Anti-Oppressive Social Work Practice: Putting Theory into Action* (London, UK: Sage, 2014), 24–25.

54 Ejeris Dixon and Leah Lakshmi Piepzna-Samarasinha, eds., *Beyond Survival: Strategies and Stories From the Transformative Justice Movement* (Chico, CA: AK Press, 2020).

55 Kim Allen, Jocey Quinn, Sumi Hollingworth, and Anthea Rose, "Becoming Employable Students and 'Ideal' Creative Workers: Exclusion and Inequality in Higher Education Work Placements," *British Journal of Sociology of Education* 34, no. 3 (2012): 431–452.

56 Sabina Siebert and Fiona Wilson, "All Work and No Pay: Consequences of Unpaid Work Experience in the Creative Industries," *Work, Employment and Society* 27, no. 4 (2013): 711–721.

57 Lev Vygotsky, *Mind in Society: The Development of Higher Psychological Processes* (Cambridge, MA: Harvard University Press, 1978).

58 David Wood, Jerome S. Bruner, and Gail Ross, "The Role of Tutoring in Problem Solving," *Journal of Child Psychology and Child Psychiatry* 17 (1976): 89–100.

6

COLLABORATIVE PRODUCTION, COMMUNITIES OF PRACTICE, AND COMMUNITIES OF CARE

On a sunny Sunday in July, Rock Camp Montreal (RCFG*) was at renowned local recording studio Hotel2Tango in Montreal, Canada. Saturday night at RCFG* featured the showcase concert in which six bands made up of girls, non-binary, trans, and gender non-conforming youth ranging in age from 10 to 17 performed. During the five-day summer camp leading up to the showcase concert, the campers learned an instrument, formed a band, and wrote an original song together. Some of them had never picked up an instrument before the camp. At the Sunday recording session, the previous night's nerves and excitement have quieted, and the atmosphere is calm and cozy. One volunteer has brought bagels and cream cheese, and another has baked a pie. Campers snack and hang out, waiting their turn to record. Some watch Demi Lovato videos on YouTube on the computer in the lounge. In the recording studio, volunteers help campers with their set up, one asking their band if everyone feels comfortable. The recording engineer who has volunteered his time to work with RCFG* communicates with campers from his booth through their headphone monitors, and I am tickled to see one camper's eyes light up in amazement as she hears his voice in her headphones. After the last band is done recording, we wait for parents to pick up the last campers, and the recording engineer leaves, telling us to close the door behind us.

This opening anecdote of the concluding day and recording session at the summer camp suggests some of the potential of moving towards more caring collaborative modes of production such that for girls, non-binary, trans, and gender non-conforming youth may have increased pathways for participation in the music industry. However, the presentation of this cozy scene belies the underlining challenges, not only of organizing a summer camp with a set goal of content production, but also of moving from individual-based to collaborative modes of

DOI: 10.4324/9781003031338-6

production more generally. Here, I operationalize and extend Jean Lave and Étienne Wenger's concept of community of practice (CoP) in order to analyze these possibilities and challenges.[1] RCFG* can be characterized as an alternative CoP that forwards collaborative modes of cultural production with clear and explicit means of participation. In opposition to the individualized navigation of informal and often inequitable routes of accessing cultural production in the mainstream creative industries, the camp seeks to reconfigure the exclusionary nature some more traditional CoPs. In this chapter, I work with the main characteristics of CoPs of mutual engagement, joint enterprise, and shared repertoire. In this case study of RCFG*, I investigate how RCFG* extends these characteristics as an alternative CoP through a number of reification strategies while also foregrounding the complexities of care that underlie this alternative mobilization. The sense of mutual engagement, joint enterprise, and shared repertoire at RCFG* stem from the desire to foster empowerment for girls, non-binary, trans, and gender non-conforming youth and widen access to music scenes. These characteristics of RCFG* as an alternative CoP can also be odds with existing policy structures, as well as individual desires and rationales for participation at the camp, posing challenges for the implementation of the tenets of RCFG* on a broader scale.

Dorothy Miell and Karen Littleton note that the rise of interest in creative collaboration stems from a desire to support these initiatives and create improved opportunities for creative work: "whilst there is an agreement about the value of trying to establish supportive contexts for collaboration, there is also a recognition that any attempts at intervention need to reflect the requirements and preferences of particular groups and communities. There is no simple agreed formula that can be applied to promote creativity."[2] In what follows, rather than attempt to determine an alternative CoP "formula," I instead seek to articulate the particular requirements and preferences of RCFG* as a CoP, and question how and if these requirements/preferences could be implemented on a wider level.

Creative Industries and Communities of Practice

As a concept, CoPs have been forwarded to capture horizontal learning-by-doing in the company of other, more seasoned practitioners. While the concept was originally articulated through examples of craft-based modes of employment, including midwifery and tailoring, it has been forwarded to map the characteristics of a wide array of groups and locales, such as virtual and online communities, second-language learners, and more formalized workplaces, including those in the creative industries.[3] Organizing features of CoPs vary across iterations of this concept, but emphasis on learning as it relates to identity formation through a community remains a key theme across conceptualizations. Indeed, a key contribution of CoP as a concept is Wenger's insistence on a "social theory of learning," which underscores relationality as learning is placed "in the context of our lived experience of participation in the world."[4]

The earliest outline of CoPs, developed by Lave and Wenger, forwards the concept of "legitimate peripheral participation,"[5] which outlines how newcomers to a community become integrated and socialized within that community through observation and initially taking on simple, low-risk tasks, and gradually taking on a more central role. Though this model of CoPs might suggest an apprenticeship-type model of learning, the concept emphasizes informal rather than formalized routes into the community, driven by the task at hand rather than set agendas. Wenger's later articulation of CoPs forwards a definition of the concept in more precise terms, identifying that CoPs are formed through mutual engagement, joint enterprise, and shared repertoire.[6] As such, CoPs are united by and driven by people doing things together with clear purpose or joint enterprise that is sustained over time through the relationships and norms of mutual engagement, and that produces a common set of resources, or a shared repertoire.

While the CoP concept remains salient and in use, Wenger's work has also been critiqued for its inattention to power dynamics and structural forces that constrain individual agency and ability to gain access and learning through a CoP.[7] In *Communities of Practice: Learning, Meaning, and Identity*, Wenger paints a rosy picture of CoPs being "everywhere":

> in garages, bands rehearse the same songs for yet another wedding gig. In attics, ham radio enthusiasts become part of worldwide clusters of communicators. In the back rooms of churches, recovering alcoholics go to their weekly meetings to find the courage to remain sober. In laboratories, scientists correspond with colleagues, near and far, in order to advance their inquiries. Across the worldwide web of computers, people congregate in virtual spaces and develop shared ways of pursuing their common interests. In offices, computer users count on each other to cope with the intricacies of obscure systems. In neighborhoods, youth gang together to configure their life on the street and their sense of themselves.[8]

Though people with diverse genders may participate in all of the activities that Wenger identifies, we can also recognize that these activities (garage bands; ham radio; AA; science; Internet and computers; youth "gangs") have been coded as masculine, and raise critical questions about access, entry, and visibility in CoPs. Wenger positions CoPs to lie at the intersection of power and meaning, similar to a familiar structure/agency dialectic. Further, he names social structures, but places them beyond his purview of analysis and positioning of CoPs.[9] As a concept, CoPs could be best operationalized through bringing social structures back in to the fold. In this chapter, my main focus is on gender, but the structural factors of race, class, disability, sexuality, age, and so on are equally important for analysis of how individuals and communities navigate the balance of power and meaning. Here, the concept of CoPs is layered with the overarching framework of feminist care ethics in this book. While both CoPs and feminist care ethics underscore relationality, care ethics contributes an analysis of structural barriers alongside a utopian commitment to new visions.

This expanded and alternative CoP concept can be readily applied to work in the creative industries, as like CoPs, routes into employment in these fields are often informal or based in networks. Power dynamics and informality creating structural barriers is also part of the critical analysis in creative industries scholarship, as informal and network-based modes of entry are understood to reproduce and exacerbate dominant patterns of workplace inequity in the creative industries.[10] While gender imbalance in the music industry has long been noted, in 2015, this inequity came to the forefront, as seen in the viral edits of U.K. music festival posters, which were photoshopped to remove all the bands that did not have any women band members.[11] The results were visually shocking: the posters went from listing dozens of bands down to handfuls. The experiment has been reproduced for Canadian and American music festivals, resulting in similarly empty posters.[12] In 2016, the Canadian Juno Awards nominees for artist of the year, album of the year, rock album of the year, rap recording of the year and dance recording of the year were all men. On Twitter, musician Grimes took note of the absence of women nominees in these categories, as well as to "engineer or producer of the year etc.," and linked the lack of recognition with lack of participation: "I can't help but feel that if women were equally rewarded for technical work they would feel inclined to participate more."[13] In response to the Juno nominations, Amy Millan of the band Stars started the hashtag #JunosSoMale, referencing the #OscarsSoWhite hashtag, which highlighted the lack of racial diversity in the 2015 Oscar nominations.[14] These conversations about lack of representation of women in the music industry suggest not only a lack of access because of the opaqueness of informality but also systemic discrimination, as women are excluded and shut out from opportunities and recognition for their contributions. Alongside increased conversation about barriers and discrimination, there is also increased commitment from communities of care to developing alternatives, removing barriers, and challenging discrimination. Here, I profile RCFG* as one such alternative in the music industry as an alternative CoP or community of care, in the historical context of the riot grrrl movement.

Historical Context: Riot Grrrl and Women in Music

The existence of girls rock camps may be one of the most long-lasting legacies of riot grrrl, an alternative and subcultural movement of the 1990s that initially centered around Olympia, Washington but diffused nationally and internationally, and that sought to claim space for women in the music industry through playing in bands alongside taking control of the means of production and dissemination.[15] Riot grrrl was a response to male-dominated punk scenes:

though these scenes may have intended to provide resistance to mainstream musical practices, they often reproduced hegemonic gender norms that created unsafe conditions for the participation of women.[16] David Hesmondhalgh's analysis of "indie" as a musical genre notes that the legacy of punk rock as a movement was a form of music that set out to organize itself around an alternative set of operating principles, and "[transcend] romantic notions of musical creativity" and move away from the "cultural myth" of "the isolated genius [as] hero" and from musical practices based in "competitive individualism." Hesmondhalgh notes, however, that even within communities intending to operate with counter-hegemonic practices, exclusionary barriers to participation were reasserted, and ultimately bands associated with the indie movement reproduced conventional norms associated with rock and roll musical performance, with "bands consisting of four or five young men playing guitars and drums."[17] In his articulation of CoPs as "social learning systems," Wenger suggests that entering into a CoP "translates into a regime of accountability" or "a way to honor the history of learning of that community."[18] As a musical formation, punk famously abandoned the notion of in-depth accountability as a rite of passage into musical production, instead suggesting that learning three chords is sufficient for starting a band.[19] Shevaughn Battle's analysis of the Montreal music scene underscores "the left-leaning, progressive and community-minded politics of indie music scenes in general, and particularly, those in the Montreal indie music community."[20] Nonetheless, Battle also notes the inaccessible and elitist nature of this scene, identifying that even when a regime of accountability is problematized by a CoP, other exclusionary barriers to participation can be erected.

Riot grrrl not only saw the rise of women playing in bands, such as Bikini Kill, Bratmobile, Heavens to Betsy, and so on, but more broadly gave rise to teen girl empowerment. Doreen Piano notes a riot grrrl do-it-yourself feminism centred around cultural production that "can be seen in the emergence of a polymorphous infrastructure of grrrl-related cottage industries that include the production of not just music, but zines, stickers, crafts, mixed tapes, and alternative menstrual products."[21] Though the riot grrrl movement worked towards the widespread involvement of teen girls in acts of creativity and the creation of networks around these forms of cultural production,[22] rather than adulation of performers in bands, media focus became centred on key individuals, in particular Kathleen Hanna of Bikini Kill, as figureheads or spokespeople for the movement, eventually leading to a refusal of riot grrrls to engage with the media and to the demise of the movement under the banner of the riot grrrl name.[23] Nyala Ali comments on the intention of Hanna and others in the movement to work towards a model of rooting the individual within a community framework, invoking Sarah Hoagland's concept of *autokeny*.[24] Similarly, in Chapter 2, I highlighted the importance of autonomy as a characteristic of emerging cultural production; *autokeny* similarly helps us understand the relational underpinning of the forms of autonomy outlined here.

CoPs offer a lens to discuss the formation of an individual self within a social or communal framework, but the maintenance of an individual/community relational balance in capitalistic systems remains challenging. Wenger's articulation of CoPs emphasizes the characteristic of sustained mutual engagement, yet sustaining relational models of identity over time is difficult. Chronicling the rise of third-wave feminism (in which riot grrrl can be situated), Leslie Heywood and Jennifer Drake comment on the difficulty of sustaining community-oriented models of the feminist self within the larger individual-centric culture: "despite our knowing better, despite our knowing its emptiness, the ideology of individualism is still a major motivating force behind many third wave lives."[25] Despite the demise of riot grrrl as a network of women-led bands, Kristen Schilt and Danielle Gillfort profile other indicators of the longevity of riot grrrl, as women involved in this movement founded and volunteered with local girls rock camps, which continue some of the community-focused mode of the riot grrrl movement through a dual focus on collaboration and personal empowerment at these camps.[26]

Background on the Case Study: Rock Camp Montreal (RCFG*)

RCFG* has existed since 2009, and emerged out of the movement of girls rock camps initiated by the Rock 'n' Roll Camp for Girls founded in Portland, Oregon in 2001. Girls rock camps now exist across the globe: Girls Rock Alliance, the international coalition of rock camps, included more than 50 camps during the time of my research project with RCFG*. I was involved with RCFG* as a volunteer coordinator and member of the board of directors from 2011 to 2013, and my case study of this organization is based in participant observation, in particular at the 2013 summer camp, and in semi-structured interviews with volunteers. I conducted some follow up interviews with RCFG* volunteers in 2016, and as such 2013–2016 is the time span of this research project, with a main focus on the 2013 camp. Participant observation involves the researcher in a dual role: engaging in activities while also observing them.[27] This type of methodology and dual role brings specific ethical concerns and necessitates openness and transparency with the intent to observe, as well as the purpose and impact of the research.[28] Prior to the beginning of the RCFG* 2013 summer camp, I sought approval from the organization's board of directors to conduct research. After the board voted in favour of my proposal, I distributed a "Letter of Information" to volunteers and parents of campers via email (access to these email lists was granted by the board). This "Letter of Information" notified RCFG* participants of my intent to conduct research with the summer camp. The letter to volunteers also stated that they may be contacted for interviews about their experiences. The camp has undergone a series of changes since the conclusion of this research project, including a change to its gender policy and the camp's name to be more inclusive for people with marginalized gender identities, including "cis women, trans women/girls, trans men/boys, gender nonconforming, trans*, two-spirited, non binary, [and] agender."[29] The camp is now called Rock Camp Montreal (RCFG*) in order to be more gender inclusive, but it was called Rock Camp for Girls Montreal (RCFG*), during the period of the research study. I have chosen to use the updated name for the camp in this book in order to recognize the movement towards greater inclusion. The previous name of the camp appears in some of my discussion of documents from the 2013 to 2016 period of the camp. Similarly, in this chapter I use RCFG*'s gender-neutral term "campers" rather than "girls" in discussion of participants at the camp; this term was in use during the period of the research study and remains in use.

The joint enterprise of RCFG* as a summer camp might be the focus on campers collectively writing an original song in bands, but more broadly, the joint enterprise of RCFG* can also be understood as the feminist project of creating more inclusive music scenes and widening access to musical production through the maintenance of an alternative CoP. Discussing the duality of CoPs as a balance of creative and constraining forces, Wenger forwards a participation/reification duality, arguing that participation in practices produces reified artefacts that CoPs draw on and co-create through shared repertoire.[30] Wenger's examples of reified artefacts include "writing down a law, creating a procedure, or producing a tool," but he asserts the reification is as much a process as it is the resulting products.[31] In my analysis here, I draw on the RCFG* *Volunteer Handbook* as a reified artifact that both reflects and shapes the mode of participation of volunteers and campers at RCFG* (Figure 6.1).

As will be discussed below, RCFG* deploys a number of reification strategies as an alternative CoP to create more access. Wenger asserts that "reification also makes up for the inherent limitations of participation … when the informality of participation is confusingly loose, when the fluidity of its implications impedes coordination, when its locality is too confining or its partiality too narrow, then it is reification that comes to the rescue."[32] Wenger's comments here can also be put into the context of social structures and gendered exclusion: music scenes can be informal, fluid, and narrow, and more accessible information through reified documents, guidelines, and working practices can be used as strategies to foster inclusion and equity.

Rock Camp Montreal as Collaborative CoP: Widening Access and Participation

The RCFG* model is based in mentorship for girls, non-binary, gender non-conforming, and trans youth, with all leadership roles, including musical instruction, songwriting, technical support, and group cohesion at the camp being led by women, non-binary, gender non-conforming, and trans volunteers. In

FIGURE 6.1 *Rock Camp for Girls Montreal Volunteer Handbook* cover image. © Rock Camp for Girls Montreal, 2012. Image by Heather Hardie

addition to instructors who facilitate learning different instruments (e.g. guitar, bass, drums, keyboards, and vocals), each band has a band coach to help facilitate songwriting and a band manager to help facilitate group dynamics and collaboration. In the 2013 camp, I volunteered as a band manager. In my interviews with RCFG* volunteers, many of these volunteers referenced existing dynamics in the music industry and their own experiences of marginalization as driving forces behind their desires to volunteer their time with the organization. As such, these experiences form one of the bases of joint enterprise in the CoP. One volunteer, Alex, comments:

> In the world we live in, there is a low number of successful minority figures in the music industry. Whether you identify as a girl, as queer, as transgender, as Black, etc. I believe it is hard to find a place in such a heteronormative and 'masculine' industry. For instance, I constantly face discrimination and judgment when doing something as simple as buying a guitar in a music store. I do believe that the music industry should be a safer space and a more open-minded and diversified sphere.[33]

Though one premise of RCFG* is to address the lack of visibility and participation of women musicians, RCFG* works towards the goal of empowerment through music rather than mastery of an instrument or performance itself. Technical skill can often be a mechanism of exclusion from participation in music scenes, and rather than only offer a corrective that merely seeks to repair this skill deficit, RCFG* also seeks to foster alternative means of participation and alternative communities.

Collaborative working practices are one strategy of working towards this goal of widening access and participation in musical production, moving away from narrow and individualistic notions of creativity. RCFG*'s mandate states that the camp "fosters the promotion of self-esteem, skill-building and critical thinking skills for girls, non binary, trans and gender non-conforming youth through collaborative music composition and performance. Rock Camp supplements the music component with workshops based on feminist and anti-oppression frameworks that provide campers with a space for critical examination and personal empowerment."[34] Media education scholars have sought to address pervasive competitive individualism in cultural production, and advocate for moving towards collaborative modes of production when working with youth as a means to widen access to cultural production.[35] David Buckingham notes the difficulties of setting up school curriculum that moves away from the Romantic notion of the individual creator, suggesting that collaborative production might be "desirable and necessary" but is also accompanied by challenges as students "come to the classroom with different levels of expertise and knowledge about the media, and with different motivations towards production." Foremost of the challenges that Buckingham addresses is gender, citing the example of boys intimidating or excluding girls with specialist musical expertise or knowledge.[36]

Reification Strategies

While rock and independent or counter-cultural forms of music sometimes operate around insider knowledge and subcultural capital, RCFG* is based in explicitness and clarity, which can be understood as a reification strategy, in order to demystify music and music-making in the attempt to create an inclusive environment to increase participation. Indeed, Wenger comments "increasing the level of participation or reification does not dispense with the other. On the contrary, it will tend to increase the requirements for the other."[37] That is, moving towards increasing participation in a CoP often necessitates increasing reification. Miell and Littleton comment that "inherent in contemporary approaches to collaborative creativity is an emphasis on studying the processes involved rather than a sole focus on examining the quality of the product of creative endeavours."[38] This movement from product to process is also found in the operations of RCFG* in the attempt to create inclusive conditions so that all campers at the camp feel empowered to participate. Fostering these inclusive conditions can also be understood as the joint enterprise of the camp: while volunteers facilitate the creation of this environment, the camp also seeks to involve campers so that there is a shared investment in the creation of this inclusive environment.

Typically, the first day of camp features a group agreement exercise, where campers suggest parameters of behaviour/conduct for the week-long camp in order to create an inclusive and respectful environment for everyone. Campers all agree to these parameters, and these terms are posted in the camp space to serve as reminders, operating as a reified document to increase inclusion and participation. In community-based settings, group agreements are used to foster co-operation, to create an inclusive space, and to make the maintenance of this inclusive space the responsibility of the group rather than the responsibility of facilitators.[39] Though the campers lead the suggestions for the group agreement, a volunteer facilitates this session and sometimes needs to intervene. Jesse chronicles that:

> I remember last year, one of their suggestions was, 'don't listen to Justin Bieber,' and I sort of flagged that one when I saw it, and said, 'well, I don't know if we can all agree [to not] listen to Bieber, because I happen to like Justin Bieber, and that's ok. And I'm sure lots of other people here also like Justin Bieber. So it's important that you can express your opinions about these things, but you don't make other people feel bad about their personal preferences.' And they were a little 'ok, yeah.' And it's that sort of thing that we set from day one that I think contributes to the idea of a safe space.[40]

This example of Bieber initially being denigrated in front of the group points to the need for intervention when creating an inclusive environment rather than merely allowing campers to self-facilitate. While Wenger characterizes much of the learning in CoPs as horizontal, occurring between peers, he also identifies the need for "vertical accountability" in the maintenance of CoPs, such as "decisional authority" and "policies and regulation." He comments "another common mistake is to demonize vertical accountability and romanticize local engagement in practice. A self-governed community is not heaven. It can reproduce all sorts of undesirable things, such as racism or corruption."[41]

In addition to a group agreement, the RCFG* *Volunteer Handbook* also sets out explicit policies to create inclusive conditions, including camp rules that prohibit racist, homophobic, or otherwise discriminatory behaviour or song lyrics. This reification strategy of explicit policy and communication of unwelcome behaviours can also increasingly be found in music venues. Outlining strategies for making venues inclusive, Jill Krajewski profiles The Vera Project, an all-ages venue in Seattle. Krajewski writes that this space

> let their community create both their rules and signage themselves through a Safe Spaces Agreement. The mural was designed by their teen-heavy volunteer steering committee. 'We value having a space where people can feel safe. Sometimes during shows, people forget this, and do things that violate what we stand for,' says Jessica Schollmeyer, participation coordinator at The Vera Project. 'It's important to have it be very clear what's okay and what's not. It stands as a visual reminder to show goers, artists, and volunteers of what this venue is about.'[42]

In this example, reification is developed not only through accountability and policies for acceptable and inacceptable behaviour in the space but also through visual communication and display of these policies.

Accessibility and inclusion can also be targeted through reification by making the tacit explicit and moving to more inclusive working practices with ways of talking and communicating. The RCFG* *Volunteer Handbook* also has suggestions for talking about music in an inclusive way by referring to types of sounds like "a fast song, a slow song, a heavy song, a noisy song" rather than genres or bands that can "make some campers with less musical experience feel alienated or not as cool."[43] This inclusive language problematizes the notion that CoPs will necessarily have or co-create a shared repertoire. Rather than organizing itself around a common musical repertoire of genres or examples of music, and seek to bring newcomers into this shared knowledge, RCFG* seeks to valorize differing levels of musical knowledge and experience. As such, this inclusive language is part of the shared repertoire of the camp, rather than an accrued knowledge of musical history or musical skills. Though skill development does happen during the summer camp, this is limited in scope due to the camp's week-long duration. Indeed, the *Handbook* stresses there is no "correct" way of playing music, suggesting "encouraging the player to find her own way" rather than demonstrating how the instrument should be played.[44]

This inclusive language also shapes the suggestions for volunteers about how to talk about the song that the campers are writing together. Musical instruction at RCFG* might advocate finding one's own way rather than mastery of a skill,

When campers say that they don't know what something means or they don't know how to do something, recognize that it can take courage to put yourself out there like that.

Some additional guidelines for BAND COACHES and BAND MANAGERS, but good for everyone:

Struggle is OK. "All awkward moments are opportunities." Not being sure of what to do and not instantly mastering something are both really important parts of experimentation. If a band, or an individual camper, is struggling with playing a certain chord or finding the note they want to play, let them search on their own. Intervene only when it seems like they are getting too frustrated to work on their own. And then only suggest how they might find something on their own. Give them the chance to work it out on their own!

Being out of tune is OK. Playing out of sync is OK. If it sounds good to the band, it IS good. The bands have a lot to do all at once – learn instruments, write a song, learn to play together. They may or may not care, or be at a place yet, to worry about fine-tuning. Put your opinions on hold unless they are actively sought; if they are, help with goals that can be easily reached at the time, and save other comments for later in the week if it seems appropriate, or keep them to yourself. "Sports-casting" what you're observing – giving non-judgmental feedback – can be a good way to go.

Band members being drowned out and/or not listened to is NOT OK. We have a responsibility to help band members make sure they can hear themselves and each other. "Hearing" each other refers to hearing each other's instruments and also hearing each other's opinions about the process and song. Try asking everyone if they can hear each other, and if there's an issue, help them get a better sound balance. Suggest having a band meeting, and act as moderator if necessary – more often than not, taking a break from playing gives band members the chance they need to express how they're feeling about the sound, the song, the process, etc.

Put your hands on an instrument during band practice ONLY as a last resort. Bands are often very tempted to "have you play it," and you may be very tempted to show how it can be done. But it not only doesn't help, it can seriously set back a band in the quest for its own sound. Try encouraging the player to find her own way. Only if she absolutely can't hold her hands in the right position to make a G chord should you demonstrate. If you have the guitar or bass strap on, or are doing whatever the equivalent on the drums might be, you have been playing too long!

FIGURE 6.2 "Best Practices for Band Coaches and Band Managers" from *Rock Camp for Girls Montreal Volunteer Handbook*. © *Rock Camp for Girls Montreal, 2012*

but there is also a desire for "everyone [to be] on the same page"[45] in the songwriting process in order to collaborate. The *Handbook* suggests that campers collectively name different parts of the song with references like "the zombie verse" or the "spaghetti verse" so all band members can contribute to the songwriting process (Figures 6.2 and 6.3). Large flipchart paper is a common

Allow campers to take the lead, provide choices and options and let them choose where they want to go and support them to get there. On the first day of band practice, you will probably have to start a dialogue about what kind of sound you want to create as a band. Acknowledge that all campers come with different tastes and experiences, and as a band you need to find ways to work together and create a song together, and that as a group you need to find a common thread of a song you all like. Some campers may also have difficulty expressing what sounds they like best and may need extra support finding ways to communicate with the rest of the band. Acknowledge that compromises may have to happen and that it's ok to disagree. Often the best way for a band to find their sound is to start playing!

When talking about music, it may be hard to avoid referring to genres and favourite bands. While it's important for campers to express what they like and to share musical inspiration, these conversations can also make some campers with less musical experience feel alienated or not as cool. To navigate these situations you may need to explain what genres sound like if you know, and find alternatives ways to talk about music that are more universal like "a fast song, a slow song, a heavy song, a noisy song...etc."

Establish a common camper led language to ensure everyone is on the same page about how to talk about song writing. For example collectively identify all parts of the songs and also give them names. For example *"First it's the zombie verse, then it's the spaghetti verse..."*.

Work on your song on big pieces of paper so everyone can see.

Establish a way to get their attention or to communicate without raising your voice.

Play the "Switch" game to help campers let go of expectations around playing an instrument "the right way" and to just simply "be" with an instrument. This exercise can also encourage risk taking and experimentation in the group, and build appreciation around what their other band members are working on.

When one camper needs attention (for whatever reason) try to ensure that the other facilitator can keep the rest of the band on the task at hand.

Make some time everyday to check-in with your co-facilitator (Band Coach or Band Manager) to talk about how you're working together, what roles and responsibilities your feel comfortable in, etc. You can also use this check-in time with your co-facilitator to see how the group dynamics are going.

FIGURE 6.3 Further elements of "Best Practices for Band Coaches and Band Managers" from *Rock Camp for Girls Montreal Volunteer Handbook*. © Rock Camp for Girls Montreal, 2012

teaching tool at RCFG*, so that everyone knows where the band is at in the composition and performance process. These mechanisms that attempt to get everyone in the band involved move away from a model of a principal individual songwriter who comes to rehearsal with parts of a song already written or a model of the vocalist being responsible for lyrical composition. The RCFG* model suggests that any or all band members might be involved in any stage of the songwriting process.

While RCFG* has the word "rock" in its title, the above list of different types of songs or sounds suggest a broader definition of musical production at RCFG*, and the camp actively encourages the exploration of other genres of music, suggesting that "it's not 'Rock Camp' in the sense of 'rock n' roll' as much as the idea that 'girls rock'!"[46] In the band I worked with in 2013, the two vocalists were heavily invested in angelic, soprano singing, while the bass player professed her love for death metal. The happy medium that was struck in this band was that the bass player would do backing vocals in the style of "death growls" or deep guttural grunts, producing a song that intermittently mixed different genres together. Apart from death metal, exploration of other musical genres at RCFG* primarily means an openness to pop music. While much of the understanding of countercultural or alternative spaces comes with a preconceived notion of an opposition to mainstream or commercialized forms of production, the RCFG* model of collaboration is based in meeting people where they are at and validating existing interests.

Validation and Pop Music

Angela McRobbie and Jenny Garber's analysis of the "bedroom culture" of girls in the 1970s suggested that giving visibility to the activities of girls within youth and subculture studies means engaging with girls' commercial and pop-oriented music sensibilities.[47] These commercial and pop sensibilities continue to be associated with feminine musical interests, and continue to be denigrated in the 21st century.[48] At RCFG*, pop music is often highlighted as part of the shared repertoire of existing musical knowledge, and is incorporated in the working practices of music instruction. Jaime, who volunteered as a keyboard instructor in 2013, chose to teach how to play the keyboard through having their group play along to Carly Rae Jepsen's song "Call Me Maybe." Jaime comments:

> It surprised me, my first year at Rock Camp, how poppy everything was … But it makes sense, because that's what those campers are listening to, right? The reason that we chose ['Call Me Maybe'], we chose it on the second or third day, we chose it just because it was so prominent at camp, and people were using it in workshops … That Carly Rae Jepsen song is fun, because it has a really prominent riff that is the tune of the song. So you don't really hear the guitars so much. You hear this really prominent keyboard riff, and

> it's actually only three notes. And you can actually play it just with one hand. So it's easy for the campers to figure out. We just help them. And then we could listen to the song and we could all play along.[49]

Here, the simplicity of the songwriting—a sometimes maligned feature of pop music—is cited as leading to empowerment due to the ease of playing and learning something that is abundantly present in the contemporary musical landscape.

Pop music may be prominent at RCFG*, but this does not mean that rock has been abandoned. Jesse comments that vocals are taught through collective singing, and as such it is important to choose songs that

> everyone knows or kind of knows or one they can listen to and be like, 'yeah, I like that' ... One of the songs we did in my first year was 'Cherry Bomb' by the Runaways, and they love that. It's a really rocking, attitude ... it's anthemic. They can scream along with that. We also do 'I Love Rock N Roll,' Joan Jett—a lot of Joan Jett happening in vocals. We did Lady Gaga, 'Telephone.'[50]

Through the week of camp, vocalists also work on learning a song at home to bring and perform for their vocal instruction group. Asked what type of songs campers pick, Jesse states,

> they are almost always top 40 type radio songs. Songs that they hear at home, on YouTube ... One of them sang 'Part of Your World' from *The Little Mermaid* last year; I couldn't even handle that. I was crying the whole time. So music soundtrack type of songs.

Danielle Giffort's case study of Girls Rock! Midwest found that volunteers recognize "multiple ways of being feminist and doing feminism," and put a feminist approach into practice through "doing" feminism with empowering activities rather than "telling" about feminism."[51] Similarly, in this vocal instruction example, a camper's decision to bring in a song from Disney—hardly a bastion of feminist consciousness raising—is celebrated rather than critiqued. The purpose of RCFG* is not to suggest to campers that the music they already know is artificial, commercial, inauthentic, or inferior, but rather to celebrate and validate their interests while broadening them with workshops like "Girl Rock History," about the history of women in music across genres.

Pop music also spills over into the way that music is sometimes created by bands at RCFG*, and in some cases, may reconfigure what "original" can mean in terms of musical composition. Commenting about mentoring their band, Morgan, a band coach, states:

> We were stuck trying to find some kind of chorus, and one of the suggestions that I made to my band is that in my own writing practice, when I get stuck, sometimes it helps for me to have a placeholder lyric or melody until I figure something else out, so I suggested that maybe they use something like that to hold the place until they found something that they liked or they thought would work, and then [Lady Gaga's 'Paparazzi'] was what they came up with. I think that for them, for many of them, pop music is the point of access into music, because it's so available, right. I think it was great. I was like, 'by all means.'[52]

Through the week of summer camp at RCFG*, this band sang the chorus of "Paparazzi" while they were writing their own song, eventually changing the lyrics but keeping some of the vocal phrasing and melody of Lady Gaga's piece. At RCFG*, the expanded and reworked notion of shared repertoire can be read as an attempt to create inclusion in the CoP, while in more traditional CoPs, shared repertoire may act as an exclusionary mechanism. Wenger comments "learning as the production of practice creates boundaries, not because participants are trying to exclude others (though this can be the case) but because sharing a history of learning ends up distinguishing those who were involved from those who were not."[53] Though Wenger suggests there is an "unavoidability" of boundaries of practice, at RCFG*, part of the terms of the joint enterprise is expanding what a shared repertoire or boundary of practice might typically look like in music scenes rather than assuming they are unavoidable, as a "shared" history of learning has historically led to the exclusion of women from these scenes.

Challenges in Collaborative Modes of Cultural Production at Rock Camp Montreal

Various reification strategies, alongside validating interests and an openness to working with existing material to reconfigure concepts of originality are all means to foster greater collaboration, access, and inclusion within a CoP, but this model and these strategies can also be challenging. Some of these challenges are interpersonal. At RCFG*, band coaches facilitate an environment where the entire band participates in the decision-making process regarding songwriting, but a predisposition towards collaborating is not always universally found across the campers; in fact, collaborating can go against the grain of dominant, internalized norms and expectations about how songwriting will happen. Charli, a band coach, comments on their experience of working with bands in which one member is blocking decision-making, "just saying no to everything and wanting to have all the ideas and absolutely blocking every other possible option," and then having to work creatively to allow this camper to see "the necessity for collaboration and for making compromises, whether this is speaking with the camper one-on-one or getting the band to allow the camper who is blocking to work on certain parts of the songwriting alone." Working with the youngest group in particular, made up of ten-year olds, Charli says,

> I would try to get the campers to come up with one thing that they wanted to be in the song and then we would work together, with the group, to find things that the other people could play while they were playing that thing that they liked, so it was like each person contributing something they felt was pretty cool and special.[54]

This requires "lots of patience, both from me and from the campers" amidst an environment of "people losing their patience, or not listening." Charli's description of the process of achieving consensus highlights the time and effort needed to foster collaboration. Discussing the work of fostering mutual engagement, Wenger comments on the labour of community maintenance, which can be invisible, "easily undervalued and even totally unrecognized."[55] This labour of achieving consensus is also care work and the work of social reproduction. Even in an explicitly feminist context where this work is targeted and emphasized, "doing feminism" can be challenging in practice. While the joint enterprise of the camp might be defined as collaborative songwriting alongside creating more inclusive conditions in music scenes more broadly, competing individual desires may still manifest in these collectively driven enterprises.

Working collaboratively is also challenging with competing expectations and interests with regards to how time might be spent during the summer camp. Charli comments,

> [songwriting] is hard, because a lot of the time a lot of the campers would spend their whole year looking forward to camp and they would become very invested in how the song was turning out, they had a lot of hopes about how it was going to be.[56]

Returning to the keyboard instructor Jaime's decision to use "Call Me Maybe" as a teaching tool, Jaime also comments that:

> Of course not everybody likes that kind of music, and there's always one camper in the group who is going to be totally resistant to the pop music, and is more into stuff that I've never heard of, or punk … more obscure stuff. That's an older camper, usually. But then there's not a whole lot we can do to accommodate their tastes. Just in my experience, those campers who are not really into the pop, and they'll just be kinda cool, and 'no, I don't want to do Carly Rae; I'm more into this really obscure punk band.' But then they don't want to suggest anything either. So I'm like, 'you're going to go along; we're going to practice this.' So it's not the most

> inclusive pedagogy, but we only have 45 minutes, so we just have to pick a song and learn it.[57]

Though pop music may have a prominent role at RCFG* and a prominent role in the lives of the campers, it is not a universal meeting ground where everyone feels included. We also see this resistance to pop music in the Bieber backlash in the example from the first day of camp above. Sarah Thornton suggests that subcultural capital manifests through asserting power with knowledge and tastes, and this dynamic can be at play at RCFG* in spite of an explicit intention of acceptance and inclusion in the joint enterprise.[58] Indeed, Wenger asserts that "a community of practice is neither a haven of togetherness nor an island of intimacy insulated from political and social relations … in real life, mutual relations among participants are complex mixtures of power and dependence, pleasure and pain…[59]" These comments also suggest the complexities of care, where care can both feel good and be a burden, is vital and messy at once.

These competing interests and messiness with regards to how time is spent is also challenging for the formation of sustained mutual engagement in the CoP. RCFG* organizes various activities year-round, and many campers return to the camp year after year, but the summer camp is only a seven-day event, and only five of these are spent on learning an instrument, forming a band, and collaboratively writing a song. In his discussion of U.K.-based music youth arts programs, Mark Rimmer gives an overview of the divergence between on the one hand, the policy structures that give rise to these programs and are often focused on performance and other quantifiable outputs that can be used for program evaluation and assessment, and on the other hand, young people's interests in joining and participating in these programs, which may not stem from a desire to compose and perform an original song.[60]

During the time of this research project, RCFG* had only been self-funded, and did not need to meet government funding requirements to produce a certain output. At RCFG*, it would seemingly be accepted if a band wanted to perform a cover song or did not want to perform at all. The pressure of time and output remain at RCFG*, even if they are not externally mandated. Charli remarks that some "campers would have anxiety attacks about not being able to finish in a week." Some campers not only sometimes struggle with collaborative songwriting but also sometimes struggle with overcoming stage fright and the internalized need to be perfect that many young girls feel, but only have five days to do so. Charli notes that "there's internal barriers to looking stupid or not being good enough to justify drawing attention to yourself. I feel like that is very girl-specific." Vocalists in particular are:

> most likely to feel scared to even start, scared to make any sound at all because the sound would be the wrong sound. They'd prefer to stay in this fantasy space where they would talk about what it was going to be like but

> would never feel comfortable to take the risk of going there. And so the work would be to break down their barriers and help their group encourage them until they felt comfortable.[61]

This limited time at RCFG* and the large task that forms the joint enterprise of the camp may compromise the formation of shared sense of sustained mutual engagement amongst the campers. Moving towards collaboration and inclusion is possible but individualized and internalized dynamics are still at play in these contexts.

Collaborative Cultural Production and Intellectual Property

Beyond these interpersonal and time challenges, collaborative modes of production that favour a model of cultural hybridity may be at odds with intellectual property laws that govern musical production and dissemination. These issues notably emerge with multi-million-dollar lawsuits or other high-profile cases when musicians feel others have used their material without permission or acknowledgement,[62] but these issues also emerged in RCFG*'s small-scale and community-based mode of collaborative production. Morgan, the band coach who worked with the band whose composition involved reworking a Lady Gaga song, notes that this issue of permission to use others' material arose in band discussions, and resulted in a discussion on the evolution of music history through appropriation of existing forms:

> I think all music is just building upon existing patterns, to use that pattern and incorporate it in a new way. I think that sometimes we get really caught up in the idea of originality, particularly when it comes to pop music. I think that's often one of the biggest criticisms of pop music, is that it all sounds the same, or whatever, it follows a particular formula, but I think the formula is just a base to jump off from. The campers were a little bit concerned about, 'well, aren't we ripping this off?' And then we ended up having a conversation about how, where does pop music come from? Contemporary pop music. It comes from rock and roll; it comes from blues; it comes from jazz. All of these things are just building on top of each other anyway. We ended up having this really great conversation about music history.[63]

RCFG* on the whole would generally support this philosophy, insofar as the camp supports its campers in their musical journeys and musical exploration. Indeed, the first day of RCFG* typically features a "Superstar Songwriting" workshop that seeks to demystify songwriting and show campers that it is possible to write and perform a song in a compressed amount of time. In this activity, workshop leaders model how to choose a song, find its karaoke track on YouTube, and rewrite its lyrics to express a new theme. This workshop is connected with the feminist mandate of the camp of empowerment through learning-by-doing and being able to create while using critical thinking, as campers are encouraged to consider the message of their chosen song and rewrite the lyrics to reflect a more positive theme. At the same time, these conversations might be best coupled with discussions about cultural appropriation and theft, and where the boundary between hybridity, empowerment, learning, and misappropriation lies.

As the ephemeral process of the five-day camp gets fixed on tape in the recording process, this approach to songwriting that validates making use of existing forms enters the industrialized and monetized arena of cultural dissemination. During the time of the research project, RCFG* initially intended to sell these recordings for fundraising purposes for the camp, but the recording engineer who was volunteering his time intervened in this process, raising questions about the potential distribution of revenues earned from the sale of these CDs. The recording engineer asked if the bands would be entitled to some of the profits, if the bands could also sell their songs, and if they did, if they would be obligated to give some of their revenues back to RCFG*. He raised the possibility of one of the songs becoming a YouTube sensation and selling 20,000 downloads through the RCFG* website—though the difficulties of both reaching an audience in a crowded digital environment and earning a sustainable income as a small-scale cultural producer are well documented, this possibility of 20,000 downloads is not altogether absurd. Beyond these concerns of revenue sharing, the recording engineer asked if the fundraising CD might compromise the sense of mutual engagement through joint enterprise at the camp if the bands felt they were being "used" to create content that RCFG* would use for its own means. Over time, these discussions eventually led to the development of a non-exclusive licensing agreement, another example of a reified artifact, so that the terms of RCFG* using campers' songs would be clear and mutually agreed upon. The organization also stepped back from the idea that the songs would be sold for its fundraising purposes, and instead would use the material for the purpose of promoting the camp.

In the licensing agreement that RCFG* used, campers have to attest that "works are original works and that these do not infringe upon any copyright belonging to any third party." While the camp works to foster collaboration and sanctions reworking existing forms, these philosophies are at odds with intellectual property laws. Martin Chanock notes that "the world of property law seeks one true version or definition of matters which the world of cultural studies acknowledges to be subject to plasticity, hybridity, and change. Bringing these two worlds together is a formidable challenge."[64] Discussing the learning that happens in CoPs, Wenger asserts that this learning forms a "practice that can be said to be the property of the community."[65] The reality of collective ownership is, however, much murkier in intellectual property structures. In her discussion of divergence between small-scale/independent music labels and existing copyright structures, Tina Piper notes that "community interest, inclusion, altruism and action out of a non-monetary interest play little role" in copyright laws,[66] but these concepts may be important to a small-scale and collaboratively based modes of cultural production, including the community-minded project of RCFG*.

The 2012 revision to the Canadian Copyright Act makes provisions to sanction "user-generated content" (UGC) such as fan fiction or other forms creative reworking of existing content. This revision specifies that the UGC must be "non-commercial" in nature to be exempted from copyright infringement. Laura Murray and Samuel Trosow comment that "as a practical matter, this may be a difficult distinction, as the commercial/non-commercial nature of use might shift over time. What happens if the UGC begins as a wholly non-commercial project, such as school project or a hobby activity, and it subsequently enjoys a measure of success?"[67] This possibility could potentially apply to a RCFG* production, starting as a non-commercial summer camp project that reworks an existing form, and that could go on to enjoy commercial success. Concerning the copyright structures that surround UGC moving into a commercial arena, Murray and Trosow remark that "we will have to watch how the practice develops in this area."[68] While a CoP might favour horizontal or collaborative learning through joint enterprise, the broader reality is that capitalism remains individually driven in terms of property law structures, ownership, and financial rewards.

In 1975, McRobbie and Garber argued in defense of the bedroom culture of girls, suggesting that studying commercial interests could be a way for the field of subculture studies to register the activities of girls, as these subjects lacked visibility in a field focused on the spectacle of supposedly resistant activities of young men. More than 40 years later, the musical interests of girls may still be overlooked and denigrated as overtly commercial. Working with rather than against these commercial interests is part of how RCFG* seeks to foster collaboration, but this process is not without its challenges, as existing policy structures can collide with practice, and the realities of a week-long summer camp with a set goal of content production may limit the transformative potential of creating alternative collaborative communities.

Though CoPs may have been conceptualized as spaces of horizontal learning, these communities can reinforce rather than dismantle dominant structural forces of power and inequity. This pattern is also found in the creative industries, which have been championed as more accessible places of employment based in talent, but in fact exacerbate labour market inequities. As an alternative CoP, RCFG*'s development of mutual engagement, joint enterprise, and shared repertoire can be understood as care labour, working to develop a community of care, fostering a relational model of collaboration that is less individual and male-centric and potentially more open and inclusive. As such, the caring and collaborative model in this alternative CoP seeks to widen participation, primarily through increased reification and validation, to include more girls, non-binary, trans, and gender non-conforming youth in musical production. However, alternative, collaborative modes of production alone cannot intervene in systemic barriers to entry to creative work or lack of equity in the creative industries writ large; as such, continued work needs to be done at the policy level and in working practices in the creative industries to move towards greater equity.

Notes

1 For discussions and uses of the communities of practice concept, see Jean Lave and Étienne Wenger, *Situated Learning: Legitimate Peripheral Participation* (Cambridge: Cambridge University Press, 1991); Éienne Wenger, *Communities of Practice: Learning, Meaning and Identity* (Cambridge: Cambridge University Press, 1998); Étienne Wenger, "Communities of Practice and Social Learning Systems: The Career of a Concept," in *Social Learning Systems and Communities of Practice*, ed. Chris Blackmore (London: Springer Verlag, 2010), 179–198.

2 Dorothy Miell and Karen Littleton, eds., *Collaborative Creativity: Contemporary Perspectives* (London: Free Association Books, 2004), 1–2.

3 Andrew Cox, "What Are Communities of Practice? A Comparative Review of Four Seminal Works," *Journal of Information Science* 31, no. 6 (2005): 527–540; Alessia Contu, "On Boundaries and Difference: Communities of Practice and Power Relations in Creative Work," *Management Learning* 45, no. 3 (2013): 289–316.

4 Wenger, *Communities of Practice*, 3.

5 Lave and Wenger, *Situated Learning*.

6 Wenger, *Communities of Practice*.

7 Cox, "What Are Communities of Practice."

8 Wenger, *Communities of Practice*, 6–7.

9 Ibid., 12.

10 Bridget Conor, Rosalind Gill, and Stephanie Taylor, eds., *Gender and Creative Labour* (London: Wiley, 2015).

11 BBC News, "How These Music Festival Line-ups Look Without All-Male Bands," *BBC News*, February 15, 2015, accessed February 18, 2016, http://www.bbc.co.uk/newsbeat/article/31629520/how-these-music-festival-line-ups-look-without-all-male-bands

12 Kristine Cannon, "What Coachella and 6 Other Music Festival Lineups Would Look Like Without Men," *She Knows*, April 6, 2015, accessed February 18, 2016, http://www.sheknows.com/entertainment/articles/1080274/coachella-and-other-music-festival-lineups-with-the-male-acts-removed-photos; M. Teo, "Here's What Canadian Festival Posters Look Like With the All-Male Acts Removed,"*Aux TV*, 2015, accessed February 18, 2016, http://www.aux.tv/2015/03/heres-what-canadian-festival-posters-look-like-with-the-all-male-acts-removed/

13 Brock Thiessen, "Grimes Blasts Juno Awards for Lack of Women Nominees," *Exclaim*, February 2, 2016, accessed February 18, 2016, https://exclaim.ca/music/article/grimes_blasts_juno_awards_for_the_lack_of_female_nominees

14 Jillian Bell, "Juno Nominations Spur #JunosSoMale Hashtag," *CBC News,* February 2, 2016, accessed February 18, 2016, http://www.cbc.ca/news/trending/amy-millan-junos-so-male-1.3430457

15 Julia Downes, "Riot Grrrl: The Legacy and Contemporary Landscape of DIY Feminist Cultural Activism," in *Riot Grrrl: Revolution Girl Style Now*, ed. Nadine

Modem (London: Black Dog Publishing, 2007), 12–51; Sara Marcus, *Girls to the Front: The True Story of the Riot Grrl Revolution* (New York: Harper Perennial, 2010).

16 Joanne Gottlieb and Gayle Wald, "Smells Like Teen Spirit: Riot Grrrls, Revolution and Women in Independent Rock," in *Microphone Fiends: Youth Music and Youth Culture,* eds. Andrew Ross and Tricia Rose (London: Routledge, 1994), 250–274; Mary Celeste Kearney, "The Missing Links: Riot Grrrl-Feminism-Lesbian Culture," in *Sexing the Groove: Popular Music and Gender,* ed. Sheila Whiteley (London: Routledge, 1997), 207–229; Marion Leonard, "Paper Planes: Travelling the New Grrrl Geographies," in *Cool Places: Geographies of Youth Cultures*, eds. Tracey Skelton and Gill Valentine (London: Routledge, 1998), 101–118.

17 David Hesmondhalgh, "The Institutional Politics and Aesthetics of a Popular Music Genre," *Cultural Studies* 13, no. 1 (1999): 34–61, 37, 35, 55.

18 Wenger, "Communities of Practice and Social Learning Systems: The Career of a Concept," 187.

19 Dave Laing, *One Chord Wonders: Power and Meaning in Punk Rock* (Philadelphia: Open University Press, 1985).

20 Shevaughn Battle, "The Beginning After the End: Independent Music, Canadian Cultural Policy and the Montreal Music Scene" (MA thesis, Concordia University, 2009), 85.

21 Doreen Piano, "Resisting Subjects: DIY Feminism and the Politics of Style in Subcultural Formations," in *The Post-Subcultures Reader,* eds. David Muggleton and Rupert Weinzierl (Oxford: Berg, 2004), 253–265, 254.

22 Rupa Huq, *Beyond Subculture: Youth and Pop in a Multi-Ethnic World* (London: Routledge, 2005).

23 Marcus, *Girls to the Front.*

24 Nyala Ali, "From Riot Grrrl to Girls Rock Camp: Gendered Spaces, Musicianship and the Culture of Girl Making," *Networking Knowledge* 5, no. 1 (2012): 141–160; Sarah Hoagland, *Lesbian Ethics, Toward New Values* (Chicago, IL: Institute of Lesbian Studies, 1988).

25 Leslie Heywood and Jennifer Drake, eds., *Third Wave Agenda: Being Feminist, Doing Feminism* (Minneapolis: University of Minnesota Press, 1997), 11.

26 Kristen Schilt and Danielle Giffort, "'Strong Riot Women' and the Continuity of Feminist Subcultural Participation," in *Ageing and Youth Cultures: Music, Style and Identity,* eds. Paul Hodkinson and Andy Bennett (London: Bloomsbury Publishing, 2012).

27 James Spradley, *Participant Observation* (New York: Holt, Rinehart and Winston, 1980), 54.

28 Kathleen Dewalt and Billie Dewalt, *Participant Observation: A Guide for Fieldworkers* (Walnut Creek: AltaMira, 2002); Russell Jones, *Research Methods in the Social and Behavioral Sciences* (Sunderland: Sinauer Associates, 1996).

29 Rock Camp Montreal, "Gender Policy" in "2020-2021 Policies and Bylaws," *Rock Camp Montreal,* n.d., accessed February 25, 2021, https://docs.google.com/document/d/1LUD7M0FSzIf6OrXgnpe8vgwb9Wn5PIDDQfxW5rZFR_I/edit

30 Wenger, *Communities of Practice.*

31 Ibid., 58.

32 Ibid., 64.

33 Alex, personal communication, 2013.
Pseudonyms have been used for Rock Camp Montreal volunteers. In keeping with Rock Camp Montreal's emphasis on moving towards gender-neutral language (e.g. using the term "campers" rather than "girls"), an effort has been made to choose gender-neutral names as pseudonyms.

34 Rock Camp Montreal, "Mission and Mandate," *Rock Camp Montreal,* accessed April 26, 2021, http://girlsrockmontreal.com/about/mission-and-madate/

35 David Buckingham and Julian Sefton-Green, *Cultural Studies Goes to School: Reading and Teaching Popular Media* (London: Taylor and Francis, 1994); Henry Jenkins, *Confronting the Challenges of Participatory Culture: Media Education for the 21st Century* (Chicago: MacArthur Foundation, 2006); Julian Sefton-Green and Rebecca Sinker, *Evaluating Creativity: Making and Learning by Young People* (London: Routledge, 2000).
36 David Buckingham, *Media Education: Literacy, Learning, and Contemporary Culture* (Cambridge, UK: Polity Press, 2003), 129–130.
37 Wenger, *Communities of Practice*, 67.
38 Miell and Littleton, *Collaborative* Creativity, 1.
39 Girls Action Foundation, "Creating a Group Agreement," in *Amplify Toolkit: Designing Spaces and Programs for Girls* (Montreal: Girls Action Foundation, 2009); Seeds for Change, *A Consensus Handbook: Co-operative Decision Making for Activists, Co-ops, and Communities* (Lancaster: Seeds for Change, 2013).
40 Jesse, personal communication, 2013.
41 Wenger, "Communities of Practice and Social Learning Systems: The Career of a Concept," 192.
42 Jill Krajewski, "The Noisey Guide to Not Being a Shithole and Making Your Venue Inclusive," *Noisey*, July 14, 2016, accessed February 11, 2021, https://www.vice.com/en/article/695e93/a-guide-for-making-your-venue-inclusive
43 Rock Camp for Girls Montreal, *Volunteer Handbook* (Montreal: Rock Camp for Girls Montreal, 2012), 37.
44 Ibid., 36.
45 Ibid., 37.
46 Ibid., 39.
47 Angela McRobbie and Jenny Garber, "Girls and Subculture," in *Resistance through Rituals: Youth Subcultures in Post-War Britain* (2nd ed.), eds. Stuart Hall and Tony Jefferson (London: Routledge, 2006 [1975]), 177–188.
48 For discussion of these gendered and devalued associations of pop music, see for example musician Grimes' comments in the media: Elisa Bray and Miranda Kiek, "Is Pop Music Sexist? Canadian Musician Grimes Thinks So," *Independent,* May 9, 2013, accessed February 25, 2016, http://www.independent.co.uk/arts-entertainment/music/features/is-pop-sexist-canadian-musician-grimes-thinks-so-8609503.html; Jenny Pelly, "Grimes Speaks out in Defense of Beyoncé, 'Gangham Style,' and Mariah Carey," *Pitchfork,* February 6, 2013, accessed February 25, 2016, http://pitchfork.com/news/49448-grimes-speaks-out-in-defense-of-beyonce-gangnam-style-and-mariah-carey/
49 Jaime, personal communication, 2013.
50 Jesse, personal communication, 2013.
51 Danielle Giffort, "Show or Tell? Feminist Dilemmas and Implicit Feminism and Girls' Rock Camp," *Gender & Society* 24, no. 5 (2011): 569–588, 579.
52 Morgan, personal communication, 2013.
53 Wenger, "Communities of Practice and Social Learning Systems: The Career of a Concept," 182.
54 Charli, personal communication, 2016.
55 Wenger, *Communities of Practice*, 74.
56 Charli, personal communication, 2016.
57 Jaime, personal communication, 2013.
58 Sarah Thornton, "The Social Logic of Subcultural Capital," in *The Subcultures Reader,* eds. Ken Gelder and Sarah Thornton (London: Routledge, 2005), 200–209.
59 Wenger, *Communities of Practice*, 77.
60 Mark Rimmer, "'Instrumental' Playing? Cultural Policy and Young People's Community Music Participation," *International Journal of Cultural Policy* 15, no. 1 (2009): 71–90.

61 Charli, personal communication, 2016.

62 For discussion of some of these high profile cases, see for example Kory Grow, "Robin Thicke, Pharell Lose Multi-Million Dollar 'Blurred Lines' Lawsuit," *Rolling Stone*, March 10, 2015, accessed May 21, 2016, http://www.rollingstone.com/music/news/robin-thicke-and-pharrell-lose-blurred-lines-lawsuit-20150310; Daniel Kreps, "Tom Petty on Sam Smith Settlement: 'No Hard Feelings, These Things Happen,'" *Rolling Stone*, January 29, 2015, accessed May 21, 2016, http://www.rollingstone.com/music/news/tom-petty-on-sam-smith-settlement-no-hard-feelings-these-things-happen-20150129; Christopher O'Connor, "The Verve Sued Again Over 'Bitter Sweet Symphony,'" *MTV*, January 11, 1999, accessed May 21, 2016, http://www.mtv.com/news/511079/the-verve-sued-again-over-bitter-sweet-symphony/

63 Morgan, personal communication, 2013.

64 Martin Chanock, "Branding Identity and Copyrighting Culture: Orientations Towards the Customary in Traditional Knowledge Discourse," in *Traditional Knowledge, Traditional Cultural Expressions and Intellectual Property Law in the Asia-Pacific Region,* ed. Christoph Antons (The Netherlands: Wolters Klumer, 2009), 177–194, 187.

65 Wenger, "Communities of Practice and Social Learning Systems: The Career of a Concept," 181.

66 Tina Piper, "An 'Independent' View of Bill C-32's Copyright Reform," in *"Radical Extremism" To "Balanced Copyright": Canadian Copyright and the Digital Agenda,* ed. Michael Geist (Toronto: Irwin Law, 2010), 423–446, 425.

67 Laura Murray and Samuel Trosow, *Canadian Copyright: A Citizen's Guide* (Toronto: Between the Lines, 2013), 146.

68 Ibid., 147.

7

INCLUSIVE SPACES FOR SMALL-SCALE CULTURAL PRODUCTION

As smoke started coming up through floorboards under their feet at an event at the Ghost Ship warehouse in Oakland, California, Ghost Ship warehouse fire survivor Ivan Mairesse remembers his friend saying to him, "It smells like a firecracker, doesn't it?"[1] Mairesse and his friends had never been to Ghost Ship before, but were in attendance on the evening of December 2, 2016 to watch a friend, Joel Shanahan, perform electronic music under the name of Golden Donna. As smoke from a fire began to fan out with "fumes … so powerful it became difficult to breathe or keep [his] eyes open," Mairesse and his friends were able to locate a staircase leading down to an exit, and stumble out through the "pitch-black" after the electricity went out. Shanahan was also able to safely exit that evening, but his friend and labelmate Chelsea Faith Dolan, who was on the line-up scheduled to perform that night, was one of the 36 people who died in the fire.[2]

The Ghost Ship tragedy represents an extreme case of death and destruction due to poorly maintained infrastructure for small-scale cultural production. Mass death can sometimes tragically occur in spaces and places that are not included in mainstream discussions of the creative industries. For example, in 2013 the Rana Plaza garment factory collapse in Dhaka, Bangladesh, killed more than 1000 garment manufacturer workers, who produced garments for brands including Benetton, Gucci, the Children's Place, and Mango.[3] The Rana Plaza tragedy highlights the extractive nature of the creative industries, with fashion companies using a globalized workforce while failing to provide safe and fair working conditions. Ghost Ship was operating as a live/ work space without residential zoning or permits. There were known electrical problems in the building, and it was a particularly cluttered environment, full of wooden furniture, which accelerated the fire and caused tragic challenges by preventing some attendees from

DOI: 10.4324/9781003031338-7

being able to locate exits once the fire broke out. While these specific circumstances contributed to the tragedy, in his account of his experience, Mairesse also comments on the similarity between Ghost Ship and other spaces: "it resembled co-ops and warehouse spaces I'd attended over the years as a young fan who supported DIY venues and experimental music."[4]

The Ghost Ship warehouse fire illuminates the contradictions and perils of overly valorizing creative economies paradigms. Creative economy and creative city discourses are often still directed to large-scale initiatives, such as downtown tourist zones or waterfront revitalizations, to the detriment of smaller-scale places where cultural production takes place. In his book *Any Night of the Week: A D.I.Y. History of Toronto Music 1957-2001*, Toronto music promoter and author Jonny Dovercourt opens by contrasting the city of Toronto's official positioning of itself as a "music city" at the policy level with a rapid string of music venue closures in 2017, some of them in the wake of the Ghost Ship tragedy, as will be discussed below. Dovercourt suggests that "'creative cities' like Toronto—which have identified music and the arts as key economic drivers—still lack the means to sufficiently protect these supportive spaces."[5] The Toronto context and music as a creative form are named here, but this "teeth-grinding irony" of the disconnect between policy and practice is often endemic in the creative industries across locations and across creatives practices. Though potentially dangerous, these supportive and small-scale/DIY spaces, like Ghost Ship, are often vital for entry-level cultural production across creative disciplines, including music, visual arts, theatre and performance, community arts, and so on. Discussing DIY or do-it-yourself culture across artistic mediums, Amy Spencer outlines that DIY culture aims to "build unique idealized networks in which anyone can participate."[6] DIY spaces can often act as launching pads in artists' careers, and are also often inclusive spaces that welcome diverse performers and audiences without the pressure to make profit or expand into larger-scale forms of creative practice.

The lack of diversity in the creative industries workforce is increasingly well documented, but it appears that earlier stages of cultural production have a better range of diversity amongst creators. Labour market profiles of creative workers reveal more demographic diversity in entry-level creative workers than in the overall population of creative workers.[7] Similarly, artistic institutions that are smaller in scope may also have better track records of fostering and representing more demographically diverse artists.[8] Spaces like Ghost Ship can foster this diversity in entry-level cultural production, but they are precarious and those who run them can be subject to fines if they do not operate according to official zoning, bylaws, and permits. Meeting the requirements of official zoning/permits for small-scale, entry-level, emerging, and DIY initiatives is often challenging. These types of ventures can sometimes operate in spaces that do not meet official codes and sanctioned uses, but meeting requirements for official uses can be enormously costly and oftentimes structurally impossible.[9] Moreover, bylaws around issues such as noise can be subjectively applied to the detriment of small-scale venues, resulting in fines and closures if new residents move into an area and then complain about venues that have long existed and have often helped make neighbourhoods in demand to prospective new tenants and owners. In the particular case of the Ghost Ship warehouse, the stakes are heightened because the tragedy of the fire at this venue in 2016 resulted in deaths and in criminal prosecution. Criminal charges were brought to two individuals, Derick Almena, described as the "master tenant" of the warehouse, and Max Harris, described as Almena's assistant, helping out with tasks such as collecting rent from the residents who lived and worked in the building. At the conclusion of the criminal trial for 36 counts of involuntary manslaughter in 2019, Harris was acquitted on all 36 counts, but Almena's charges resulted in mistrial.[10] At the time of the writing of this book, Almena had yet to be retried, but my purpose here is not to delve into the criminal proceedings or to assign individual guilt or innocence in this particular matter. More broadly, this tragic incident illustrates the complexities, vital need, and perils of physical space for emerging forms of cultural production and for reimagining the creative industries.

Beyond Artist-Led Gentrification

Emerging artists and cultural producers are sometimes identified as the first layer of an artist-led model of gentrification. This model highlights the role of artists moving into affordable areas to live and work and making these areas trendy, resulting in increased costs of real estate in these areas. Simply put, analyses of gentrification examine the transition of particular neighbourhoods from lower-income to sought-after areas for development, and artist-led gentrification analyses examine the role of art and artists in this transition. Discussing the art world boom in the 1980s in the Lower East Side in New York City, art historians Rosalyn Deutsche and Cara Ryan assert that "participants" in the art scene, whether "consciously or unconsciously" approach a "neighborhood with dominating and possessive attitudes that transform it into an imaginary site. Art journals, the mass media, galleries, established alternative spaces, and museums manipulate and exploit the neighborhood, thereby serving as conduits for the dominant ideology that facilitates gentrification."[11] Here, art-scene participants are defined broadly, including both cultural producers in those in intermediary roles, including alternative spaces. Deutsche and Ryan suggest that real-estate development and large-scale investment in the Lower East Side was preceded by, and contingent upon, artists' mass movement into the area. It is important to acknowledge that this pattern of artist-led gentrification exists. However, this model narrowly examines the role of the artist in catalyzing change, rather than more broadly examining the lack of policy protections around real estate speculation or for affordable and stable housing.

Geographer David Ley examines the role of artists as "agents" of gentrification through comparative empirical data, concluding "the relationship between artists and gentrification is not inevitable but it is frequent."[12] Ley points to the entire process of social valorization of artists that results in the "socio-spatial change."[13] Sociologist Meghan Rich examines how artists are seen as a "tool" for gentrification, but suggests that artists "are often the victims of the neighborhood 'success' and subject to displacement when neighborhood real estate values escalate."[14] Rich concludes, "what artists want and need is ownership over legal, up-to-fire-code spaces."[15] Artists, other classes of workers, and residents all need secure, stable, and affordable housing and work spaces. In this book, I suggest a creative ecology approach is best suited to address the importance of both large-scale and small-scale spaces for the creative industries. In this chapter, I register the complexity and the broader processes embedded in socio-spatial change through the creative industries, acknowledging but moving beyond the role of individual artists or arts collectives in catalyzing gentrification.

Above, I discussed both the specificity and extreme nature of what happened in the Ghost Ship fire, but also the similarity of this space to many others like it. Similarities can also be found across gentrifying cities where economically driven motives push forms of small-scale cultural production to the physical margins of cities. The Ghost ship warehouse was located in Oakland, California, across the bay from San Francisco, the most expensive city in the United States; San Francisco and the Bay Area have seen soaring rents and real estate costs through the advent of Silicon Valley, home to technology companies like Apple, Google, and Facebook (sometimes also included in definitions of the creative industries when the IT sector is included). Oakland also has some of the most rapidly rising rents in the United States; in an article for the *Guardian*, Sam Levin reports that "long-time Oaklanders and tenants' rights activists … said the tragedy was a symptom of a major affordability crisis and the long-term failure of urban housing policy to protect the most vulnerable people."[16] Maria Poupet, executive director of a housing rights group called Causa Justa in Oakland comments that the aftermath of the Ghost Ship fire saw some people "blaming the victims."[17] Raising concerns about safety can lead to eviction and closure of spaces, rather than resulting in assistance for artists to gain affordable housing or work/exhibition space or assistance to make their spaces safer. Closures further accelerate increased real estate costs, creating a "pathway for real-estate developers to remove a low-income arts community and replace it with more profitable, market-rate housing," Levin writes. In Levin's article, musician Tarik Kazaleh comments "that's a slumlord landlord's best-case scenario … They'll just get a tech firm and get more money."[18] In an article in the *Village Voice* about the Ghost Ship tragedy, Sophie Weiner suggests tackling "the root cause of inequality," highlighting that "aggressive rent control, higher wages, and widespread support for marginalized groups would take away some of the fuel that drives the creation of physically unsafe arts spaces."[19] This multi-prong approach to systemic inequality moves beyond the reductive simplicity of the artist-led gentrification model.

Community Architects and Civic Salvagers

In contrast to identifying artists as the source of these problems of safety, gentrification, and displacement, in her book *Make Some Space: Tuning into Total Refreshment Centre*, Emma Warren casts the work of creating and maintaining physical spaces for emerging forms of cultural production as the work of "citizen salvage." She outlines that this work refers to "the way that people can find and make space in a city where the opportunities to do so have diminished on all fronts."[20] Similarly, Dovercourt casts the people involved in creating music scenes as "community architects."[21] Warren profiles the history and activities of a particular space in the Hackney borough of London, England, called Total Refreshment Centre (TRC), that was active as a music performance and recording space under that name between 2012 and 2018, but Warren also has an expansive understanding of the importance of physical spaces for cultural production, including but spanning beyond music. She includes under her purview of citizen salvage "expressions of culture that comes from people gathering to do stuff, whether that's community gardening or cooking or any kind of making or doing. It's about people, and it's about the relationships we can make in these spaces, whatever our age or background."[22] Important to note here are the forms of connection and community that emerge through culture and through physical spaces. The "salvage" that Warren names is directed towards salvaging these qualities of community building, rather than "salvaging" or restoring/renovating physical spaces, though this physical salvage also can sometimes occur. For Warren, places like TRC are "more than just receptacles of youthful hedonism, more than transient meat markets. They have intrinsic value, culturally, communally and for us individually, throughout our lives, and we need suitable physical space in which this can happen."[23] Many forms of creative practice need sustained access to physical space to ensure their existence: spaces for rehearsing, making, creating, and collaborating alongside spaces for presenting, exhibiting, performing, vending, etc., but access to space is often difficult to obtain and sustain. There is a sharp contrast between the positively positioned "community architect" or "civic salvager" and the more disdained "artist-gentrifier," and at worst, the "artist-criminal." This latter designation is of course an extreme occurrence, and while the Ghost Ship criminal cases examined criminal negligence, this "artist-criminal" designation can also emerge through noise fines or other bylaw infraction penalties that small-scale and DIY venue operators can face.

Space for Marginalized People and Forms of Cultural Production

Here, I cast forms of citizen salvage as care work, as individuals and groups exhibit the typology of care thinking outlined in Chapter 2: manifesting and enabling relationality, being impacted by and recognizing structural barriers, and creating space to enable new visions of inclusive cultures for the creative industries. DIY spaces can act as "safe spaces," where marginalized people may feel more enabled to express a range of identities or exhibit creative work that falls outside of mainstream or hegemonic forms of creating and being. Correspondent April Aliermo's video profile of DIY spaces for *CBC Arts* outlines the role and importance of these spaces. In this video, Cathleen Calica, co-founder of art space 187 Augusta, says, "187 Augusta is a community arts space. This space is for women of colour and people who are marginalized. It's catering to the people who need it, because I need it, and my community needs it." Just John, director of Blank Canvas gallery says, "it's one of the most important things we do … making sure this space is a conduit for art and culture happening in the city of Toronto. It's a safe space for every person coming from different places in the community, whether BIPOC, artists of diaspora, all walks of life, queer youth. This is a place where you can present your work and express yourself. Yes, there can be prestigious galleries out there. But there also needs to be a place where artists feel safe, feel comfortable, artists can grow. DIY spaces serve that need."[24]

These comments outline the vital and often transformative role of "safe spaces" for people from marginalized and underrepresented communities at the intertwined levels of identity formation, cultural production, and social/community engagement. Further, Just John's comments suggest the need for an ecological approach to the creative industries to ensure the existence of both small-scale and large-scale spaces and institutions to support cultural production—both "prestigious galleries" and DIY spaces. The Ghost Ship warehouse fire incident illuminates the tragic irony that these so-called safe spaces can often be physically unsafe, as they can exist in abandoned or makeshift spaces that do not adhere to regulated building or safety codes. Discussing this contradiction in the aftermath of the Ghost Ship fire, Oakland-based musician Kimya Dawson wrote, "if I hadn't had people inviting me to their unconventional venues over the years I would have been dead a long, long time ago … We're not trying to put each other in danger. We are trying to save each other's lives."[25] Reflecting on the experience of running a DIY venue called Fort Thunder in Providence, Rhode Island, Brian Chippendale names "the paradox of life affirming death traps." Discussing the Ghost Ship tragedy, Chippendale states, "I think everyone involved in booking shows at this deep underground level of culture—where money isn't really being generated for the venue or the booker—at some point starts to wonder why they are doing it. Why book performers and bring people into your private space and disrupt your day to day rituals and your productivity? An urgency to enhance the community? To bring people together? A thirst for some revelation found only in communal experience? Perhaps people who do it are paying a karmic debt for some show they went to as a kid that changed their life."[26] These broad questions speak to mixed but community-based impulses to organize these types of spaces, in the absence of economic rewards.

From Surveillance to Community Care: Responses to the Ghost Ship Tragedy

The Ghost Ship fire presented a moment of reckoning for cities, space, culture, creativity, and community. At the municipal level, the mayor of Oakland, Libby Schaaf, announced $1.7 million of funding for affordable spaces for artists and arts organizations.[27] Alongside this increased funding, there was also a law-and-order response. Pressing criminal charges against Derick Almena and Max Harris, district attorney Nancy O'Malley said Almena and Harris' actions "amount to disregard for human life" as they "knowingly created a fire trap with inadequate means of escape."[28] This law-and-order response also included increased surveillance of DIY spaces and venues in Oakland and in its surrounding area but also across North America. Discussing building hazards and fire code violations, Oakland city councilman Noel Gallo commented, "it's throughout these neighborhoods ... We need to enforce the rules. This is the not the first and maybe not the last."[29] This situation of "enforcing the rules" took a particular twist through the involvement of 4chan, an online platform that has been a haven for alt-right troll groups. After the Ghost Ship fire, 4chan users led a campaign to call fire marshals to report DIY venues, often resulting in inspections and closures. On the "Politically Incorrect" 4chan board, known as a platform for racism and sexism, one commenter identified DIY venues as "open hotbeds of liberal radicalism and degeneracy and now YOU [sic] can stop them by reporting all such places you may be or may become aware of to the authorities, specifically the local fire marshel [sic]." Commenters on this post offered insight on how to locate these types of spaces: "look on college communities, facebook groups, and music forums. Try searching for keywords like queer and safespace [sic]." Referring to the Ghost Ship tragedy, one commenter notes "fate has presented us this opportunity to strike the left at its core and destabilise [sic] them ... Don't waste it!"[30] These tactics were effective and resulted in venue closures across North America. In spite of their misguided tactics and their hateful messaging, the 4chan message board in some ways accurately identified the importance of DIY spaces for fostering inclusive cultures.

The short documentary film *In the Wake of Ghost Ship*, directed by Jason Blalock, highlights the accelerated inspections of live/ work warehouses in the days after the Ghost Ship fire, and profiles one space called Burnt Ramen in Richmond, California, which was investigated after the mayor received an anonymous tip. Burnt Ramen was one of many venues listed as "places to report" on the 4chan "Politically Incorrect" message board. The film follows Burnt Ramen owner Mykee Ramen, residents, and community members working to get the warehouse up to code after it is reported. After city inspectors visit the space, it receives 58 code violations and is closed; owner Mykee Ramen resorts to living in his van. At a subsequent protest at a Richmond city hall meeting, one impassioned speaker references the Ghost Ship fire and cries, "my friends died, and you cannot evict people in the name of my friends who died," highlighting the human cost of the Ghost Ship tragedy, and the injustice of mobilizing this loss to further marginalize community members.[31] In Toronto, an article in *CBC Arts* chronicles that "this vigilante wave hit Toronto: one of the city's rare DIY spaces was shut down. A 4chan member called the fire department, citing the art hub as unsafe; the fire department came for inspection and prohibited the organizers from continuing operations." This article concludes, "we need to create better infrastructure for small-scale art and emerging artists to thrive."[32]

Alongside these official responses, including surveillance and crackdowns, community-led responses worked on the continued existence and support of small-scale spaces. I suggest care as an alternative to tragedy/response: an alternative that works towards sustained existence outside of moments of crisis. Discussing diversity and inclusion efforts in online and hackerspaces, Christina Dunbar-Hester characterizes the "painstaking construction of safer and closed spaces" online as "attempts to build infrastructures of care."[33] Dunbar-Hester articulates care as a form of social infrastructure, enabling forms of sociality and social practice. Physical infrastructure also scaffolds these infrastructures of care: care enables the existence of these spaces, and care flows also back through their maintenance and support, here particularly visible in this post-Ghost Ship moment.

After the Ghost Ship warehouse fire, designer and curator S. Surface started a community-compiled Google Document called *DIY Venue Harm Reduction*, sharing strategies to increase physical safety in these spaces. This document is careful to outline its own limitations while suggesting tips to increase safety, opening by stating "*DIY Venue Harm Reduction* is a resource for people who manage spaces, host events, and/ or attend events. This is an incomplete, evolving draft of suggestions for fast, free and low-cost changes that can be implemented immediately. This is **not** a comprehensive safety manual or replacement for involving licensed experts and meeting fire/building codes" (emphasis in original).[34] In contrast to funding and punishment, this community-based response emphasizes action and accountability. Following from the discussion of inclusion action plans in Chapter 3, in this document we can identify the elements of naming and defining a problem, and then moving forward with concrete suggestions for action. *DIY Venue Harm Reduction* opens by naming problems of safety in venues. There is not a substantive emphasis on defining what is or is not safe; instead, the document mobilizes harm reduction and disability justice frameworks in its definitions of the problem and identification of pathways towards greater safety, emphasizing reducing harm and inequitable access to space, noting "communities of color, low-income communities, immigrant communities, and vulnerable communities who are likely to inhabit spaces at risk of fire, eviction, or gentrification, is a high priority for the editors of this document."[35] Actions that are outlined include "Immediate, Low-Cost, and Free Building and Safety Modifications," such as decluttering the space, clearing obstructions, and not using flammable materials for art installations. The document follows these first-tier recommendations with "Secondary and/ or Higher-Cost Building Improvements and Information," including posting floor plans, have access to multiple exits, replacing DIY walls with sheetrock and insulation, and keeping heat-generating lighting equipment to a minimum. This document addresses both organizers and attendees at events in DIY spaces. The "Actions to Take for Venues and Promoters" section includes limiting the numbers of attendees at events, and provides an easy-to-grasp formula for calculating a venue's maximum capacity of attendees. The "Actions to Take for the Public" section includes having awareness and a plan for exiting a venue, and being aware of others with mobility concerns at events. This section concludes with extending the framework for "safe space" from discussions of inclusive environments to physical safety, noting that "we have begun to establish a culture where it is considered helpful and welcome to demand safer spaces that are free of *behavioral* threats, such as gender-based and sexual harassment, abuse, assault, misogyny, homophobia, transmisogyny, transphobia, racism, xenophobia, ableism, fatphobia, ageism, classism, and bigotry in all its forms. We must also include *literal* building and life safety in our demands to keep our spaces safer" (emphasis in original).[36]

Theorizing Space

Here, I explore a range of definitions of safe space and concepts that identify what space enables, including *safe space*, *homeplace*, *brave space*, *space of appearance*, and *Thirdspace*. These concepts can establish a broad framework for understanding the importance of physical space, both for physical safety and for inclusive cultures. Instead of evaluating any one term over another, exploring the multiplicity of these terms can underscore the role of physical space in creating opportunities for pedagogical and relational spaces of encounter in the creative industries. In order to register this role, we need concepts to help think about and articulate the importance of space.

From Safe Space to Space of Appearance

The concept of "safe space" is commonly used to designate a space that is inclusive or not violent or hostile towards people from marginalized or underrepresented communities. For example, the Safe Space Network defines safe space as "a place where anyone can relax and be able to fully express, without fear of being made to feel uncomfortable, unwelcome, or unsafe on account of biological sex, race/ethnicity, sexual orientation, gender identity or expression, cultural background, religious affiliation, age, or physical or mental ability. A place where the rules guard each person's self-respect and dignity and strongly encourage everyone to respect others."[37] This definition underscores both comfort and guidelines, "rules" to establish the creation of a safe space. In her book *Mapping Gay L.A.*, Moira Kenney traces a history of gay activism and community building in L.A., and highlights the origins and usage of the term "safe space" in the women's/ LGBTQ movements of the 1960 and 1970s. Kenney examines the role of gay and lesbian bars as gathering spaces when homosexuality was criminalized, alongside the role of consciousness-raising groups in fostering safe space. Kenney writes, "safe space in the women's movement, was a means rather than an end and not only a physical space but a space created by the coming together of women searching for community."[38] Kenney highlights the role and importance of physical space in relationship building and enabling community connections. Even if safe space is a means towards accomplishing broader ends or goals in this definition, its vital importance for community building is underlined.

As a term, "safe space" has perhaps both become overused and unfairly stigmatized. Betty Barrett identifies that the term is an "overused but undertheorized metaphor."[39] Here, I survey various definitions and iterations of this term in order to contribute some nuance to its use. Critique of this term has stemmed from its use in university campuses and classrooms, with some universities moving to condemn this concept or not sanction safe spaces at their institutions due to the perception that safe space contradicts freedom of expression. For example, in 2016, the University of Chicago sent a welcome letter to incoming undergraduate students, outlining that the university does not "condone the creation of intellectual 'safe spaces' where individuals can retreat from thoughts and ideas at odds with their own."[40] As the concept of safe space expands and becomes more commonly employed, it can include elements like content or trigger warnings to inform participants in advance about difficult content being discussed or screened, or preferred gender pronouns being stated, and these elements have drawn reactionary pushback. Proponents of safe space suggest that it cultivates a space where participants can expect to be free from harassment or hate, but this does not preclude debate or discussion of difficult ideas, or retreat from differing thoughts. In their article "Safe Space: Towards a Reconceptualization," Heather Rosenfeld and Elsa Noterman of the Roestone Collective outline the history of the term "associated with keeping marginalized groups free from violence and harassment."[41] Yet they emphasize that safe space is ongoing "relational work" and as such, "discursive, pedagogical safe space is therefore not static, but a constant movement between safe and unsafe, individual and collective, agreement and disagreement."[42] Rosenfeld and Noterman largely consider educational settings, especially classrooms, but also offices and community centres in their analysis and discussion. These authors' analysis of pedagogical space can be extended to include culture and creativity in this relational space of "constant movement." The authors assert "safe space is a space of uncertainty and change—reactively and proactively responding to and interacting with an insecure world," suggesting not only relationality with other individuals but also relationality through being in dialogue with society, rather than retreating from it.[43]

In their discussion of safe space, Rosenfeld and Noterman highlight bell hooks' concept of "homeplace" from her book *Yearning: Race, Gender and Cultural Politics*, where hooks underlines the "construction of a safe place where Black people could affirm one another and by so doing heal many of the wounds inflicted by racist domination."[44] hooks invokes spaces of family and comfort that enable some relief from dominant, discriminatory norms. For hooks, the affirmation and healing of homeplace is in dialogue with embracing "the margins." Returning to the discussion of centring difference from Chapter 4, the work of fostering inclusion is not necessarily "safe," in that it can entail discomfort and critical conversation. Discussing choosing the margins, hooks foregrounds risk rather than safety: "this space of radical openness is a margin—a profound edge. Locating oneself there is difficult yet necessary. It is not a 'safe' place. One is always at risk. One needs a community of resistance."[45] Here, hooks outlines the importance of others and of fostering difference through collectively undertaking discomfort, and the necessity of a community to help shoulder this risk and discomfort—community affirmation and healing are vital in supporting the ability of individuals to bear some of this risk and discomfort.

Another extension of the concept of safe space is the term "brave space," which social justice educators Brian Arao and Kristi Clemens suggest is an environment that encourages "taking risks on the topic of race and racism" though critical conversations.[46] Arao and Clemens suggest that "safe space" can sometimes enable people who hold privilege to shy away from uncomfortable or critical conversations that examine their own role in maintaining hegemonic systems of power under the mantle of "safety." In contrast, they outline that brave space enables controversy with civility by owning one's intentions and impact. Though brave space offers a repositioning of safe space to emphasize risk rather than security, these elements are also present in the definitions of safe space outlined above, even if this term has been diluted through its overuse.

These concepts of safe space and brave space invite reflection on how to be in dialogue with others through space; other concepts of space further underscore the individual identity formation that happens through space. Philosopher Hannah Arendt introduces the concept of the "space of appearance" via the idea of the *polis*, akin to the concept of public space, or a space of collective action. In *The Human Condition*, Arendt writes: "the *polis*, properly speaking, is not the city-state in its physical location; it is the organization of the people as it arises out of acting and speaking together, and its true space lies between people living together for this purpose, no matter where they happen to be."[47] Through this definition, Arendt articulates a shifting locus for power: away from the agents and intuitions of the state, and towards people and their interactions. Indeed, Arendt articulates power as "the human ability not just to act but to act in concert," suggestive of a capacity for collective agency.[48] Arendt further defines the polis as a space of appearance, "a mode of being together," and a space for the formation of the self in dialogue with others. The space of appearance is not a physical location, but is a space where this mutual recognition can materialize, the space between people. Arendt hinges the existence of a sense of self and of the surrounding world on the ability to have spaces of appearance: "to be deprived of [the space of appearance] means to be deprived of reality."[49] In short, we need others and places to show up to see others in order to be a self. For Arendt, the space of appearance is not bound to any one location, and "can find its proper location almost any time anywhere" but "does not always exist."[50]

Different spaces of appearance produce different expectations and possibilities for being and relating, in that different spaces are produced by and give rise to differing social and ontological possibilities: an office building, an opera house, and a DIY venue could all function as spaces of appearance, or these spaces may not enable modes of "being together." DIY venues can enable a space of appearance for marginalized forms of identity, sociality, and cultural production. Though the space of appearance is not site-specific and does not inevitably follow from physical encounters, meeting and gathering still need physical space. We can further identify cultural production as a space of appearance, allowing for the meeting and unfolding of the self. Identifying the importance of the space of appearance enables asking critical questions for the creative industries. If mainstream creative industries reproduce and exacerbate hegemonic patterns of exclusion, what alternatives exist? What spaces of appearance exist for the emergence of underrepresented identities and communities?

Thirdspace and Spatial Justice

These critical questions about space and the creative industries can further be fruitfully conceptualized through Edward W. Soja's work in his book *Thirdspace: Journeys to Los Angeles and Other Real-and-Imagined Places*. Soja outlines an approach to cultural analysis that he terms "thirding-as-Othering," moving past binary oppositions that are common and pervasive in Western thought, emphasizing space and spatial analysis as a mediator of socio-historical analysis. Soja suggests that the role of space has been undertheorized, but theorizing space offers a third point of analysis alongside social and historical analysis. For Soja, space is both material and immaterial, real and imagined, touching on elements of how space is experienced and is perceived, and moving beyond these binaries. He articulates that Thirdspace is a "mode of thinking about space that draws upon the material and mental spaces of the traditional dualism but extends well beyond them in scope, substance, and meaning."[51] This mode of analysis neither relies on "the reduction of the real solely to material objects, to things in themselves," nor is "reality confined to 'thought things' (*res cogito*) and comprehended entirely through its representations." Instead, socio-spatial analysis is presented as an "open alternative" of "both/ and also…" that is "radically open to additional otherness, to a continuing expansion of spatial knowledge."[52] This mode of analysis suggests that "the social and the spatial are seen as mutually constructed … Sociality, both routinely and problematically, produces spatiality, and *vice versa*," given that "material geographies and spatial practices shape and affect subjectivity, consciousness, rationality, historicality, and sociality."[53] Informed by configurations of power, how people interact shapes space, and space shapes how people interact.

To trace a lineage of a socio-spatial or Thirdspace approach to cultural analysis, Soja draws on the history of Black intellectual thought, emphasizing bell hooks and Cornel West's theorizing of political movements. In Soja's analysis, hooks and West both emphasize the importance of "linking together many radical subjectivities and creating new 'meeting places' and real-and-imagined 'spaces' for diverse oppositional practices."[54] Soja's reading of hooks' work emphasizes her reworking of binary oppositions, "into a re-envisioned spatiality that creates from difference new sites for struggle and for the construction of interconnected and non-exclusionary communities of resistance. In doing so, she opens up in these real-and-imagined other spaces a Thirdspace of possibilities for a new cultural politics of difference."[55] Soja also finds commonality in Henri Lefebvre's concept of "spaces of representation" and Michel Foucault's concept of "heterotopias," in that both of these concepts emphasize the "trialectics" of space, power, and knowledge. To state this importance simply, Soja cites a 1982 interview with Foucault, in which Foucault states, "Yes. Space is fundamental in any form of communal life; space is fundamental in any exercise of power."[56] Space is needed to gather and form community; space is a needed platform to materialize power, but space is also needed to open alternatives and exercise agency. Soja's analysis of Lefebvre's concept of spaces of representation highlights "capitalism, racism, patriarchy, and other material spatial practices that concretize the social relations of production, reproduction, exploitation, domination, and subjection," pointing to how ideology manifests itself and take shape in space. These "dominated spaces" can also be "chosen spaces for struggle, liberation, and emancipation" full of "perils as well as possibilities."[57] This space is "alive: it speaks" and "may be directional, situational, or relational, because it is essentially qualitative, fluid, and dynamic."[58]

Foucault has a similarly expansive conceptualization of space with his term "heterotopia." Soja highlights the publication of Foucault's lecture notes under the title of "Of Other Spaces" in 1986, after his death, where he underlines heterotopias in his search for "other spaces" and "other sites" that "have the curious property of being in relation with all the other sites, but in such a way as to suspect, neutralize, or invert the set of relations that they happen to designate, mirror, or reflect." Heterotopias are spaces where alternatives to dominant norms may be possible. Foucault suggests that heterotopias are "real places" that "do exist and that are formed in the very founding of society—which are something like counter-sites ... Places of this kind are outside of all places, even though it may be possible to indicate their location in reality."[59] As such, drawing on Lefebvre and Foucualt, for Soja, Thirdspace is not any one place but an approach to conceptualizing a socio-spatial analysis, hinging on the capacity of meeting grounds to open up possibilities for relational being and becoming. Soja comments, "all spaces can be seen as

Thirdspaces or heterotopias depending on the scope of one's critical geographical imagination, the perspective one has on how far one can reach with a critical spatial perspective. Heterotopias are what you open up to view when you look at space heterotopologically, whether you are looking at an asylum, a garden, a boat, or Los Angeles."[60] As such, I am conscious of not identifying any one space or DIY venue as a Thirdspace, and instead highlight the inclusive social practices that inform and emerge from these spaces.

Thirdspace can be a useful concept to assert the importance of space and spatial analysis in a material sense, especially at a time where physical meeting spaces and creative spaces are evaporating, in particular spaces dedicated to or earmarked for emerging and underrepresented forms of creative practice. For Soja, considering access to space and the complexities of space is in the purview of social justice:

> spatial justice specifically points to the important spatial dimensions of (social) justice. It does not refer to something different than social justice, except in the sense that emphasizing the specifically social dimensions of justice often occurs with relatively little sensitivity to space, territory, location, boundary, geographical distributions, etc.[61]

As such, in their capacities to assess the vital role of space, concepts like Thirdspace and space of appearance can highlight spatial justice as social justice, inviting questions like: who has access to space? Which activities are valorized and which are marginalized in different spaces? How can space enable and reveal these patterns of inclusion and exclusion?

These spatial justice questions can be applied to the creative industries to query what forms of cultural production are visible in space, and which forms of cultural production exist on the physical margins. As discussed in Chapter 1, a creative ecology framework for the creative industries widens the lens beyond the most visible, large-scale forms of cultural production in order to also register, valorize, and investigate spaces on the margins. This ecological framework is best accompanied by care ethics. As discussed in Chapter 2, Bernice Fisher and Joan Tronto's first stage of care is *caring about*, meaning paying attention. Below, I profile the advocacy work of Acme Studios in London, England, and this organization's care work directed to paying attention to space for artists alongside the hands-on caregiving work of creating and maintaining low-cost live/ work spaces.

Advocacy for Small-Scale Spaces: Acme Studios, London, England

Founded in 1972 in London, England by Jonathan Harvey and David Panton, Acme Studios is a housing charity dedicated to affordable and secure studio and live/ work spaces for artists. Currently, Acme is the largest single provider for affordable artist studios in England, renting space to over 800 individual artists in 16 buildings in the Greater London area, seven owned outright by Acme and the others held mostly on long-term leases. In their document called *Securing the Future*, Acme comments on the gap between a creative industries economic boom and the challenges facing individual artists: "the success of the contemporary art world in London in recent years has not trickled down to the majority of individual artists who continue to struggle to afford time and space to devote to their work. It is these artists that create the 'product' on which the rest of the contemporary art world relies. Studio provision in London and throughout the U.K. is vital, but continues to be undervalued, partly because it is less visible than the more public-facing elements of the wider visual-arts ecology."[62] Here, a creative ecology model can be useful to register and valorize working artists and practitioners whose labour contributes to the development of a larger creative industries landscape. Acme addresses this gap between economic success and labour challenges by working to secure space for artists to live and work, operating with a mission that underlines the intrinsic social and cultural importance of art and artists: "artists are essential to society, and we place them at the heart of everything we do. Through our activity, we are committed to ensuring that artists can continue being artists."[63]

In its early days of existence in the early 1970s, Acme began by approaching the Greater London Council (GLC) for use of empty houses that were pending demolition. In exchange for working on repairs on these properties to bring them back to working order, artists were given very low rents to use these spaces. Acme co-founder David Panton recalls the utopian impulses and the "incredible flowering of new ideas about culture, society, egalitarianism" through his student days of the late 1960s, enabling a disposition of wanting to be "part of changing the world."[64] Upon graduation in 1971, David and his peers encountered a different reality in the U.K., one of strikes, a decline of optimism, and an economic environment of "no work and no prospects." David contrasts the "swinging sixties" atmosphere of West London during his student days with the environment in East London, which had been badly hit and not recovered from bombing through WWII. This abundance of empty and boarded-up property in East London enabled Acme to act like a "pipeline, a conduit" for artists to gain housing, "creating community" through working to access these properties for themselves and others by seeking a "reasonably legal framework." After the GLC granted access to an initial handful of properties, it continued to contact Acme, offering further empty houses for conversion, as this abundance of empty properties was perceived as a problem to which Acme could offer a solution. David chronicles that through the period of 1972–1978, Acme handled upwards of 500 houses, acting like a property manager for many houses. Some of these short-term leases were returned to the GLC for demolition or re-development, and some of these short-life buildings were permanently transferred to Acme if they were deemed no longer required for development schemes.

David describes a "massive change" to British politics with the election of Margaret Thatcher's Conservative government in 1977, causing an evaporation of the ready supply of these abandoned and short-life properties. David chronicles an "atomization of society" through the mainstreaming of neoliberal values, including changing attitudes about the importance of individual home ownership. Thatcher's "Right to Buy" legislation enabled tenants living in Council housing (social housing) to buy their units. This change caused both the supply of properties available to Acme to dry up, and also enabled some of the artists living in properties that Acme was managing to purchase their homes. Through this period, Acme's focus changed from residential properties to industrial ones, and as Acme received charitable status, the organization was able to obtain funding for building conversion work for abandoned spaces such as a banana warehouse and a former meat-processing factory, becoming a "wholesaler and organizer" of artist studios.

In the 1990s, after the introduction of the National Lottery in the U.K. and funds from the Lottery becoming available for arts funding, Acme was able to shift from a short-life housing organization focused on building repair, conversion, and management to become a building owner. In 1996, Acme purchased two buildings outright, and the "purchase of these two buildings provided the beginnings of an asset base against which the organization could borrow. Acme could now plan a long-term capital development programme to secure the future of its support for artists."[65] As noted above, Acme owned and operated 16 buildings at the time of the writing of this book. Acme continues to rent studio and live/ work spaces to artists at below-market rents; in 2012, Acme estimated that they were renting their spaces to artists at a third of market value. In addition to affordability, Acme offers the security of long-term leases to their artist tenants.

Beyond securing arts funding to build their own spaces, Acme Studios advocates for a partnership model of "cultural planning gain" between commercial developers, local government, and artists for the construction of new buildings, such that artists are given space in new developments and developers are permitted by local authorities to break ground. David developed an advocacy model of the "dynamic triangle" for Acme, highlighting the confluence of society, business, and culture based in "triple wins" or benefits for all parties (Figure 7.1). For local government, the gain is a fully occupied building with long-term mixed tenants, creating a resource base for local employment. For developers, "in addition to achieving planning, developers gain from the process because the quiet activity of artists' studios is perfectly compatible with housing and provides a guaranteed use of commercial space which is often difficult to fill. Living alongside artists is a powerful marketing tool."[66] Artists gain affordable long-term studio or

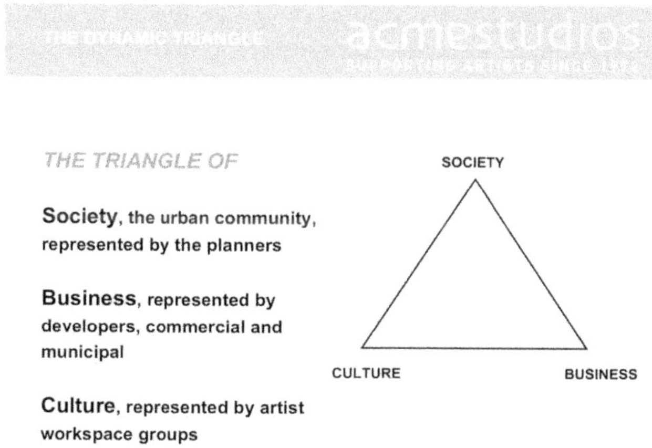

FIGURE 7.1 The Dynamic Triangle by David Panton, Acme U.K. © David Panton

live/ work spaces, built to suit artists' specifications in the deals brokered by Acme. Between 2006 and 2012, Acme participated in four development partnerships in four buildings, supported by Arts Council England, creating more than 130 studios with long-term leases, ranging from 75 years to 999 years. In 2013, this partnership work with commercial and social housing developers continued with the opening of another 100 studios in three further buildings. Acme notes the "continued demand for affordable and secure studios" and maintains a waiting list of 200 artists seeking to rent space.

Given the ongoing criticisms of artists as catalysts for gentrification, David speaks to the "politics of regeneration" and Acme's advocacy work to underscore the importance of art and artists in cities, ensuring artists can be anchored into central locations and "stay put," rather than face waves of displacement. He also notes the artwashing or the "camouflage" of developments having a trendy artistic look or visual appeal, without social housing provisions or "genuine supports." He says these "camouflage" deals "look like cultural planning gain, but actually, they are just business." David casts these types of artwashing developments as gentrification not regeneration. He says, "to try to do something that is genuinely permanent and that is affordable is very, very difficult." As noted, the Acme triple-win strategy works best for visual and other types of artists who are relatively quiet; David notes adapting and retrofitting some of Acme's units to accommodate visiting musicians, noting that "music is a different sort of process."

Rather than suggest that Acme's model should be applied to all categories and types of creative workers, a creative ecosystem approach to advocacy alongside developing policy frameworks can envision and enable different scales and different types of workers to co-exist, instead of overemphasizing corporate interests and exclusively large-scale approaches to the creative industries. Acme offers one approach to this advocacy work, embedded in and born out of post-WWII spatial history. Other approaches need to be tailored to different forms of cultural production, different communities, and different contexts. In Toronto, in 2020, the Nia Centre for the Arts, a not-for-profit organization founded in 2008 to support, showcase, and promote Black arts from across the African diaspora, announced plans to build Canada's first professional Black arts centre, supported by $7.5 million of capital funding from municipal and federal levels of funding alongside funding from the charity United Way. Chronicling the "rich, if little-known, history of Black arts and cultural spaces" in Toronto, Amanda Parris highlights that "a critical and consistent thread throughout this history of space for Black art and culture in Toronto has been the question of ownership. Stories abound of tenants being evicted, commercial rents being raised to exorbitant levels and condos replacing buildings that hold so much significance and meaning for the community."[67] Given these contemporary and historical challenges of accessing space, the future work for critical creative industries scholarship is vast: to better chronicle these histories of spaces that incubate underrepresented forms of cultural production, while also contributing the lenses and vocabulary for advocacy work, such that these spaces can be anchored through ownership rather than face ongoing waves of displacement. In this book, I aim to contribute a piece of this vocabulary through creative ecology and care ethics, enabling attention to forms of cultural production that have been historically less visible due to systemic discrimination and lack of vision for social and cultural values, alongside economic value.

Notes

1 Ivan Mairesse, "Oakland Warehouse Fire: A Survivor Shares What He Saw and How He Escaped," *Billboard*, December 9, 2016, accessed November 17, 2020, https://www.billboard.com/articles/news/7616991/oakland-warehouse-fire-survivor-account
2 Philip Sherburne, "As Golden Donna and Auscultation, Joel Shanahan Explores the Far Reaches of Electronic Music," *Bandcamp*, October 8, 2020, accessed November 17, 2020, https://daily.bandcamp.com/features/joel-shanahan-frozen-clock-hovering-interview
3 Tansy Hoskins, "Reliving the Rana Plaza Factory Collapse: A History of Cities in 50 Buildings, Day 22," *The Guardian*, April 23, 2015, accessed April 29, 2021, https://www.theguardian.com/cities/2015/apr/23/rana-plaza-factory-collapse-history-cities-50-buildings
4 Mairesse, "Oakland Warehouse Fire."
5 Jonny Dovercourt, *Any Night of the Week: A D.I.Y History of Toronto Music 1957-2001* (Toronto: Coach House Books, 2020), 7.

6 Amy Spencer, *DIY: The Rise of Lo-Fi Culture* (London: Marion Boyars, 2005), 11.
7 Hill Strategies. *A Statistical Profile of Artists and Cultural Workers in Canada* (Hamilton, ON: Hill Strategies Research, 2014); Miranda Campbell, "'Shit Is Hard, Yo': Young People Making a Living in the Creative Industries," *International Journal of Cultural Policy* 26, no. 4 (2020): 524–543.
8 Anne Dymond, *Diversity Counts: Gender, Race, and Representation in Canadian Art Galleries* (Montreal: McGill-Queen's University Press, 2019).
9 See in particular my chapter "Montreal: City of Noise" in *Out of the Basement: Youth Cultural Production in Practice and in Policy* (Montreal: McGill-Queen's University Press, 2013).
10 Laura Anthony and Amanda del Castillo, "Ghost Ship Verdict: Max Harris Acquitted, Released from Jail, Mistrial for Derick Almena Due to Hung Jury," *ABC News*, September 6, 2019, accessed November 12, 2020, https://abc7news.com/verdict-reached-in-deadly-ghost-ship-warehouse-fire-trial/5433897/
11 Rosalyn Deutsche and Cara Gendel Ryan, "The Fine Art of Gentrification," *October* 31 (1984): 91–111, 105.
12 David Ley, "Artists, Aestheticisation and the Field of Gentrification," *Urban Studies* 40, no. 12 (2003): 2527–2544, 2540.
13 Ibid., 238.
14 Meghan Ashlin Rich, "'Artists Are a Tool for Gentrification': Maintaining Artists and Creative Production in Arts Districts," *International Journal of Cultural Policy* 25, no. 6 (2019): 727–742, 730.
15 Ibid., 739.
16 Sam Levin, "Oakland Warehouse Fire Is a Product of Housing Crisis, Say Artists and Advocates," *The Guardian*, December 5, 2016, accessed November 17, 2020, https://www.theguardian.com/us-news/2016/dec/05/oakland-warehouse-fire-ghost-ship-housing-crisis
17 Ibid.
18 Ibid.
19 Sophie Weiner, "Preventing Another Oakland Warehouse Tragedy Means Supporting Artists, Not Punishing Them," *The Village Voice*, December 5, 2016, accessed November 17, 2020, https://www.villagevoice.com/2016/12/05/preventing-another-oakland-warehouse-tragedy-means-supporting-artists-not-punishing-them/
20 Emma Warren, *Make Some Space: Tuning into Total Refreshment Centre* (London: Sweet Machine Publishing, 2019), 12.
21 Dovercourt, *Any Night of the Week*, 7.
22 Warren, *Make Some Space*, 12.
23 Ibid., 12–13.
24 April Aliermo, "Dance Circles and a Radical Haircut: How Marginalized Artists Find Home in DIY Art Spaces," *CBC Arts*, June 6, 2017, accessed November 6, 2020, https://www.cbc.ca/arts/exhibitionists/dance-circles-and-a-radical-haircut-how-marginalized-artists-find-home-in-diy-art-spaces-1.4148333
25 Anna Cafolla, "Why DIY Creative Spaces like Oakland Are So Precious," *Dazed*, December 9, 2016, accessed November 6, 2020, https://www.dazeddigital.com/artsandculture/article/33987/1/why-diy-creative-spaces-like-oakland-are-so-precious
26 Brian Chippendale, "The Paradox of Life Affirming Death Traps," *The Creative Independent*, December 15, 2015, accessed November 12, 2020, https://thecreativeindependent.com/people/the-paradox-of-life-affirming-death-traps/
27 Jon Blistein and Sarah Grant, "Oakland Mayor Pledges $1.7 Million for Art Spaces After Deadly Fire," *The Rolling Stone*, December 8, 2016, accessed April 8, 2021, https://www.rollingstone.com/music/music-news/oakland-mayor-pledges-1-7-million-for-art-spaces-after-deadly-fire-114382/

28 Eliott C. McLaughlin and Phil Gast, "Two Arrested in Oakland's Deadly Ghost Ship Fire," *CNN*, June 5, 2017, accessed November 12, 2020, https://www.cnn.com/2017/06/05/us/oakland-ghost-ship-warehouse-fire-charges/index.html
29 Sam Levin and Alan Yuhas, "Oakland 'Ghost Ship' Warehouse Had a History of Violations Before Deadly Fire," *The Guardian*, December 4, 2016, accessed November 17, 2020, https://www.theguardian.com/us-news/2016/dec/03/oakland-ghost-ship-warehouse-fire-violations
30 Gabrielle Canon, "4chan Users Launch Campaign to Shut Down DIY Venues in Aftermath of Oakland Fire," *Vice*, December 15, 2016, accessed November 17, 2020, https://www.vice.com/en/article/d7jwdj/4chan-trolls-diy-spaces-oakland-fire
31 Jason Blalock, "In the Wake of Ghost Ship," *Vimeo*, June 12, 2017, https://vimeo.com/221287627
32 CBC Arts, "Do-It-Yourself Art Spaces Are Under Siege—and We Need to Do Everything We Can to Protect Them," *CBC Arts*, January 18, 2017, accessed November 17, 2020, https://www.cbc.ca/arts/do-it-yourself-art-spaces-are-under-siege-and-we-need-to-do-everything-we-can-to-protect-them-1.3941733
33 Christina Dunbar-Hester, *Hacking Diversity: The Politics of Inclusion in Open Technology Cultures* (Princeton, NJ: Princeton University Press, 2020), 53.
34 "D.I.Y. Venue Harm Reduction," n.d. accessed November 17, 2020, https://docs.google.com/document/d/1KPEURnlCPjedaSSPhpq6hvigkXbbXxDvv1gvrwRLrTQ/edit
35 Ibid.
36 Ibid., 20.
37 "What Is Safe Space," *The Safe Space Network*, accessed November 11, 2020, https://safespacenetwork.tumblr.com/Safespace
38 Moira Kenney, *Mapping Gay L.A* (Philadelphia, PA: Temple University Press, 2011).
39 Betty Jo Barrett, "Is 'Safety' Dangerous? A Critical Examination of the Classroom as Safe Space," *The Canadian Journal for the Scholarship of Teaching and Learning* 1 (2010): 1–12, 1.
40 David Schaper, "University of Chicago tells Freshman It Does Not Support 'Trigger Warnings,'" *NPR,* August 26, 2016, accessed November 11, 2020, https://www.npr.org/2016/08/26/491531869/university-of-chicago-tells-freshmen-it-does-not-support-trigger-warnings
41 The Roestone Collective, "Safe Space: Towards a Reconceptualization," *Antipode* 46, no. 5 (2014): 1346–1365, 1346.
42 Ibid., 1347, 1355.
43 Ibid., 1362.
44 bell hooks, *Yearning: Race, Gender and Cultural Politics* (Toronto: Between the Lines, 1990), 42.
45 Ibid., 149.
46 Brian Arao and Kristi Clemens, "From Safe Space to Brave Space: A New Way to Frame Dialogue Around Diversity and Social Justice," in *The Art of Effective Facilitation,* ed. Lisa M. Landreman (Sterling, VA: Stylus Publishing, 2013), 135–150, 141.
47 Hannah Arendt, *The Human Condition* (Chicago: The University of Chicago Press, 1998 [1958]), 198.
48 Hannah Arendt, *On Violence* (Boston: Houghton Mifflin Harcourt, 1970), 44.
49 Arendt, *The Human Condition,* 199.
50 Ibid., 198, 199.
51 Edward J. Soja, *Thirdspace: Journeys to Los Angeles and Other Real-and-Imagined Places* (Malden, MA: Blackwell, 1996), 11.
52 Ibid., 64, 63, 61, 60, 61.
53 Ibid., 72, 77.
54 Ibid., 84.

55 Ibid., 96.
56 Quoted in Soja, *Thirdspace,* 149.
57 Ibid., 68.
58 Ibid., 69.
59 Ibid., 157.
60 Quoted in Christian Borch, "Interview with Edward W. Soja: Thirdspace, Postmetropolis and Social Theory," *Distinktion: Scandinavian Journal of Social Theory* 3, no.1 (2002): 113-120: 114.
61 Ibid., 119.
62 Acme Studios, *Securing the Future: Celebrating the Past* (London, UK: Acme Studios, 2012), 2.
63 Acme, "Our Values," *Acme*, accessed November 24, 2020, https://acme.org.uk/about/mission-and-values/
64 David Panton, personal interview, December 16, 2020.
65 Acme, *Securing the Future*, 3.
66 Ibid., 4.
67 Amanda Parirs, "Nia Centre and the Legacy of Black Arts and Culture Spaces in Toronto," *CBC Arts*, November 9, 2020, accessed March 19, 2021, https://www.cbc.ca/arts/nia-centre-and-the-legacy-of-black-arts-and-culture-spaces-in-toronto-1.5795044

CONCLUSION: TOWARDS A COLLABORATIVE FUTURE

In November 2020, my research lab, Creative Communities in Collaboration (CCC), held a small online research festival and workshop series called "Towards a Collaborative Future." The purpose of "Towards a Collaborative Future" was to tackle imagining a future where collaboration is more possible through increased avenues for co-creation, teaching and learning, and community engagement. Workshops involved discussion and hands-on skill development for mixed audiences of academics, students, practitioners, and the general public. Topics ranged from cultural mapping methods and the arts-service organization ecosystem in Canada; food sovereignty and sharing stories and experiences with growing food; storytelling through archival research from a social justice perspective; and speculative translations through creative writing, pushing the linguistic boundaries of hegemonic English (Figure 8.1). This expansive focus pushes the boundaries and limits of what the "creative industries" might mean; indeed, the CCC seeks this expansion so that the topics of the arts, social justice, gardening and food sovereignty, history, and the politics of language might be possible areas investigated by creative industries scholarship and creative industries practice. The CCC investigates how creativity and cultural production enable resilience and strength in communities. Not only a driver of 21st century economies, culture and creative expression also enhance the wellbeing of individuals and communities. This understanding of the role of cultural production in society includes but also expands the main economic framework for the creative industries, discussed in Chapter 1.

Expanding the definition of the creative industries and rearticulating social, cultural, and economic value is also needed in light of the urgent challenges of diversity, equity, and inclusion in the creative industries. These challenges include diverse representation in creative industries, both for those "on stage" in cultural

DOI: 10.4324/9781003031338-102

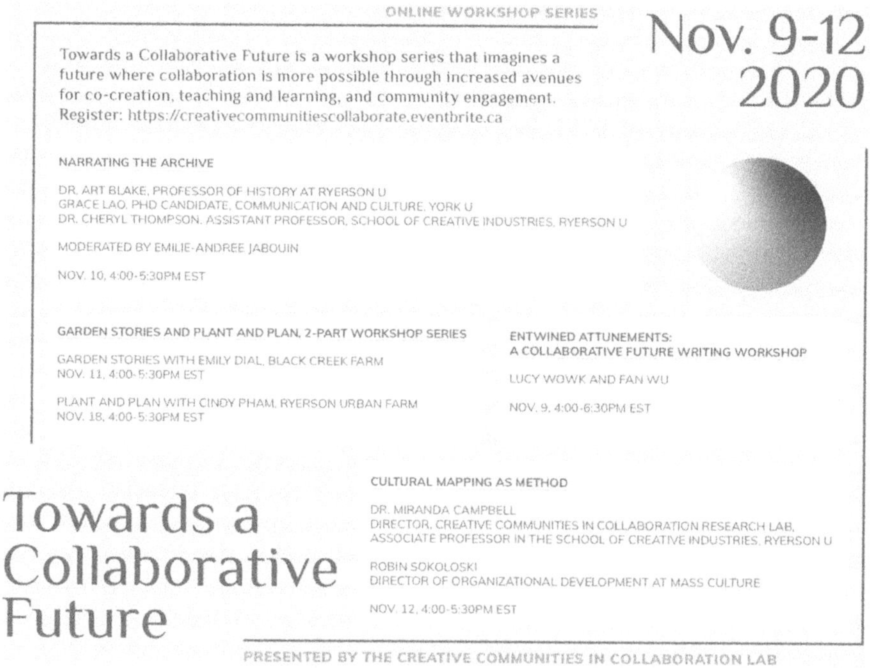

FIGURE 8.1 "Towards a Collaborative Future" Flyer from CCC Research Lab. © Creative Communities in Collaboration research lab, image design by Lucy Wowk

production, across industries, and for those working behind the scenes, as well as safe and inclusive working environments. Through this book, I have sought to establish that this expansion means addressing systemic barriers and systemic discrimination. I echo Joshua Vettivelu's language of "historical overrepresentation" due to white supremacy, from Chapter 4; this overrepresentation needs to be addressed, alongside creating space and visibility for underrepresented forms of cultural production and communities. These conversations about diversity, equity, and inclusion are increasingly in the spotlight in the creative industries, but progress is not linear. In the Introduction, I profiled the cyclic nature of the #OscarsSoWhite conversation in 2015, 2016, and 2020, with overrepresentation of white nominees in many categories of the Academy Awards. In 2021, these conversations emerged yet again, with a lack of Golden Globe nominations for Black writer, director, producer, and actor Michaela Coel's landmark television series, *I May Destroy You*. This critically acclaimed show depicts the nuances of surviving sexual assault, race, friendship, the life of the creative, and the role of social media with complexity and verve. Amongst the outcry about this Golden Globes snub, film director Alma Har'el pithily summed up the outrage with her tweet, "sometimes racism is the only explanation."[1] Coel also responded simply, with a tweet on the day that the Golden Globes nominees were released linking to an article from *Deadline* titled "Damning New

Report Reveals that BAME [Black, Asian, and Minority Ethnic] Representation Went Backwards in British TV Last Year," and no further comment.[2] This article opens by profiling that "diversity went into reverse in the British television industry last year, a damning new report has revealed, despite a global reckoning over racism and the rise of the Black Lives Matter movement following the death of George Floyd." The report from the Creative Diversity Network found a decline in creative content produced by racialized people for British TV non-white from 22.7% in 2019 to 21.2% in 2020. In behind-the-scenes work, "BAME representation … stood at 11.8% [in 2020], down from 12.3% in 2019."[3] Suffice to say, these findings are disappointing and much work remains to be done, so that the creative industries better reflects the public, tells diverse stories, and challenges systemic bias that undermines diverse representation.

Care ethics offers an expansive framework to do this continued work of recognizing structural barriers and systemic bias while recommitting to new visions. Alongside care ethics, an expansive definition of the creative industries, that also highlights the relationships between social, cultural, and economic values, can enable more diversity. With this expansion, scholarship in the creative industries should also aim for specificity, recognizing specific contexts, possibly through disaggregating the creative industries into different disciplines or different categories of workers, participants, and other stakeholders for investigation and analysis. Here, I conclude this book with a profile of a Toronto-based collective called Tea Base that centres artistic expression from the Asian diaspora. I return to the typology of care thinking from Chapter 2 of relationality, recognizing structural barriers, and transformative visions. I also return to the importance of physical space, discussed in Chapter 7, and investigate how space can enable these forms of care, and how these forms of care materialize through access to space. I suggest the type of work being done by collectives like Tea Base is a vision for more caring and collaborative creative industries. I offer this snapshot of a more collaborative future for the creative industries, one that I want to inhabit, as a fan, a teacher, and a researcher.

Tea Base: Relationships, Joy, and Collaboration

Reimagining, Relationally: "Giving Each Other More Resources"

Tea Base is a community arts space housed in the Chinatown Centre shopping mall in downtown Toronto. Specifically, Tea Base is located in the Chinatown Centre basement in the former Kem Xuân Hương Ice Cream shop, which was run by a Vietnamese couple for almost 20 years, until 2013. The Tea Base website notes "this shop started out as a gathering place of sorts and we are *honoured* to inherit and continue its legacy" (emphasis in original).[4] In 2018, the Toronto Art Book Fair was held in Chinatown Centre, and the Angry Asian Feminist Gang, a Toronto collective founded by Amy Wong, did a pop-up event at Kem Xuân Hương Ice Cream for the book fair, drawing attention and interest to the space. Tea Base co-founders Hannia Cheng, John Smith, and Michael Vu signed a lease with this shop later in 2018, and launched with the "Support Your Local Tea Base" music festival in October 2018 with artists, vendors, karaoke, arts and crafts, and a street-dance battle, amongst other activities. Tea Base formally opened in January 2019 after renovating the space. The Tea Base team has expanded beyond its co-founders to include co-creative director Christie Carriere, co-director Florence Yee, and technical director Jay Phillips, amongst others. Tea Base operates as a gallery, workshop space, and a hang-out spot that, true to its name, also started out serving tea. Tea Base's website describes the space as "sort of a tea shop, sort of an office, sort of a garden club, sort of a venue, sort of a Mahjong hall, sort of a library, but we're mostly a living room."[5] Co-founder Hannia Cheng comments on the possibilities that emerge from this relaxed and supportive environment, "I'm just really interested in community building and art as a place for people to hang out and share stories and be tender."[6]

Hannia underscores that space is needed for relationships and collaboration to emerge, noting that "access to space is just so rare in this city and it's so hard, and public space isn't even free. Public space doesn't really exist, and it's not really for the public. So I think the biggest piece for me is having a physical space that people can gather around without having to consume or buy things."[7] Though shopping malls are private, not public space they can sometimes operate as indoor gathering space. As Hannia notes, physical space is difficult to come by in Toronto due to high costs of commercial rents, and often rapid cycles of real estate speculation and subsequent displacement. Interestingly, for Tea Base, accessing commercial space in a mall offers some small relief from these broader capitalistic pressures, as Tea Base offers a space to gather where the public does not have to purchase anything. Hannia outlines:

> Back in the mall's heyday, aka 90s till early 2000s, it was a very bumping place! However, since a majority of the city's Chinese population has moved to the suburbs, the mall has since become semi recluse and quiet these days. It's missing a lot of the qualities of what we normally conceptualize as a mall. Chinatown Centre was built as a condominium mall (modelled off the Hong Kong style) and operates as such but with its current context of many abandoned/empty units in a mall that's smack-dab in the middle of the downtown core, it opens up a new opportunity to reimagine what a 'mall' can be outside of a capitalist structure. Instead of a mall that's transaction and consumer based what about a mall that's service and community-based? There's so much space in that mall that's being under-used, part of the bigger vision is to have influence on who moves into the mall and help brand the mall as a place where people can gather not just to buy things but also for the Chinatown community to participate and engage with itself.[8]

This reimagining of how space might be used also extends to the collective's vision for community arts. Tea Base is an art space, but co-director Florence Yee notes that Tea Base has "a different audience than usually comes to galleries. We're very far away from a gallery; we have no white wall space." Florence describes Tea Base as "kind of a living room, kind of a tea shop, kind of an open art show."[9] This difference in physical space also enables a different ethos and form of exchange. More than just an art space for exhibition, Florence notes that Tea Base is a platform for community mentorship, where members and participants are "giving each other more resources," not just showing work. In their study of creative entrepreneurship, Alia Weston, Alexandra Hong, Karli Ferriolo, and Jacqueline Shaw highlight the context of access to space in Chinatown: "as Chinatowns across North America are threatened by gentrification leading to displacement and unaffordability, Tea Base's presence within Toronto's Chinatown takes up space—which may otherwise go unused. It maintains a physical presence and representation of cross-generational efforts to maintain Pan-Asian diasporic cultures." In this analysis, accessing and providing space enables Tea Base to act as a "grassroots artist run incubator for community activism."[10]

On its website, Tea Base's mandate states that "we aim to make accessible space for intergenerational activists and artists who support social justice movements in and around Chinatown. Tea Base is a space that develops solidarity across marginalized groups through relationships, joy, and collaboration," highlighting the pleasure and fun of care.[11] Many of Tea Base's activities happen through working relationally with friends, family, local community members, cultural heritage, and an embeddedness within the Chinatown neighbourhood. Hannia describes past and present relationships with other shop owners in the mall, also noting, "My mom used to work in the mall and I grew up in that mall. Some of the shopkeepers recognize me, they're like, 'I remember you.'" Some of Tea Base's emphasis is on Chinese culture and language; their most popular event was "Mahjong Mondays," a weekly gathering to play the traditional Chinese tile-based game. Tea Base also holds mother-tongue "language cafés" in Cantonese, Mandarin, and Vietnamese to practice language skills. Florence comments that a lot of second-generation speakers do not hear their mother-tongues being spoken, but at the same time, "a lot of my peers value what we learn from our family, our grandparents, especially language." Hannia also speaks to family connection in Tea Base programming, highlighting soup-making and macramé workshops with her mom as some of the favourite events she has done.

Structural Barriers and Challenges

Tea Base is a volunteer-run organization, funded through membership drives that financially support operational costs like rent. While Tea Base has applied for and receives some programming funding for its activities, all staff work as volunteers. Additionally, as a collective Tea Base works with a non-hierarchical, flat structure, which Hannia characterizes as a "double edged sword." This can be a more inclusive and equalizing organizational structure and while "you don't have a boss, you're also not an employee," meaning that "the boundaries [around the work and the roles] are complicated, it's kind of messy."

This flat structure and community engagement at the core of Tea Base's values opens up possibilities. Co-director Chris Carriere comments on an openness to community collaboration and programming. She says, "people would use Tea Base as a platform" in that "other collectives, groups, or individuals would come to us with an idea. And if we thought it went along with our programming, we would co-construct it, and showed it, or made it happen in the space somehow. That way it is not all about us and all the things we come up with. The community is involved not just by participating or attending events, but by creating them and collaborating on them."[12] With this approach, in its first year of existence in 2019, Tea Base put on 157 events, both with its own programming and others renting the Tea Base space. COVID-19 interrupted Tea Base's programming in 2020, but Tea Base still put on more than 80 events in that year, many of them virtual. Commenting on the unpaid labour needed to mount this high volume of events, whether internal or external, Hannia says, this labour is "for the people, for each other." And yet this scope of labour can also lead to burnout; Tea Base organizers comment that in some ways, the 2020 COVID-19 lockdowns brought a needed break and rest from this heavy activity.

Florence notes challenges of access to knowledge and learning from similar organizations and past work in similar communities. In our October 2020 interview, Florence noted recently having learnt about a similar organization, Asian Arts Freedom School, that existed 15 years prior, commenting, "It seems like we have the exact same mandate and the exact same hopes. I think there's a lot to be uncovered and we don't want to keep remaking the wheel." In light of this lost knowledge, Florence underscored the importance of the "intergenerational" element of Tea Base's mandate and fostering connections with parents, Elders, and older generations.[13]

Despite the energy and time of the Tea Base organizers and the relatively affordable space they were able to access through renting a mall unit, Tea Base also faces challenges around access to space. At the end of October 2020, Tea Base closed in the Kem Xuân Hương Ice Cream mall unit after being evicted by their landlord to renovate and open a high-end seafood stall (Hannia jokes that the new incarnation of the space could be called "Sea Base"). Due to lack of protections and regulations in commercial and residential real estate markets, these problems of "renovictions" are quite common in Toronto. Because of the restrictions on physically gathering due to COVID-19 in 2020, Tea Base planned to transition to virtual programming and find a new physical space in the same mall, the Chinatown Centre in Spring 2021, noting on the Tea Base Instagram that "saying goodbye to our first physical space has been such a lovely and sad experience."[14] Still, Tea Base organizers remained optimistic and committed to the organization's continued existence, developing plans to incorporate as a not-for-profit co-operative in their October 2020 Town Hall meeting, alongside announcing the closure of their physical space.

Beyond organizing events and activities in their own physical space, Tea Base also participates in broader counter-gentrification and anti-displacement movements through the Friends of Chinatown (FOCT) initiative. This community organizing group's focus is to keep Toronto's Chinatown affordable and inclusive. One focus in 2020 was on a redevelopment project, located at 315–325 Spadina, planned to be redeveloped into a 13-storey rental building, without community consultation or translation of information about the proposed redevelopment in Chinese. FOCT advocated for meaningful consultation with Chinatown community members, alongside pushing for affordable housing to be built. As an alternative to externally imposed redevelopment, FOCT began researching community-controlled land through community-land trust models, learning about past success with this not-for-profit land stewardship model from work in this area in Toronto by the Parkdale Land Trust and Friends of Kensington Land Trust.

New Visions: "Art + Action"

Tea Base's advocacy work and commitment to equity is also infused its programming. Hannia recognizes the role of art organizations in "inherently gentrifying the space[s]" they occupy, and says that Tea Base is "very intentional about fostering community relationships." To this end, Hannia says, "we want to create a mutual ecosystem where our presence actually benefits the neighbourhood and the people who live in it." Reflecting on some of the most memorable events that Tea Base has programmed, Florence highlights "Butterfly Hands," an art exhibit and activist mobilization to support sex workers in May 2019 (Figure 8.2). This event was developed in response to a City of Toronto proposal to increase licensing fees for massage parlours and holistic centres, "which are known to be also places where sex workers work."[15] The "Butterfly Hands" Facebook event description provided the context that "Tea Base and all the artists involved stand on a united front to raise the voices of massage parlour workers and all sex workers to help protect their right to safety and right to work. The voices of these workers knows what is best to ensure their access to safe and dignified working conditions. The current proposal largely misrepresents migrant workers as trafficked victims despite hundreds of workers having expressed they are neither trafficked victims nor traffickers. This job provides financial stability and supports the families of these workers."[16]

Billed as an "art show + action," this exhibit was co-curated by Tea Base and Butterfly: Asian and Migrant Sex Workers Support Network, and featured the work of four photographers, Mary Chen, Kelly Lui, Lily Yunru Lü, and May Truong, who took photographs of massage parlour workers and their hands. This

FIGURE 8.2 "Butterfly Hands" Event Flyer from Tea Base Collective. © Tea Base collective, graphic design by Ananda Gabo

exhibit also featured visual art and stop motion videos made by the workers themselves. Guests were asked to trace, cut out, and decorate drawings of their own hands to add to the installation in support and solidarity of all the workers. Florence highlights the beauty of the installation, with mall infrastructure amplifying nice spring weather and lighting during the May exhibit, "it was really sunny and there is a great skylight in the mall that illuminates everything." The opening exhibit was the first part of a series of actions, followed by a rally to attend the City meetings discussing proposed bylaw changes, which resulted in the City not moving forward with the proposal.

This intersection of art and community-engaged action was also present when Tea Base was invited to program an event for the "All Hours" showcase at the Art Gallery of Ontario (AGO), a monthly late-night art/music party event at the gallery. Florence notes that this "All Hours" event is billed to be welcoming and all-ages, but still has admission fees, and the institution itself still can have a certain

FIGURE 8.3 "AGO Is in Chinatown, Chinatown Is on Stolen Land" Banner from Tea Base Collective. © Tea Base collective. Photo by Charisse Fung. Banner by Florence Yee

"glow of elitism." The date that Tea Base was invited to participate fell on Lunar New Year, and was also at the height of conflict on Wet'suwet'en land about pipeline expansion in Northern British Columbia and Alberta in Canada in 2020. In response, Tea Base installed programming from their own space in the AGO, creating a Mahjong hall within the AGO, accompanied by a 20-foot banner that read "the AGO is in Chinatown. Chinatown is on stolen land," while also raising funds for the Wet'suwet'en legal defense fund (Figure 8.3). The "glow" that the AGO has as an art institution in the art world that Florence references may not typically be based in its geographic situatedness, and Tea Base sought to intervene in this dynamic in its installation, encouraging a different and more embedded relationship between neighbourhood residents and the AGO. Tea Base asked the AGO to print complimentary tickets, and with what Florence terms "radical outreach," delivered these tickets through a list of Chinatown family associations, which are "an informal way of giving mutual aid in many Chinese and East Asian cultures, based on your family name, but nowadays whoever lives nearby or in the building."[17] Florence and Hannia knocked on doors, explaining in Cantonese that they were giving out free tickets to a Lunar New Year event with free food and free Mahjong, which resulted in some seniors coming to the AGO for the first time, though they may have lived in the neighbourhood for their whole lives. Reflecting on this event and this community mobilization, Florence says, "that to me is the spirit of Tea Base."

Notes

1 Alma Har'el, Twitter post, February 3, 2021, https://twitter.com/Almaharel/status/1357097371704823809

2 Michaela Coel, Twitter post, January 28, 2021, https://twitter.com/MichaelaCoel/status/1354803151010816002?s=20

3 Jake Kanter, "Damning New Report Reveals that BAME Representation Went Backwards in British TV Last Year," *Deadline*, January 28, 2021, accessed March 19, 2021, https://deadline.com/2021/01/cdn-bame-representation-backwards-tv-1234682277/
4 Tea Base, "Origin Story," *Tea Base*, n.d., accessed November 24, 2020, https://www.myteabase.com/story
5 Tea Base, "About," *Tea Base*, n.d., accessed November 24, 2020, https://www.myteabase.com/aboutteabase
6 Hannia Cheng, personal interview, October 9, 2020.
7 Ibid.
8 Hannia Cheng, email correspondence, January 31, 2021.
9 Florence Yee, personal interview, October 9, 2020.
10 Alia Weston, Alexandra Hong, Karli Ferriolo, and Jacqueline Shaw, *Critical Perspectives on Creative Women's Entrepreneurship* (Toronto: OCAD University, Centre for Emerging Artists and Designers, 2020), 31–32, 30.
11 Tea Base, "Home," *Tea Base*, n.d., accessed November 24, 2020, https://www.myteabase.com/
12 Chris Carriere, personal interview, October 9, 2020.
13 Florence Yee, personal interview, October 9, 2020.
14 Tea Base, "Saying Goodbye to Our First Physical Space," *Instagram*, November 2, 2020, accessed April 9, 2021, https://www.instagram.com/p/CHGZRy8gl1M/?utm_source=ig_web_copy_link
15 Florence Yee, personal interview, October 9, 2020.
16 Tea Base, "Butterfly Hands— Art Show +Action Event," *Facebook*, May 11, 2019, accessed April 4, 2021, https://www.facebook.com/events/tea-base/butterfly-hands-art-show-action/1875796375854725/Accessed 26
17 Florence Yee, personal interview, October 9, 2020.

INDEX

187 Augusta, Toronto 178
224 Wallace, Toronto 35–37
2SLGBTQIA+ artists 83, 143, 182
  barriers for 11, 60, 156, 178–79
  spaces for 60, 43, 77–78, 123, 128
  underrepresentation of 6, 66, 75, 85; *see also* gender
4chan trolling 179–80
abuse, workplace 5, 85, 181
  conflict versus 4–5
  normalization of 5, 6, 50, 71, 111
  underreaction to 5, 73, 77; *see also* harm
Academy Awards 7, 75
access, creative industries 51, 61–62, 96, 131, 143–44, 163
  to advancement 30, 56, 129, 137, 142
  barriers to 40, 49–52, 130–32, 142, 151–52, 190
  to resources 14, 99–100, 107, 177, 186–87, 196–200
  scaffolded support 121, 129–31, 139–42, 180
  widening 57–58, 80–81, 105–6, 122–26, 133–35, 149–60
Acme Studios, London, England 186–90
advertising 3, 54
  as creative industry 25
  marginalized communities and 100
African studies 15, 16
Agenda for Change Report (Equity UK) 82–83, 86–89
Ahmed, Sara
  diversity discourse 68–69, 76–77, 79
  politics of reattachment 89, 98
Akhavan, Abbas 108–9
Alberta's Future Leaders (AFL) Program 128
Almena, Derick 175, 179
Annenberg Inclusion Initiative 66, 75, 80–81
anti-oppressive practice (AOP) 130–32, 142, 156
antiques 25–26
apocalypse, narratives of 15
architecture
  community architects; *see* community
  as creative industry 25
  otherwise 15; *see also* otherwise movement
Arendt, Hannah 183–84
art 17, 54, 83, 101, 103, 156
  community programs; *see* community arts programs
  critics 58, 98
  design appropriation; *see* cultural appropriation
  institutions; *see* institutions, creative industries
  justice 17, 70, 98, 127; *see also* creative justice, social justice model
  politics of 33–34, 39, 70, 95, 101, 108, 185
  practices 33, 37–38, 62, 106–7, 110, 122–30, 174–77
  status quo and 17, 67, 77, 108
  visibility of 33–34, 39, 59–61, 95, 100–1, 168, 195
  world of 83, 106, 108, 122, 175, 187, 202
Art Gallery of Ontario (AGO) 201–2
artists 3, 12
  autonomy; *see* autonomy
  barriers for; *see* barriers to cultural participation
  Black 8, 38, 52–53, 101, 107, 124

of colour 6, 57–59, 66, 70, 98, 101–2, 107, 178
deaths of 1, 173, 178–80
demographics of 2, 11, 56–57, 71–72, 174
emerging 11, 53, 60, 105, 134–36, 140–44, 175–80
evictions of 35–36, 176, 179–80, 190
gender-diverse 83–85, 88, 106
gentrification and 35–36, 175–80, 189, 198–200
hip hop; *see* hip hop
Indigenous 15, 29, 37–38, 52–53, 94–95, 107, 123
queer; *see* 2SLGBTQIA+ artists
racialized 38, 52–53, 107, 110, 123–24, 178
representations of; *see* representation
resources; *see* resources, cultural
spaces for 53, 106–13, 137, 174, 178–80, 196–98; *see also* spaces for cultural production
young; *see* creatives, young; youth
ArtReach 123–24, 133–35, 140–41
"Art Work," 35–36
AT&T Diversity & Inclusion Annual Report 76–77, 80–81
Australia 25, 28–29, 37, 82, 125–26
autokeny 152
autonomy
artistic 51–54, 56, 70–71
creative 51–52, 55, 62, 152
economic imperatives versus 52–55
funding versus 70–71
relational 44, 51–54, 105
workplace 48, 51, 57, 62
Avengers, The 103

Baker, Sarah 48, 51
Ball, Mark 3, 122
Balmas, Maciek 37–38
BAME (Black, Asian, and Minority Ethnic) representation 195–96
Banks, Mark (*Creative Justice*) 13–14, 30–31, 68–70
barriers to cultural participation 29–30, 97, 177
addressing 11, 14, 51, 62, 151–52, 165–66, 196–200
incubator model and 130, 136–37, 142
structural 40, 49–52, 57–58, 80, 99, 132–33
Barry, Ben 39–40
Bassel, Leah 48–49
Belfiore, Elenora 18, 97
Belle, Viktoria 110–16
Bikini Kill 152
BIPOC (Black, Indigenous and people of colour)
artists 6, 57–59, 66, 70, 98, 101–2, 107, 178
underrepresentation 111
blackfishing 8
Black Light 101
Black Lives Matter movement 7, 16, 101–2, 196
Blackness
anti- 7–8, 102
commodification of 8, 79, 101–2
postmodern 98
Black people 6, 74, 77
artists 8, 38, 52–53, 101, 107, 124
cultural appropriation; *see* cultural appropriation
imagining futures and 16–17
intellectual thought 19, 95–96, 105, 185
invisibility of 40, 102
prioritizing 52, 101
queer 60, 111, 124
racism against 7–8, 12, 16–17, 101–2
underrepresentation 16–17, 27, 52, 57–58, 101–2, 194–96
women 52, 60, 97, 101
writing about 7, 101
books; *see* publishing
Bourcheix-Laporte, Mariane 29
Bowen, Deanna 108–9
brave space (Arao and Clemens) 181, 183
British Council Creative Economy Unit 25
brown, adrienne maree 11–12, 17, 49, 123
"brown girls to the front," 94–95
Burke, Tarana 6
burnout, activist 77, 110, 116, 143, 199
Burnt Ramen 179
"Butterfly Hands" exhibit 200–1

Cammarota, Julio 127–28
Campbell, Mark V. 8
Canada
arts industry 12, 34, 101, 121–22, 190, 194
caremongering phenomenon 43
creative industries 28, 36, 101–2, 111, 148, 151
cultural and economic development 29, 36, 168

capitalism 15, 26, 57
care work versus 44, 46, 48, 197
conditions underpinning 39, 44, 168
economic versus social reproduction 46, 59, 108–10, 153, 185
racial 108–10
rethinking 18, 33, 61
care (work) 50, 180
barriers in 49, 61, 110
capitalism and 46, 110, 116
community and; *see* communities of care
definitions 44–45, 48–50
disability justice 48–49, 98–99
etymology of 49–50
inclusion action plans and 89–90
phases of 45–46, 186, 196
teaching and 104–5, 107–8, 116
valuation of 34, 45–49, 53–54, 104–5, 143
webs 47–49, 55, 62, 95, 114, 141, 180; *see also* social reproduction
care deficit 43–44, 90
career development 88, 106, 110, 174
challenges with 5, 11, 57, 68
incubator model and 121, 124, 129–31, 135–44
care ethic, feminist 10, 13, 186
creative industries and 4, 48–52, 57, 62, 95, 132, 149–51, 196
feminist scholarship and 38, 44, 196
relational ontology and; *see* relational ontology
self, notions of 44–45, 61, 104–5, 143, 165
social reproduction and; *see* social reproduction
trouble, staying with the 39
Caremongering–TO Facebook group 43
care thinking 177–78
notion of 49, 57, 59, 62
racialized people and 48, 98
Care Work (Lakshmi Piepzna–Samarasinha) 46, 48–49, 99
CBC
Jian Ghomeshi; *see* Ghomeshi, Jian
news reports 34–35, 101, 178, 180
Centering Marginalized Communities: A Framework for Intersectional Money in Politics Events (Gomez and Boldt) 100
centring difference 48, 50, 183
dialectic of 61, 96–99, 111
representations 96–97, 101–2
valuation and 94–97, 100, 116; *see also* marginalization, marginalized perspectives
Cheng, Hannia 197–200, 202
chief diversity officer (CDO) positions 74–75
Chinatown, Toronto 107, 196–200, 202
Chippendale, Brian 178
civic salvagers 177
class 73
analysis 67, 96, 100, 131, 150
creative; *see* creative class
privilege and 44, 55–58, 181
working; *see* working class
Clear Expectations: Guidelines for Institutions, Galleries and Curators Working with Trans, Non-Binary and Gender Diverse Artists in Australia (National Association for the Visual Arts) 82–85, 88
climate crisis 16, 18, 44
Coel, Michaela (*I May Destroy You*) 195–96
Cohen, Nicole 47
cohesion, social 10, 24–28, 35, 38, 121, 126, 154
collective action 164, 176, 183
creative industries and 10–13, 16, 46–47, 56
healing and 6, 15, 43, 182–83
neoliberalism versus 47, 49, 51–52, 61
pedagogy and 104, 106, 128
social imaginary 17, 32, 45, 52–54, 154
social justice 127–32
support structures 43, 46–49, 107
collectives 4, 16, 44, 62, 105–16, 123
Precarias a la Deriva 47
Tea Base; *see* Tea Base
College Street Bar, sexual assault 111
colonization 17, 128–29
care work versus 48–49
knowledge extraction and 34, 38, 44, 48, 80
legacy of 29, 39, 44, 82–83, 88, 132; *see also* decolonization
communities of care 13–14
COVID–19 and 43, 49
definitions 47–48, 57
developing 151, 168, 180, 186
importance of 45–46, 59–62, 115
organizing work and 46–49, 53, 98–100, 114–16
status of care work 47, 58–62, 114
communities of practice (CoP) 19–20, 106, 149–50, 156–58

alternative 151–54, 163–68
collaborative 154–55
joint enterprise 149–50, 154, 156–57, 163–68
mutual engagement 133, 149–50, 153, 164–68
shared repertoire 149–50, 154, 158, 161–63, 168
community 15, 53, 99, 114–16, 131, 176
architects 177
art 19, 30, 35–36, 59–61, 105–7, 178; *see also* community arts programs
of care; *see* communities of care
economic needs versus 58–62, 108–10, 122–23, 129–31, 187
engagement 137, 178, 194, 199–201
knowledge 34, 37–39, 58, 99
organizing 15, 46–49, 59–62, 98–100, 151–60, 200
recognition 30, 34, 52, 59, 78–80, 99, 108–10
responses to violence 6, 180–82
space 183–87, 190, 196–200
wellbeing 9–10, 17, 43, 52, 109–10, 126–27, 143, 183
youth and 10, 29, 51–52, 126–30, 137–38
community arts programs 174
affirmation 134–41
benefits 122–24, 127, 129–30, 134–40
best practices 124–25, 131–35, 139
challenges facing 142–44, 163–66
definition 122
mentorship; *see* mentorship
models of 125–31, 163–68
open exploration 139–40, 142
scaffolded support 121, 129–31, 139–42, 180
study of 120–21, 124, 126–44
community-based organizations (CBOs) 131
"Community Youth Arts Programs as Creative Industries Incubators" research project 9, 121, 137
companies, creative industry 25, 36, 176
abuse at 5, 62, 71–73, 77, 85, 173
"diversity" in 19, 62, 67–68, 73–81
power relations in 30, 33, 78–81
toxic environments 8, 62, 85–86, 114
competition 32, 99, 133, 141
collaboration versus 51, 54, 58–59, 95, 106, 123
for work 30, 47, 50, 152, 156
Composite Diversity Index (CDI) 71–72
concentric rings model 31–32, 39
Conflict is not Abuse: Overstating Harm, Community Responsibility, and the Duty of Repair (Schulman) 4–5
conflict prevention 4, 131–33, 135
consent 6, 114
cultural appropriation and 88–89
co-operatives, worker 47, 174, 200
corporations 28, 100, 190
diversity reports and programs 66–67, 73–74, 76–81
gentrification and 35–36; *see also* companies, creative industry
COVID-19 12, 16, 113
community mobilization 43, 49, 199
crafts 25, 197
cultural production 18, 149, 152
workers 54–55, 58–59
Crawhall, Nigel 34
Crawley, Ashon 15
Creative Canada Policy Framework 29
creative cities 34
celebration of 1–3
costs of 3, 35
policy, local 24, 28, 174
creative class 71–73
Creative Communities in Collaboration (CCC) 194–95
creative ecology framework 186
care ethics in 39, 44, 190
rearticulating value within 14, 51–52, 187
research methodology and 38, 46, 176
creative economy 10, 14
as economic driver 25, 29–30, 36
model 32, 35, 174
creative industries
celebration of 1–3, 10, 12, 27, 30–31, 71, 102, 162
contradictions in 10, 50, 61, 96, 174, 178, 182
costs of 3–4, 107, 110, 176, 198
cultural versus 10, 31
curation 50, 57–58, 82–85, 105, 110, 200
definitions of 10–11, 32
disciplines 25–26, 34
as a discourse 24, 30–32
as ecosystem; *see* creative ecology framework
entity of 24, 31–33

ERIBA model 32
four models of 31–32
mapping 25–29, 33–34; *see also* cultural mapping
national identity 26–27, 35
policies; *see* policy, creative industries
power and; *see* power
profitability of 8, 14, 26–28, 53–55, 76, 176
creative justice 14, 70
creatives, young 48, 105, 111, 165
autonomy of 51, 152; *see* autonomy
coping strategies 50–62, 150, 165
public perceptions of 2, 56, 126, 129, 139, 176
support for 36, 103, 122–30; *see also* youth
creativity 38, 50, 99, 149, 152, 194
discourse 28, 30, 32, 69, 101, 156
as economic input 28, 32, 59
incubating 121, 125, 129–31
crisis 71
capitalism and 44, 46, 55, 176
climate; *see* climate crisis
possibilities within 15–16, 180
critical civic practice 127–28
critical creative industries scholarship 30–33, 69–71, 98–101, 107–8, 190
critical discourse analysis (CDA) 24, 28–30, 76
critical diversity
discourse 67–70, 76
framework 69–71, 89–90
critical pedagogy 96
humanization 104
margins and 103–5
relational social practices and 103
CRITpaper 54
cultural appropriation 132, 167
Black culture and 8, 38, 52
design work 37, 82–83, 88–90
Indigenous culture 52, 82–83, 88–90
Urban Outfitters 37–38
cultural mapping 17–18
as alternative discourse 33–34, 39
community mapping versus 38–39
definition 34
ethics of 38–39
geo-referenced 34–35
methodology 24, 34–35, 37–38, 51, 194
policy 25, 29, 33
storytelling 34–35, 38
tensions of scale 35–36
visibility, politics of 34
Cultural Mapping as Cultural Inquiry (Duxbury, Garrett-Petts, MacLennan) 34
cultural participation
barriers to; *see* barriers to cultural participation
cultural production and 4, 14, 95, 106
non-economic value of 29, 54–55, 57–58
parity of 70
cultural production 29, 36, 103–4, 186
access to; *see* access, creative industries
characteristics of 26–27, 31, 48, 50, 59, 178
collaborative 149–52, 156, 163–69, 190
craft-based; *see* crafts
emerging; *see* emerging cultural production
everyday versus high 3, 96; *see also* everyday culture
small-scale; *see* small-scale cultural production
social justice work and 120, 149–52, 190, 195
spaces for; *see* spaces for cultural production
underrepresented forms of 12–13, 17–18, 26–27, 37, 95–102, 195
youth 10–12, 46–47, 52–56, 105
cultural studies 3, 96, 167
as "ordinary,"; *see* everyday culture
Cunningham, Malaika 3, 122
Cunningham, Stuart 25, 29, 31–32
Curl Project 8

"Damned If You Do: Conversation on the Politics of Refusal," 108–10
Dandelion Initiative 105
origins of 110–11
pedagogy 114–16
policy development 111, 113
programming 113, 116
training 111–13, 116
decolonization 15, 70, 123, 129
democracy 44
collective care and 46–47
cultural work and 14, 88
deficit of 14, 44, 100
Department of Culture, Media and Sport (DCMS), U.K. 28

Creative Industries Mapping Documents 25–26
de Peuter, Greig 47
design
as creative industry 11, 25, 31, 54
cultural appropriation 37, 40, 82–83, 88
design justice 98–99
Design Justice: Community-Led Practices to Build the Worlds We Need (Costanza-Chock) 98
disability justice work 19, 43, 48–49, 150, 180
deficit model versus 96, 98–100
disabled people 58, 75, 78
barriers for 6, 11, 131
invisibility of 40, 66–67
justice scholarship; *see* disability justice work
leadership 17, 43; *see also* design justice
disaster, pedagogy of 15–16
discourse 2–4
of centring; *see* centring difference
creative industries 28, 51
discursive focuses 24, 27, 182
diversity; *see* diversity discourses; *see also* critical discourse analysis (CDA)
discrimination 73, 158
culture of 7–8, 17, 60, 62, 77, 183
gender 58, 151, 156
racial 58–59, 156
systemic 59, 69, 71–73, 80, 151, 190, 195
diversity 1, 12, 142
affirmative action 68, 72
benchmarks 57, 75, 78, 106
business case for 14, 74, 99
as buzzword 72–73, 99
celebration of 67–72, 76, 78–81, 88–89
as demographic difference 66–68, 72
discourse of; *see* diversity discourses
fostering 60, 67–68, 80–81, 180, 196
inclusion rider 75–76
inclusion versus 6, 16, 73–81, 95, 122, 139; *see also* inclusion action plans
integration and learning perspective 99–100
lack of 6–10, 57–59, 70, 80, 144, 151, 174
power, critiques of 76, 83
reports; *see* diversity reports
"tolerance,"; *see* Composite Diversity Index (CDI)
women, just add 73–75
diversity discourses 12
acronymization 77
challenges with 6, 39, 68–72, 194–96
critical diversity versus; *see* critical diversity
descriptive and normative 12, 62, 68–71
proliferation of 68–69, 76–78
systemic inequalities versus 12, 27, 69, 73, 77–83, 90
diversity reports 66, 88
common elements of 71, 74, 76–79, 82
company branding 74, 76–77
products and programs 79–82
profit motive 76
"top six," 76–82
DIY (do-it-yourself) spaces 3–4, 174, 184, 186
music 54, 152
safety and 177–81; *see also* Thirdspaces
DIY Venue Harm Reduction (S. Surface) 180–81
Dovercourt, Jonny (*Any Night of the Week: A D.I.Y. History of Toronto Music 1957–2001*) 174, 177
Dunbar-Hester, Christina 73, 76, 79, 88, 180
Duxbury, Nancy 27, 34
dynamic triangle (Acme Studios) 188–89

Eastmond, Kiana "Rookz,"; *see* Rookz
economic factors
advancement 122–23, 129–32, 136
community needs versus 44, 58–60, 108–10
cultural industries 25, 31–32, 53–58
cultural production 8–9, 83, 108–10
resources, access to; *see* resources, cultural
social change and 70–71
economic growth 10, 187
cultural mapping and 25, 32–33, 36, 72, 174
decoupling from 9, 14, 47, 61–62, 70, 136, 178
imperative 4, 9–11, 13, 53–55, 176
indicators, cultural industries 25–28, 32–34, 176
social reproduction and 46–51
economic value, cultural industries 194–96
community versus 9, 32–34, 48–52
mapping metrics 25, 29, 33, 106, 136

model emphasis on 29–34, 53, 97
social realm versus 17, 33, 37–38, 61–62, 190
Edmondson, Amy 68
education 32, 47, 80, 199
critique of 57, 61, 107, 139, 156, 182
domination versus freedom 100, 104–5
informal 50, 52, 56–57, 102–4, 116, 125–32, 139
post-secondary 1, 4–5, 40, 55–56
role of 88–89, 104, 113
self- 56, 111
youth 56, 125–28
Elba, Idris 27
emergence 11–12, 33, 51, 54, 184
emerging cultural production 8, 10, 14, 59
importance of 2, 16, 39
skills for 11, 15, 152
employment, creative industries 56, 151
abusive; *see* abuse, workplace
diversity in 67, 70, 75–80, 99
growth of 10, 55, 188
indicators 25–26, 32–33
fair pay 3, 58, 70, 79, 81, 144
quality of 32–33, 50–51, 112–13, 199
rhetoric versus working conditions 51, 55, 75–81, 168
self-; *see* self-employment
un-; *see* unemployment
youth 124–31, 134–37, 142–44; *see also* companies, creative industry, jobs, creative industries
enslavement 40, 44
entrepreneurship 36, 55, 198
norm of 11, 31, 44–45, 52, 75
skills 11, 44, 58–60, 99
supporting 121–22, 129–31, 137
equity 98, 114, 194–95
emphasis on 7, 12–16, 57–58, 81, 102, 200
employment 39, 67–70, 73–74, 135, 151
groups deserving 6, 27, 50, 154
lack of; *see* inequality
Equity UK; *see Agenda for Change Report* (Equity UK)
everyday culture
ideology and 4, 96
perceptions of 3–4
Every Day We're Hustling (blog/ podcast) 2
exploitation, creative industries 39, 175
labour 44, 68, 77, 99, 185
self- 48, 56, 68; *see also* creatives, young, internships, unpaid, labour, creative industries, workplaces, youth
exports, economic value of 25–26, 28–39
extractivism, cultural 38–39, 97, 173

Fairclough, Norman 24
fashion 173
as creative industry 8, 11, 25, 31, 56
education 39–40
notions of 27, 40
visibility in 39–40, 59
feminism 44, 79, 95–96, 162, 164, 167
liberal 8, 73
work of 6, 47, 49, 73, 123, 152–56, 196; *see also* care ethic, feminist
Feminist Theory: From Margin to Center (hooks) 97
Feminism for the 99% (Arruzza, Bhattacharya, Fraser) 73
filmmaking 112
4% challenge 66–67, 76, 81
community 55, 122, 128, 179
as creative industry 5–6, 11, 25, 29, 31
diversity discourse and 30, 70, 75, 79–80
representation, need for 27, 30, 66–67, 70
women directors of colour 66–67; *see also* Annenberg Inclusion Initiative
Fisher, Bernice 44–45, 49–50, 57–58, 95, 186
Flew, Terry 28, 36
Florida, Richard 71–72
Floyd, George 81, 101–2, 196
Ford, Ashley C. 8
Fox News 73–74
Fraser, Nancy 44, 46, 70, 73
Freedom Dreams: The Black Radical Imagination (Kelley) 16–17, 105
Freire, Paulo 16–17, 19, 104
friendship 116, 195
importance of 54, 59–61, 106, 123, 179–80
work and 48, 59–61, 125, 198
full-time work 25, 111, 136
lack of 11, 55
funding 131
challenges finding 54, 122, 188, 198
crowd- 122, 202
government 179–80, 188, 190
micro- 28, 123–24, 137

politics of refusal 108–10
structural conditions on 70–71, 126, 165
youth program 133–43
futures 27, 80, 125, 187
imagining 17, 49, 188, 194

Garber, Jenny 161, 168
GDP contribution, cultural industries 25–26, 29, 36
gender 46, 72, 182
-based violence 105, 110–16, 181
discrimination 8, 50, 58, 83, 96, 131, 154
non-conforming people 62, 82–85, 88, 133, 148–56, 169
norms 39–40, 45, 68, 97, 152
parity 28–30, 66–67, 73, 82, 151; *see also* women
gentrification 35–36, 189, 198–200
artists and 175–76, 180
Gerges, Merray 54
Ghomeshi, Jian 111
Ghost Ship 1–3, 173–80
Gieseler, Carly 6
Ginwright, Shawn 127–28
girls rock camps 151, 153
globalization 28, 33, 79, 173
Global South, labour of 44, 173
"good work," notion of 48, 51, 126
Gross, Jonathan 14

Halifax Pop Explosion (HPX) 94–95
Hall, Stuart 96, 102
Haraway, Donna 12, 39
harm 38, 103
cultural appropriation and 83, 89
overstating 5
reduction 70, 100–2, 126, 133, 180
workplace 5, 17, 51, 62, 68–77; *see also* abuse, workplace
Harris, Max 175, 179
Hesmondhalgh, David 14–15, 48, 51, 103, 152
heteronormativity 100, 156
heteropatriarchy 57
heterotopias (Foucault) 185–86
Higgs, Peter 25, 29
hip hop 8, 59–60, 101
homeplace (hooks) 181, 183
hooks, bell 48
on cultural production 104, 185
on margins and resistance 97–98, 103–4, 110, 183
Yearning: Race, Gender, and Cultural Politics 103, 183
humanization (Freire) 13, 17, 104, 132

immigrants 11–12, 71–72, 95, 180
inclusion action plans
as care work 89–90
defining 82–87, 180
D & I reports versus 82, 88–90
forward movement 82, 87–90, 180
naming 82–83, 180
inclusion, creative industries 18
action plans; *see* inclusion action plans
community arts programs and; *see* community arts programs
diversity versus 6, 16, 73–81, 95, 122, 139
lack of 5–7, 27, 39, 51, 62, 67–70, 142–44
politics of 67–69, 98–100, 105–10, 194–95
rhetoric, corporate reports 34, 74–78
rider 75–76
spaces of 174–81, 185–86, 199–200
striving for 13–16, 44–47, 52–54, 57–60, 103, 154–57
supposed 3, 10, 75–80
incubator model 9, 198
notion of 124–25
PEERS program; *see* PEERS
scaffolded support 121, 129–31, 139–42, 180
SKETCH Working Arts; *see* SKETCH Working Arts
underrepresented groups and 80, 137, 143, 190
youth arts programs 120–25, 130–31, 136, 138
Indigenous peoples 29
AFL Program; *see* Alberta's Future Leaders (AFL) Program
artists 37–38, 88–89, 94–95
dispossession and 15, 38–39, 40, 52–53, 82–83
Effects on Aboriginals from the Great Lakes Environment (EAGLE)
project 38
methodologies 38–39, 48

programming for 123–24, 128–29
residential schools 15, 34–35
resurgence 38–39, 83
underrepresentation 48, 57–58; *see also* decolonization
inequality 3, 12
addressing 7, 10–11, 66, 180
care work and 46, 49, 57–58
diversity discourse versus 12, 27–30, 69, 73, 77–83, 90
gender 8, 50, 58, 83, 94–96, 131, 154
racialized 50, 55, 81, 94, 102, 180
social 14, 29–30, 50, 81, 149–51
systemic 50–52, 70–73, 131–32, 168, 176
informal networks, creative industries 50, 103, 122, 131, 149–51, 154
marginalized people and 62, 116, 137, 141, 202
innovation 30
diversity and 69, 72, 99
pedagogical 11, 48, 121, 124
technological 28, 32, 72
institutions, creative industries 71
care work and 49, 106, 128, 182
challenges with 28, 44, 49, 95, 107–10, 201–2
racism and sexism in 75, 102, 107
re-envisioning 16, 49, 82–86, 103, 126, 174–78
intellectual property 26, 82, 166–68
internships, unpaid 10, 56, 60–61, 135
intersectionality 12–13, 60, 95–96
IT (information technology); *see* software

jobs, creative industries 46, 111
menial 54–55
multiple 10, 58, 106
number of 25, 32–33, 36
support 62, 126, 137; *see also* employment, creative industries, labour, creative industries
Juno Awards, Canadian 151
Just John (Blank Canvas gallery) 178

Kantor, Jodi 5
Kaptownwala, Nafisa 59
Kardinall Offishall 8
Kelley, Robin D. G. 16–17, 105
Kenney, Moira (*Mapping Gay L.A.*) 181–82
Krajewski, Jill 158

labour, creative industries 67
aspirational 56–57, 59–62, 131, 143–44, 174, 200
care; *see* care (work)
community 59–61, 100, 163–65, 187
conditions 3–6, 10, 47–48, 51, 56–57, 70–76, 99, 111, 135
contradictions of 10, 99, 168
precarious 3, 10, 47, 50, 79–80, 108, 113, 173–74
reimagining 10, 14, 51–52, 55–56
unpaid 3, 10, 56, 60–61, 135, 199
youth and 10, 50–60, 128, 135, 174; *see also* jobs, creative industries
Lady Gaga 162–63, 166
Lakshmi Piepzna-Samarasinha, Leah 43, 46, 48–49, 99
land trust models 200
Lave, Jean 149–50
leisure software; *see* software
Levin, Sam
Ley, David 175–76
LGBTQ+ people; *see* 2SLGBTQIA+ artists
liberation 17, 140, 185
critical pedagogy and 104–5
line of flight (Deleuze) 55–56
Littleton, Karen 149, 157
Loveless, Natalie 12
Luckman, Susan 18, 54–55, 58–59

Magnussen, Humboldt 53–54
Mairesse, Ivan 173–74
mapping, creative industries; *see* creative industries
marginalization
creatives' 57–58, 133, 143
cultural production and 11, 16–17, 38–39, 102–4
diversity reports 75, 77
institutional 12, 75, 102, 107, 143
perspectives of; *see* marginalized perspectives
systems of oppression and 43, 95, 98–101, 176
youth 120–33, 142
marginalized perspectives 154–55
cultural production and 38–39, 57, 97, 102–4, 108
spaces for 177–84, 186, 198

value of 16, 48, 97, 98–100
McRobbie, Angela 47, 55–56, 161, 168
media 31, 76, 98
cultural representations and 70, 94–95, 103, 122, 152
danger of 3–4, 56, 175
diversity, need for 27
influence of 6, 14–15, 27, 29, 175
studies 14–15, 30, 55, 156
youth and 56, 105, 120, 127; *see also* social media
mentorship 126, 139, 154, 162, 198
informal 58–59, 61–62, 131
programs 52, 58, 80, 105–6, 128, 131, 141–42
meritocracy paradigm 69, 71–73, 88
#MeToo movement 5–6, 67, 81, 111
metrics, creative industries 37
diversity 71–73, 77–78, 153
economic; *see* economic value, cultural industries
policy 25, 29, 33–34, 106, 168
Miell, Dorothy 149, 157
Milano, Alyssa 6
misrepresentations, symbolic violence of 97, 200
Montreal, Quebec 1–2, 12, 148, 152–55, 163
multiculturalism 12, 68, 79
music 131, 140, 197, 200–2
British industry 26–27
Canadian industry 1–2, 8, 58, 94–95, 101, 154–56, 174
as creative industry 1–2, 11, 25, 31, 54, 75, 163, 177–79
as male dominated 52–53, 62, 94–95, 112, 151–56
riot grrrl movement; *see* riot grrrl movement
as white dominated 52–53, 66, 94–95
youth solidarity in 58, 62, 120, 126, 168–69, 189; *see also* RCFG*, hip hop
mutual aid 15, 43, 133, 202
definition of 48

neoliberalism 16, 188
communities of care versus 47–53, 130–32
creative industries policy and 28–29, 31, 34–36, 95
individualism and 31, 44, 47, 57–58
politics of refusal 108–10, 123
Netflix 74, 76, 81
Noddings, Nel 44–45, 104–5
non-binary people
community care 43, 111, 148–49, 154
representation 82–85, 88, 169
norms, hegemonic 39, 88–89
affirming 51, 69, 95, 99, 103, 152
resisting 44, 98, 101–3, 116, 152, 163, 183–85
Noterman, Elsa 182–83

Oakland, California 1, 3, 173, 176–79
Oakley, Kate 3, 27–28, 122
Oasis 26
O'Connor, Justin 27–28, 30–31
Ontario 36, 105, 107, 201
cultural industries policy 29–30, 35, 113
#OscarsSoWhite 7, 151, 195
otherwise movements 15
Out of the Basement (Campbell) 2

Panton, David 186–89
Parris, Amanda 101–2, 190
participatory action research 10, 38, 128
patriarchy 51, 57, 185
pedagogy
as bridging concept 13–14, 103, 106
centring difference 94–96, 100–1, 105–6, 116
creative industries and 13–17, 34, 82–83
critical; *see* critical pedagogy
cultural repair 106, 114–16, 182
encounters 94–95, 99, 104, 110, 181
informal 102–3, 116, 131
practice 139–42
programming and 120–24, 128, 164–65
public 102–3, 125, 128
Pedagogy of Hope (Freire) 16–17
PEERS
guest speakers 108–10
organizational structure 106–7
purpose of 105–6
performing arts 88–89, 174
as creative industry 11, 25, 31, 152, 177
employment in 33, 106
sexual violence in 82–87, 112
youth programming 152, 156, 161
photography 11, 31, 94, 200
diversity discourse and 59, 75, 79–80
Pimienta, Lido 52–53, 94–95
Plieninger, Tobias 34
police 2, 110, 133

policy, creative industries 12, 43, 46, 113–16
discourse 31–36, 56, 68–71, 78, 85, 190
East Asia 27–28
model of 28, 31–32
national 24–25, 29–30
proliferation of 24–28, 174
small-scale spaces 2, 142–43, 174–76
value, notions of 2, 18, 25–26, 31–33, 99, 174
youth program 144, 149, 153–54, 157–58, 165, 168–69
political economy 14, 70
popular culture 8, 26–27
Blackness in 66, 101–2
hegemonic norms and 30, 56, 66, 95–97, 103
Potts, Jason 31–32
power
care work and 45, 48–49, 165–68, 183
community 16–17, 100, 131–32, 150–53
configurations of 28–30, 40, 70–71, 100, 165, 183–85
creative industries and 50, 95–98
cultural escalator 96–97
discourse on 24, 79, 82–83, 150
diversity reports, critique of 76, 82
gendered 50, 83, 85, 113–16
margins versus centre; *see* centring difference; marginalized perspectives
opacity of 24
reclaiming 67, 102–6, 142–44, 149, 156–57
society and 5–6, 24, 79, 96–98, 127, 131–32
privilege 40, 96–98, 114, 183
class 55, 73
creative industry workers 2, 55–56, 106
provincial governments 113
cultural and economic development 29, 36
publishing
as creative industry 11, 25, 29, 31, 54
whiteness of Canadian 7–8
Puig de la Bellacassa, Maria 39, 45, 49

racialized people (people of colour) 94
barriers for 11, 50, 97
cultural appropriation; *see* cultural appropriation
labour, creative industries 55, 108–10, 143
programming for 123–24
representation of 6–7, 51, 66–70, 80, 97, 196
racism, creative industry 40, 50, 74, 158, 179–81
anti- 68–69, 114
anti-Black 7–8, 16–17, 97–98, 101–4, 183, 195–96
in Canada 94, 102
systemic 16, 46, 52, 57–60, 75–76, 100–2, 185
radio 25, 58, 111, 150, 162
Rana Plaza garment factory 173–74
RCFG* (Rock Camp Montreal) 148
as alternative CoP 149, 151, 154, 168, 169
reification strategies 149, 154, 156–58, 163, 169
validation 135, 155–56, 161–63
Volunteer Handbook policies 154–55, 158–60
widening access 149–60, 169
Recollet, Karyn 15
Refinery 29, 8
reflexivity 106–7, 124, 132
in creative industries 12–13, 16, 47, 68, 100, 121
research methods and 36, 38, 139
relational ontology 44–45
care work in 49, 52
representation 12, 27, 48, 78–79, 111, 169
diversity and; *see* diversity; diversity discourses
media 25, 70, 94–95, 103, 122, 152
mis-; *see* misrepresentations
negative 70, 76, 83, 97
as placeholder 108–10
tokenized 74–75, 82–83, 88, 110
under- 6–8, 13–17, 57–58, 66–67, 82–85, 101–2, 194–96
researchers, social science 33–34, 128–29
participant observation 9, 124, 153
role of 13, 20, 38, 144, 196
resources, cultural 28, 83
access to 43, 47, 58, 95, 99–100, 107, 131–33
community 34–35, 38–39, 43–48, 188
employee groups 76–77, 81, 88
sharing 14, 38, 123–24, 133, 150
values for 14, 74, 180, 196–98

revenues, creative industries 14, 74, 99, 167
 economic impact of 26, 33
 quantification of 25, 29
riot grrrl movement 94, 151
 cultural production 152–53
Rise of the Creative Class (Florida) 71–73
Rookz (Sandbox Studios) 59–60
Rosenfeld, Heather 182–83
rupture, pedagogical 15–16
Ryerson University 1, 4, 9

safe spaces 3
 notions of 157–58, 181–83
 youth programming and 134, 178–80
Saha, Anamik (*Race and the Cultural Industries*) 70–71
Scenescapes: How Qualities of Place Shape Social Life (Silver and Clark) 37
scholarship, creative industries 51, 194–96
 celebratory tone 10, 12, 27, 30–31
 critical; *see* critical creative industries scholarship
 critique of neoliberalism 30–31, 151
School of Creative Industries (Ryerson University) 1, 4–5
self 50, 184
 -employment 11
 -exploitation 48, 56, 68
 learning and the 104–5, 122
 -realization 29, 48, 51, 55–56, 122–23, 129–38
 relational ontology and 44–45, 49, 52–53, 104, 143, 153
 technologies of the 125
 Western, individualized 16, 44, 52, 57, 61, 75
sexism 50, 75, 105, 114, 179
Sex Pistols 26–27
sexual violence 8, 10, 76
 credibility and 6
 pervasiveness of 5–6, 46, 50, 81, 94
 speaking about 5–6, 82–83, 85–87, 110–11
 survivors, support for 67, 105, 110–16
 white women and 6, 74
 workplace 67–68, 73, 76, 110–16
sex workers, support for 200–1
She Said: Breaking the Sexual Harassment Story That Helped Ignite a Movement (Kantor and Twohey) 5
Simpson, Leanne Betasamosake 38–39
SKETCH Working Arts 123–24, 129–35, 139
slavery; *see* enslavement
small-scale cultural production 166
 challenges of 51, 167–68
 importance of 1–2, 18, 53–55, 104
 safety and 3, 173, 176–83, 186–87
 spaces for 173–80, 186–87
 visibility of forms 33, 36–38
Smith, Stacy L. 66
social change
 community and 48, 122–23, 129–30
 imagination and 16–17
 power dynamics 79, 100
social imaginary
 creative industries and 17, 26–27
 pedagogy and 15–16
social justice model 120, 124–25, 127–31, 143, 186, 194
social media 56
 "centring" discourse 94–95, 102
 movements 5–6, 95, 102, 195–96
social reproduction 49, 141
 in capitalism 44, 46–47
 definition of 46
 economic versus 46–47, 49, 135, 164
socio-economic barriers 8, 73
soft skills 11
software industry 25–26, 33
Soja, Edward (*Thirdspace: Journeys to Los Angeles and Other Real-and-Imagined Places*) 184–86
solidarity 6, 43, 62, 201
 youth 57–59, 198
spaces of appearance 181, 183–84, 186
spaces for cultural production 173–76, 179–80, 186–87, 196–98
 inclusivity of 3, 7, 60, 105, 122–24, 177–78
 physical safety in 1–4, 173, 176–83, 186–87
 precarity of 2, 10, 47, 79–80, 108, 113
spaces of representation (Lefebvre) 185
spatial justice 184–86
Spice Girls 27
survival strategies 6, 35, 105, 111–16, 195
 under capitalism 5, 15, 53, 97–98, 108–10

Talking Heads 1–2
Tea Base 20, 196–202
television 59, 103, 195–96

as creative industry 25, 29, 55, 73
underrepresentation in 27, 66–67, 70, 75, 97
Think Before You Appropriate: Things to Know and Questions to Ask in Order to Avoid Misappropriating Indigenous Cultures—A Guide for Creators and Designers (Intellectual Property Issues in Cultural Heritage Project) 82–83, 88–90
Thirdspaces 181, 184–86
Thompson, Cheryl 7–8
Throsby, David 31–32
Time's Up 66–67, 80–81
Tokumitsu, Miya 56
Toronto, Ontario 1, 12, 43, 111, 133, 138, 174
community arts spaces 35–36, 105–7, 120–24, 180, 190, 196–200
diversity and 8, 12, 101, 178
Total Refreshment Centre (TRC) 177
training, creative industries 6–7, 62, 74, 86, 110–16, 135, 154
trans people 156
community programming for 124, 148–49, 154–56, 169
erasure 40, 83, 85, 88
trauma 17, 116
Tronto, Joan 44–46, 48–50, 55–58, 95, 186
Twitter 6, 67, 151, 195
Twohey, Megan 5

Ubisoft 35–36
unemployment, youth 16, 61–62, 126–27
unions 47, 82
United Kingdom 82, 151
Acme Studios 187–89
community arts programming 26, 122, 125, 165
economic contribution, creative industries 25–26
national identity, creative industries 26–29
United Nations
Conference on Trade and Development (UNCTAD) 28
creative industries policy and 27–28
United States 7, 37, 69, 74, 78, 103; *see also* Oakland, California

Varvarousis, Angleos 15–16
value 13–14
aesthetic 18, 54, 97
community 10, 35, 39, 59
cultural 9–10, 31, 52, 81, 96–98, 190
economic versus other forms 4, 8–9, 24–25, 28–32, 49, 52, 59
margins versus centre and 96–98
power relations and 24, 96–98, 190
recuperating 4, 15–16, 61, 70, 96–98
social 9, 32–33, 35, 39, 47, 52–55, 118n48, 190
Vera Project 158
Vettivelu, Joshua 106–9, 195
VIBE Arts 120, 123
Vikram, Anuradha (*Decolonizing Culture*) 70–71
violence
collective responses to 6, 105, 110–16
gender-based 77, 115–16
safe spaces and; *see* safe spaces
sexual; *see* sexual violence
symbolic 97
women's experiences of 4–8, 110–13
workplace 5–6, 110–16
youth experiences of 122, 129
visual arts 174, 201
as core creative art 11, 31, 187
volunteerism 80, 94, 115, 127–35, 139, 198
paid work versus 59–61, 100, 124
RCFG* 153–62, 167; *see also* labour, creative industries

Walt Disney Company 67, 76, 162
Belong diversity report 78, 80–81
Warren, Emma (*Make Some Space: Tuning into Total Refreshment Centre*) 177
Weinstein, Harvey 5–6
wellbeing 29, 77
arts programs and 9, 114, 116, 122–23, 142–43
community 9, 109–10, 139, 194
Wenger, Étienne 149–50, 152–54, 157, 163–65, 167
Wet'suwet'en legal defense fundraising 202
Whippersnapper Gallery 12, 105–7, 110
white supremacy 57
Williams, Raymond, "Culture is Ordinary," 3–4, 8, 96
Wilson, Nick 14
women 8, 114
barriers for 30, 68, 94–95, 97, 137
"just add," 73–75, 77

labour of 45, 51, 113, 143
#MeToo movement and; *see* #MeToo movement
representation and 4–7, 11, 57–58, 66–67, 78–80, 151–53
support for 52, 62, 94–95, 111, 154–56, 162–63, 178
white 6, 40, 94–95
workers, creative industries 33, 71, 82, 173–76, 196
abuse of; *see* abuse, workplace
entry-level 56–58
support for 47, 58, 102, 112, 144, 190
youth 51, 53–58, 128
working class 3–4
cultural production 8, 55, 96
workplaces 149
abuse in; *see* abuse, workplace
autonomy 51, 71
policy and 56, 67–69, 74, 77–80, 86–87
safety, right to 5–6, 67–68, 110–16, 173–76, 200–1
support in; *see* workers, creative industries
toxic culture 5, 8, 68, 111–13, 151
violence; *see* sexual violence; violence
writers 15, 66
barriers for 11, 56, 195
emerging 11, 54

Yaovi, Johanna 8
Yee, Florence 197–202
Younger Than Beyoncé (YTB) gallery 53, 56
youth
arts programs 9, 120–25, 130–31, 136, 138
communities of care 13–14, 46–49, 51–53, 98–100, 114–16
creative labour and 10, 50–60, 124–31, 134–37, 142–44, 174
cultural production 10–12, 46–47, 52–56, 105
definition of 11–12
engagement 123–33, 136–40, 143
suicide 9
underrepresentation 56–58, 62, 105, 120–33, 142, 168–69, 189
unemployment 16, 61–62, 126–27
workers; *see* workers, creative industries
Youth Video OUTreach (YVO) 128

For Product Safety Concerns and Information please contact our EU representative GPSR@taylorandfrancis.com
Taylor & Francis Verlag GmbH, Kaufingerstraße 24, 80331 München, Germany

www.ingramcontent.com/pod-product-compliance
Ingram Content Group UK Ltd.
Pitfield, Milton Keynes, MK11 3LW, UK
UKHW022353190926
475702UK00015B/2259
* 9 7 8 0 3 6 7 4 6 8 1 5 6 *